SENSATION AND MODERNITY
IN THE 1860s

This is a study of high and low culture in the years before the Reform Act of 1867, which vastly increased the number of voters in Victorian Britain. As many commentators worried about the political consequences of this 'Leap in the Dark', authors and artists began to re-evaluate their own role in a democratic society that was also becoming more urban and more anonymous. While some fantasized about ways of capturing and holding the attention of the masses, others preferred to make art and literature more exclusive, to shut out the crowd. One path led to 'Sensation', the other to aestheticism, though there were also efforts to evade this opposition. This book examines the fiction, drama, fine art and ephemeral forms of these years against the backdrop of Reform. Authors and artists studied include Wilkie Collins, Dion Boucicault, Charles Dickens, James McNeill Whistler and the popular illustrator Alfred Concanen.

NICHOLAS DALY is Chair in Modern English and American Literature, School of English, Drama and Film, University College Dublin.

CAMBRIDGE STUDIES IN NINETEENTH-CENTURY
LITERATURE AND CULTURE

General editor
Gillian Beer, *University of Cambridge*

Editorial board
Isobel Armstrong, *Birkbeck, University of London*
Kate Flint, *Rutgers University*
Catherine Gallagher, *University of California, Berkeley*
D. A. Miller, *University of California, Berkeley*
J. Hillis Miller, *University of California, Irvine*
Daniel Pick, *Birkbeck, University of London*
Mary Poovey, *New York University*
Sally Shuttleworth, *University of Oxford*
Herbert Tucker, *University of Virginia*

Nineteenth-century British literature and culture have been rich fields for inter-disciplinary studies. Since the turn of the twentieth century, scholars and critics have tracked the intersections and tensions between Victorian literature and the visual arts, politics, social organization, economic life, technical innovations, scientific thought – in short, culture in its broadest sense. In recent years, theoretical challenges and historiographical shifts have unsettled the assumptions of previous scholarly synthesis and called into question the terms of older debates. Whereas the tendency in much past literary critical interpretation was to use the metaphor of culture as 'background', feminist, Foucauldian, and other analyses have employed more dynamic models that raise questions of power and of circulation. Such developments have reanimated the field. This series aims to accommodate and promote the most interesting work being undertaken on the frontiers of the field of nineteenth-century literary studies: work which intersects fruitfully with other fields of study such as history, or literary theory, or the history of science. Comparative as well as interdisciplinary approaches are welcomed.

A complete list of titles published will be found at the end of the book.

SENSATION AND MODERNITY IN THE 1860s

NICHOLAS DALY

CAMBRIDGE
UNIVERSITY PRESS

CAMBRIDGE UNIVERSITY PRESS
Cambridge, New York, Melbourne, Madrid, Cape Town,
Singapore, São Paulo, Delhi, Mexico City

Cambridge University Press
The Edinburgh Building, Cambridge CB2 8RU, UK

Published in the United States of America by Cambridge University Press, New York

www.cambridge.org
Information on this title: www.cambridge.org/9781107630208

First published 2009
First paperback edition 2013

A catalogue record for this publication is available from the British Library

Library of Congress Cataloguing in Publication Data
Daly, Nicholas.
Sensation and modernity in the 1860s / Nicholas Daly.
p.   cm. – (Cambridge studies in nineteenth-century literature and culture ; 70)
Includes bibliographical references and index.
ISBN 978-0-521-76022-5 (hardback)
1. English literature–19th century–History and criticism.   2. Sensationalism in literature.
3. Social change–Great Britain History–19th century.   4. Literature and society–Great
Britain–History–19th century.   5. Art and society–Great Britain–History–19th century.
6. Great Britain–Intellectual life–19th century.   7. Modernism (Literature)–Great Britain.
8. Modernism (Art)–Great Britain.   I. Title.
PR468.S6D36   2009
820.9'355–dc22   2009028521

ISBN 978-0-521-76022-5 Hardback
ISBN 978-1-107-63020-8 Paperback

For Stephanie

Contents

Illustrations

Acknowledgements

This book has changed career a number of times: beginning as a study of women in white, it became for a period a broad and even survey of culture in the 1860s, before assuming its current shape as an account of elite and popular cultural forms in the run-up to the 1867 Reform Act. This final version has been influenced by the thoughtful comments of a number of audiences who listened to excerpts and early avatars of various chapters: at the British Association of Victorian Studies conferences at Keele in 2004 and in Liverpool in 2006; the MLA in Washington, DC, in 2005; the Locating Subjects conference at the University of Calabria in Cosenza in 2005; the Research Seminar for Victorian Literature at Oxford University in 2006; the North American Victorian Studies Association/ Victorian Studies Association of Western Canada Conference at Victoria, BC, in 2007 and at Yale in 2008; the Research Seminar series at NUI Maynooth in 2008; and the Performing the Material Text Symposium at Florida State University in 2008, as well as at the Research Seminar Series in the UCD School of English, Drama and Film, where my colleagues have listened tolerantly to versions of at least two chapters. Participants in my 'Feeling Modern' MA seminar at UCD also deserve thanks for being the guinea pigs for some of these ideas.

Among the individuals to whom I am indebted for suggestions, support, hospitality, criticisms or literary and historical truffles are Nancy Armstrong and Len Tennenhouse, Claire Connolly, Fintan Cullen, Fionnuala Dillane, Tracy Davis, David Glover, Virginia Jackson, Darryl Jones, Meegan Kennedy, Margaret Kelleher, Ivan Kreilkamp, Chris Morash, Katy Mullin, Deaglán ó Donghaile, Francis O'Gorman, Marilena Parlati, Paige Reynolds, Lyn Pykett, Caroline Reitz and Lisa Surridge. My thanks to Lawrence Rainey, who gave me a chance to air an early version of Chapter 3 in *Modernism/Modernity*. The anonymous readers for the *Journal of Victorian Culture* offered sound advice on an earlier version of Chapter 2, and the anonymous readers at Cambridge University Press made many helpful suggestions about the original manuscript. Also at Cambridge, thanks to Ray Ryan, and to Linda Bree and her colleagues for their help, and thanks to Wendy Toole for her meticulous copy-editing.

The modern research university is often subject to the same time compression as the rest of the late capitalist economy, and is thus not always an easy place in which to do research. This book would have taken much longer to finish without a number of breaks from everyday teaching and administration. In 2003 I spent three months in Hanover, New Hampshire, as part of the academic exchange between Trinity College Dublin and Dartmouth College. My time there, and the excellent resources of the Olin Library, allowed me to write an early draft of what is now Chapter 2. My thanks to the Dartmouth English Department, and to Peter Cosgrove, Tom Luxon and Ivy Schweitzer, Brenda Silver and Paul Tobias, and Peter Travis for the hospitality I enjoyed. Much of the writing of the other chapters was enabled by the award of a year-long Senior Fellowship from the Irish Research Council for the Humanities and Social Sciences: at a time when research funding is increasingly aimed at trans-institutional networks and collaborative projects, they are to be commended for continuing to fund the single-authored book project.

I am grateful to a number of libraries and librarians: the libraries and librarians of UCD, TCD and Dartmouth College; Sue Crabtree, Special Collections Librarian, and Angela Groth-Seary at the Templeman, University of Kent, Canterbury, for their help with the Boucicault materials; and Fiona Barnard, Rare Books Librarian at the University of Reading, for her assistance with the Spellman Collection of Victorian Sheet Music Covers. The British Library also helped with rare sheet music covers, as did Joe Tooley and David Paramor. My thanks to the National Gallery in Washington, DC, for permission to reproduce James McNeill Whistler's *Symphony in White No. 1: The White Girl*; and to the Musée d'Orsay for permission to use an image of Gustave Courbet's *L'Origine du monde*.

There are networks other than those based on research, and I am, as always, grateful to my friends outside the academy for a range of encouragement and scepticism. Among a larger cast, particular thanks to Peter and Nicola Byrne, Mike Darcy, Madeleine Darcy and Andrew Lane, Peter Heffernan and Joan Hickson, Moggs Kelleher and Michael Vallely, Margaret Kelleher and John Tarpey, Catherine Kirwan, Brian Murphy and Miriam O'Brien, Fintan and Irene Murphy, and Paul O'Donovan.

Pride of place goes to my family in Cork, the Dalys, and my family in Dublin: Stephanie and Pola.

Introduction: White Years

This is a book about culture in an age of crowds, specifically the culture – popular and elite – of Britain in the 1860s, which is marked by a recurring interest in crowds and how their attention might be solicited, held and managed. Such an interest can be related to the general forces of modernization at work in Britain in those years, but it can also be tied directly to the political transformations that saw their formal expression in the 1867 Reform Bill, which transferred a significant measure of power to the urban working class. This was the so-called 'Leap in the Dark' that some political commentators saw as tantamount to giving power to that allotrope of the crowd, the mob. I will be arguing that there is a connection between this political modernization and the cultural phenomenon of 'sensation', which runs through the 1860s. London, that other capital of the nineteenth century, is the focus for much of the discussion, though a number of the figures we will consider – popular playwright Dion Boucicault and fine artist James McNeill Whistler, for example – had transnational careers, and many of the cultural phenomena, from sensation melodrama to blackface minstrelsy, escape the borders of any one national culture.[1]

This is also in part a book about a recurring image, the woman in white, a vulnerable, even ethereal figure who yet has the power to spellbind the crowd, which is rarely represented as either vulnerable or ethereal. The first such Woman in White appears not in Britain, but in France. On 11 February 1858, a fourteen-year-old French girl, Bernadette Soubirous, her sister, Toinette, and a neighbour's child, Jeanne Abadie, went out to gather firewood. They wandered out of the Pyrenean town where they lived until they came to the Massabielle Grotto, by the river Gave. Here, the other two crossed the river, but when Bernadette began to remove her stockings to cross, she went into a trance-like state, and saw something out of this world. In early accounts she seems to have described this entity simply as 'quelo', the Occitan word for 'that' (Bernadette did not learn standard French until some years later), or as 'dama' or 'demaisela', a White

Lady or fairy queen of the kind that appears in the folklore of the region. Questioned afterwards by a local priest, she described her vision as of 'something white, which had the appearance of a lady'.[2] Later she would describe it as a figure in white, carrying a rosary and wearing a blue sash, all part of the traditional iconography of the Virgin Mary.

There would be further visions. By 1 March, groups of 1,500 or so people were coming with her to the cave, and the authorities decided to fence off the site to control the crowds. People came in the belief that the entranced Bernadette was seeing Mary, the mother of Jesus, or, as she reportedly styled herself to the visionary, the Immaculate Conception.[3] The London *Times* soon picked up the story, not least, perhaps, because it was pleased to observe that for all the splendour of Napoleon III's Paris, France still laboured under a 'strange mixture of irreligion and superstition'.[4]

The Times greeted the reports from Lourdes with something close to contempt, but in the decade following Bernadette's experience a number of similar apparitions manifested themselves throughout the city. 'Pepper's Ghost', the vitreous spectre that was all the rage as a theatrical special effect in 1862–3 is, perhaps, the best known of these secular spirits. At the Royal Polytechnic Institution, the Adelphi Theatre and a number of the music halls, this optical illusion created for the audience

the impression of a person clearly visible and capable of appearing as one of a party, but wholly impervious to the sense of touch. The manner in which the figure suddenly vanishes, literally seeming to go nowhere, is most startling; still more surprising is its disappearance, when it gradually melts away, assuming a more filmy look, till it has attained absolute nonentity.[5]

The less commercially inclined 'Woburn Square Ghost' was to emerge in 1867. According to the 1860s memoirs of Alfred Rosling Bennett:

It was reported that the figure of a woman in white was appearing nightly amongst the trees at the northeast corner of the enclosed garden in Woburn Square, and had been seen of many. The Press noticed the matter, with the result that crowds invaded the Square after nightfall, blocked the thoroughfare and refused to be moved on. But the ghost became coy under such conditions, and although some declared they saw her plainly, the majority – including myself – were not so fortunate, and some felt considerably aggrieved. The sensation persisted for a week or two and then died away. What the true facts were never transpired, but the evidence in favour of some sort of apparition was very strong … Our Lady of Woburn Square had a good and lively (for a ghost at least) innings.[6]

But there were also more subtle aftershocks of the events at Lourdes in the literature, drama and fine art of the 1860s. In *The Woman in White*, Wilkie Collins's seminal 'sensation novel' of 1859–60, drawing master Walter

Hartright becomes embroiled in a complicated plot by villains Sir Percival Glyde and Count Fosco to steal a young woman's identity. The first of many narrative jolts comes in the form of his chance moonlit encounter on the road to London with a mysterious young woman, clad from head to toe in ghostly white. This 'extraordinary apparition' seems 'as if it had that moment sprung out of the earth or dropped from the heaven'.[7] The success of the novel when published in serial form in *All the Year Round* (Dickens's tuppenny weekly magazine) reached beyond the usual middle-class novel-reading public, though it may have only touched upon that more heterogeneous 'Unknown Public' that Collins uneasily describes in an essay of 1858 in *Household Words*, 'a public to be counted by millions; the mysterious, the unfathomable, the universal public of the penny-novel-Journals'.[8]

The first of the 1860s 'sensation plays', special-effects-driven melodramas, was Dion Boucicault's *The Colleen Bawn* (1860), in which the son of the manor wants to extricate himself from a secret marriage to a poor young woman, Eily O'Connor. The crowds came to see the great 'sensation scene', in which Eily is saved from drowning in a moonlit water cave, a secular grotto in which the play's hero, Myles, also distils illegal spirits. Boucicault borrowed most of his plot from Gerald Griffin's novel *The Colleen Bawn* (1829), the title of which phonetically reproduces the Irish *cailín bán*, sometimes translated 'darling girl', but literally meaning white or fair girl. Myles makes his famous 'header' to save Eily when he sees 'something white' in the water. Like *The Woman in White*, Boucicault's *Colleen Bawn* was a great popular success, and inspired a wide range of spin-offs, including an opera, *The Lily of Killarney*, whose title continues the white theme. (This floral title suggests how the immaculate apparition of Lourdes shades into the more generic, secularized figures of purity and virtue in distress that are at the heart of most nineteenth-century melodrama: these heroines are delicate blossoms, orphans of the storm that is modernity, or angels cast out of the house into a cold world.[9])

Women in white were also popping up in the fine art galleries, notably the Berners Street Gallery, off Oxford Street, where a large painting by James Abbott McNeill Whistler, *The Woman in White*, was exhibited in the summer of 1862 to a rather mixed reception. Better known now as *Symphony in White No. 1: The White Girl*, or simply *The White Girl*, it represents a woman in white against a white background. The first of his attempts at a new type of 'painterly' painting, an art that would eschew narrative content for pure form, it boldly advertises its own materiality as paint on canvas. Refused by the Royal Academy, *The Woman in White* was to become a *succès de scandale* when it appeared the following year at the *Salon des Refusés*, the famous alternative exhibition ordered by Napoleon III to accommodate the many works that had been excluded from that year's official Salon, including a number of paintings that were to become icons of Impressionism. Fernand Desnoyers, in his pamphlet on the Salon, described Whistler as 'le plus spirite des peintres' and the painting as a portrait of a spirit, a medium.[10] Gustave Courbet, it was reported, was also struck by the work's spiritual quality: '[He] calls your picture an apparition, with a spiritual content (this annoys him); he says it's good.'[11] With the benefit of hindsight we can recognize Whistler's painting as a foundational work of what would become aestheticism, the movement that rejected the moral mission of Victorian art and literature for a commitment to the pursuit of form, dusting off an earlier French slogan (attributed to Théophile Gautier), *l'art pour l'art*: art for art's sake. As developed in the writings of Walter Pater from the late 1860s, this emphasis on beauty and autonomous sensuous experience would come to be one of the dominant notes of late Victorian cultural discourse. To court new impressions would be one's duty to oneself; and the question to ask of a book or painting would be: 'What effect does it really produce on me?' Whistler's aesthetic apparition would help to train a select audience in this new way of seeing.

What links these disparate cultural artefacts, other than their resonance with Lourdes, is that at the time they were all seen to be part of the new phenomenon of 'sensation'. Pepper's Ghost and the Woburn Square apparition were popular sensations; *The Woman in White* was read as a sensation novel; *The Colleen Bawn* was regarded as a sensation play; and Whistler's *Woman in White* was viewed as a daring sensation picture. I will return to a more detailed discussion of what 'sensation' means in the chapters that follow, which look at the popular and high culture of the 1860s. For now it might be helpful to think of sensation as the cultural dominant of the 1860s; it was a way of describing cultural artefacts that deployed a variety of shock and suspense effects, but more generally its use seems to mark a perceived shift in the cultural market, a disruption of culture consumption stratified by class.[12]

For some commentators, the novels, plays and paintings of the age of sensation seemed to appeal too much to the crowd, providing a series of shocks and frissons rather than any more elevating aesthetic experience. 'Sensation' is a term that denotes a physiologically based theory of reader/viewer response, and it appears in counterpoint to the growth of the mass market as a component of the spread of social modernity. But political modernity is also relevant here: as Jonathan Loesberg pointed out some twenty years ago, it is not a coincidence that the decade that witnesses the appearance of sensation is also marked by debates about the Reform Act that for the first time enfranchised large numbers of working-class men.[13] It will be my contention here that the years of women in white, and indeed of sensation more generally in the cultural realm, are the same years in which the crowd comes to be seen as usurping social and political authority. In an earlier study, *Literature, Technology, and Modernity* (2004), I suggested that sensation novels and sensation drama produced a sort of 'training' in modernity, acclimatizing people to the pace of industrial, urban life through homeopathic doses of shock and suspense. Here I want to argue that such training was not a politically neutral phenomenon. The novels and plays of the 1860s cannot be seen in any straightforward way as simply disciplinary apparatuses in the Foucauldian sense, but I would argue that their use of sensation to capture and hold the attention of heterogeneous audiences can be linked to largely reactionary fantasies about the crowd in the years of Reform. That these novels and plays also often seem to suggest the impossibility of holding the self or the crowd together complicates this connection, but it does not cancel it.

We often reserve the term the 'age of crowds' to describe the end of the nineteenth century and the beginning of the twentieth, the period that is marked by the publication of Gustave Le Bon's *La Psychologie des Foules* (1895), Gabriel Tarde's *L'Opinion et la Foule* (1901) and Gerald Stanley Lee's *Crowds: A Moving Picture of Democracy* (1913), as well as by Frederick Winslow Taylor's *Principles of Scientific Management* (1911).[14] However, it is possible to bring the age of crowds forward, anchoring it instead to, say, Edgar Allan Poe's prescient 'Man of the Crowd' (1840), Charles Baudelaire's *Les Fleurs du Mal* (1857) and Matthew Arnold's *Culture and Anarchy* (1868) in the cultural realm; the Great Exhibition of 1851 in the economic; and the 1867 Reform Bill in the political. Closely bound up with the interest in crowds is the issue of consumption. In this period we see the further consolidation of the mass consumerism that had been signalled by the commodity-driven phantasmagoria of the Great Exhibition of 1851, and its many sequels, that saw people embark on secular pilgrimages, 'on the move to look at merchandise', as Hippolyte Taine put it.[15] This shift in Britain from self-definition in terms of production to self-definition in terms of consumption makes leisure a problem as well as a pleasure for the middle classes. As Peter Bailey describes, from mid-century there appears a new concern with the issue of leisure, in part because the middle classes simply had more of it, but also because it was an area of social life that presented new problems of distinction. Bailey cites the comments of journalist Matthew Browne, who wrote that 'social boundary lines are not so sharply drawn as they used to be ... the old cordon sanitaires have snapped under the pressure of the multitudes and we have not succeeded in twisting new ones'.[16] If the countryside still represented a relatively transparent social world, in which such leisure activities as fox-hunting allowed for participation according to rank, the leisure sphere in the cities, towns and seaside-resorts was socially opaque (we might see the enormous popularity of hunting yarns and hunting prints as symptoms of nostalgia for a more stable world of organic hierarchy). The lifting of the 'taxes on knowledge' as well as improvements in printing technology meant that cheaper newspapers and literature were part of this new landscape of leisure.

The coming of the mass market involves, by definition, a blurring of the lines of stratified consumption – it becomes difficult to label things as 'middle-class goods', or for that matter 'working-class goods', and this applies to cultural commodities as much as it does to more tangible ones. When access to entertainment is by purchase – of an excursion ticket, or theatre ticket, say, or of a book or mass-reproduced image – it is much harder to police participation. Pricing, of course, provided one attempt to regulate such consumption, but it was not by any means a reliable method. In this light the growth of a professionalized leisure industry, providing a wider and more variegated range of entertainments, is an important factor. But if the leisure sphere becomes a more contested area, and one in which commentators are increasingly concerned about who is watching, reading or listening to what, this is also complexly related to developments in the political realm, where older class certainties were facing collapse. At the beginning of the 1860s there was no interest among the Tories in extending the franchise, and even one of the most prominent Whigs, Lord John Russell, was known as 'finality John' because of his view that the 1832 Reform Act was the last word on the subject: the more prosperous echelons of the middle class had political power to match their economic might, and this was quite enough for even the liberals in the political establishment, with a few notable exceptions. And yet Reform was very much in the air, and by the end of the decade radical changes were to take place: the 1867 Act for the first time gives the vote to substantial sections of the working class. From the point of view of the ruling classes, it looked as if the masses were taking over.

When we recognize that democracy was the spectre haunting Britain in the late 1850s and 1860s, it becomes easier to understand not just the politics of culture in the period, but also more general political dispositions. In the sphere of culture, some of the more heated rhetoric around 'sensation' can be recognized as part of a war of position around Reform. The shrill response in some quarters to sensation drama, sensation novels, sensation songs, sensation paintings, and so on, encoded fears that at a time when political power appeared to be shifting towards the working class, the sphere of culture was not functioning to secure class distinction, as West End audiences and middle-class readers yielded to the pleasures of vulgar transpontine effects (viz. those associated with the working-class theatres of Westminster and beyond). As Andrew Maunder notes, among the recurring attitudes in the reviews of the period is that sensation novels 'were the offspring of the debilitating influence of modern commercial culture, and working-class culture'.[17] One of the most famous contemporary reviews, that of H. L. Mansel, sees the highly coloured publications of the penny and halfpenny press (i.e. 'penny dreadfuls') as 'the original germ, the primitive monad, to which all the varieties of sensational literature may be referred, as to their source'.[18] In July 1866 the *Westminster Review* saw sensation as a contagion spreading 'in all directions from the penny journal to the shilling magazine, and from the shilling magazine to the 30-shilling volume'.[19] Cartoons that show servants taking a keen interest in sensation fiction embody similar views, and such assumptions persist after Reform: for example, the *Saturday Review* in 1878 confidently declares that sensation provides 'toys for the class lowest in the social scale as well as in mental capacity'.[20] But of course the tricky thing was that these 'toys' strongly appealed to other classes too, making taste a very inaccurate index of social position.

The spectre of democracy in these years helps to explain attitudes to domestic cultural consumption, but it also helps us to understand British opinion on overseas events. The American Civil War dominates the headlines for much of the decade, and Britain's sympathy for the South has often been noted, alongside the misery created by the 'Cotton Famine' in Lancashire. But the hostility in many quarters to the North and sympathy for the South may have had less to do with cotton, or economics more generally (the North was protectionist), than with the perception that the Northern States of the Union represented democracy run riot. The North was perceived as a brash place in which power had been allowed to fall into the hands of immigrants and the half-educated – was not even the President a bumptious country lawyer who had once worked with his hands? By contrast, the South could be seen to represent a traditional, hierarchical, organic society, with the plantation as an image of paternalistic pastoral order, enlivened by comic or sentimental song. In this context, the slave revolt, or 'servile insurrection', that many in Britain prophesied in the South as a consequence of the war can be seen not only as a fantasy about race but as a displacement of fears of an analogous revolt at home among the urban working class; the vogue of blackface minstrelsy, with its celebration of orderly plantation life, can at least in part be seen as the corollary of such fantasies and fears.

If the popular and high culture of this period introduces a number of secular avatars of the Lourdes apparition, that is, I will argue, because events at Lourdes offered a suggestive scenario for those who were trying to re-imagine the place of culture in relation to an age of crowds. The trance-like state of Bernadette provides a version of the states of reverie that, as Jonathan Crary has shown, are the flipside of a modernity increasingly concerned with attention, punctuality and disciplined subjectivity. But, more importantly, perhaps, Lourdes offered a paradigm of how the distracted crowd might be kept spellbound: the crowds that came to see Bernadette seeing the Virgin Mary, and later just to stare at the Cave of Apparitions, indicated that the attention of the masses could be seized if only a powerful enough substitute for religious spectacle could be found. Attention, in other words, could be engineered.[21] If one aspect of 'sensation culture' is a preoccupation with the tide of crowd-pulling novelties and spectacular entertainments that threatened to overwhelm the lines of good taste, the other is an interest in just how the wandering gaze of a mass subject might be held. In the chapters that follow I want to look at the way in which a number of cultural artefacts of the 1860s – novels, plays and paintings, as well as other more ephemeral forms – took up the issue of attraction, or how attention might be solicited in an age of crowds. The imagination of alternative versions of community was also important as we will see, many of these artefacts incorporate heterotopian fantasies of a non-modern, non-urban, pastoral world, whether that of the ante-bellum South or of rural Ireland.

* * *

That the 1860s are years of social and political transformation is a fact registered not just in the popular and high culture of the period, but in the solidly middlebrow political novels of the period. Equidistant from sensation and aestheticism alike, the realist novels of Anthony Trollope clearly document the seismic shifts that were under way. In the Palliser novel sequence, Trollope's Irish hero, Phineas Finn, begins his political career in *Phineas Finn* (1869) by standing for a pocket borough in rural Ireland, Loughshane, a seat very much in the gift of his father's friend, the Earl of Tulla. His second seat, Loughton, is also more or less handed to him on a plate by the aristocracy, this time by the father of his friend

Lady Laura: the Earl of Brentford, a Whig grandee. But in *Phineas Redux* (1874), the passing of the 1867 Bill means that such pocket boroughs have all but disappeared, and Phineas has to make efforts to woo the working-class voters of Tankerville, a dreary coal-mining town near Durham (in fact, despite his eloquence he loses the election, but is awarded the seat when his Tory rival is found to have bribed voters). Phineas's efforts to be a popular orator are not the only signs in the Palliser novels of the changing base of power: the prominence of the penny press is evident in the frequent appearances of Quintus Slide, assistant editor and later editor of the *People's Banner*, who not only has the effrontery, as Finn sees it, of considering himself a gentleman, but even contemplates running for office.

Other, less clear-cut, forms of transition also underlie the appearance of sensation. Considered physiologically, sensation does not appear in a vacuum, but in the context of more general debates about the nature of sensory experience in a world transformed by industrial technologies, by urbanization, and by the nascent consumer culture that appears embryonically in the great international exhibitions and in more mature form in the new department stores. Lieven de Cauter has argued that the mid-nineteenth century gives rise to a strand of cultural criticism that links the visual excess of modernity to the impossibility of the classical unified subject. This line can be traced from Baudelaire's kaleidoscopic subject in the age of exhibitions, reflecting back the chaotic visual abundance around him, to Benjamin's distracted crowd, to Fredric Jameson's account of the postmodern subject, for whom cognitive mapping is all but impossible as he or she tries to find the elevator at the Bonaventure hotel.[22] In a different but related account of the sensory impact of modernization, Jonathan Crary, in *Suspensions of Perception*, argues that after mid-century there arises a conception of the normative modern subject as not just isolated and cellularized, as Michel Foucault has told us, but also focused and alert even in a dazzling and mobile world. Attention and attentiveness are the keywords of a new discourse that imagines a focused subject who can withstand the sensory saturation of modernity, and be trained to maintain a productive focus. But this discourse was troubled by 'the realization that attention had limits beyond and below which productivity and social cohesion were threatened'; that forms of focused attention on one stimulus can tip over into states of distraction, daydream and reverie.[23] Tony Bennett has likewise argued that from the mid-nineteenth century the state begins to entertain hopes that exhibitions and museums could be used to harness attention in productive ways, and that the wandering modern subject of

Sunday leisure might be disciplined into forms of national subjectivity: the exhibition of material culture could function in a sort of reverse pan-opticon.[24] The artefacts of sensation culture share this ambivalence about the modern subject. It is possible, as D. A. Miller showed us in *The Novel and the Police* some twenty years ago, to read the sensation novel as part of the disciplinary apparatuses of modernizing Britain; but it is also possible to see that these novels often dwell on the failure of the stable, centred subject – states of reverie are as prevalent as the alert consciousness of the detective, that focused private eye. In sensation fiction, and more obviously in sensation drama and painting, the dyad of riveted attention and distraction is not only thematized, but is made the animating principle of the entertainment: the reader or viewer is gripped, but what grips us is often the display of distraction or madness; tightly plotted narratives that turn on particular sensation scenes mean that much of what we read or see is consumed almost blindly. If these novels, plays and paintings are machines of attention, they also regularly seem to despair of the possibilities of control of either the self or others.

In this study of the politics of culture in the 1860s, whiteness and sensation may be seen as two threads that take us through some of the decade's key cultural artefacts. As it appears in *The Woman in White, The Colleen Bawn* and *Symphony in White, No. 1*, whiteness operates as an index of spectacle and attentiveness across three media (at least), and appears in complex conjunction with the issue of sensation. Sensation may in turn be seen to involve a number of overlapping ideas: (a) a physiological, and politically neutral, concept of reader/audience response; (b) a rather less neutral discourse regarding the dilution of real culture by a culture of shock, sensation and 'effect' – as Martin Meisel has shown, the term 'effect' evokes an opposition between organic/classical form and cultural artefacts where that form is broken up, sacrificed to cheap thrills of immediate response; and (c) an assumption, linked to (b), that such 'effects' ultimately derive from across the river Thames, from working-class theatres, an assumption that presumably rests on a more fundamental equation of the working class with body rather than soul – and which suggests in turn that (a) is not so politically neutral after all. Class is not the only axis of difference here: whiteness and sensation also open onto a separate if related context for self-definition in these years, race and ethnicity, and women in white always exist in contrast to other imagined figures – darker, more corporeal figures. Thus in the years leading up to the 1867 Reform Act the newspapers and magazines give extensive coverage to the American Civil War (1861–5), debates around race in the wake of Darwin's *Origin of Species*

(1859), the Fenian activities of 1867, and the gorilla craze that attends the writing and lectures of Paul Du Chaillu. If Lourdes offered a model of spectral attention-engineering, of the numinous put to more secular use, there were also concerns, animated by the new science of race, that crowds might not be susceptible to control at all. We will also see, though, that the crowd is not a passive entity incapable of self-representation; in the 1860s a new cultural venue, the music hall, comes into its own, producing competing images of modern life that owe little to the discourse of sensation or of aestheticism.

ENGLAND IN THE 1860S

It may be helpful at this point to provide a brief overview of Britain in the 1860s. In terms of national politics, as I have mentioned, the great topic was Reform. In 1860 Britain was not a democracy as we would now understand that term, since somewhere in the region of 80 per cent of the adult population did not have the right to vote. For some of the ruling class, Reform was a 'leap in the dark' that would see them ruled over by this unknown and unknowable mass. Ultimately, in the face of the mass meetings addressed by John Bright and others, Reform could not be avoided. When the Whigs failed to pass a bill, rather curiously it fell to the Tory administration of Lord Derby to do so in 1867.[25] (Universal male suffrage did not appear until 1884; women, of course, would not obtain the vote until 1918, and then only to a limited extent.)

In terms of international politics, it can be hard to separate the political and the economic: the decade opens, for example, with the looting and burning of the Summer Palace by Lord Elgin's troops, marking the end of the Second China War (1856–60), a war that had largely been waged because Britain felt that China had not been co-operating with sufficient zeal in the trade opened up by the Opium War of 1839–42.[26] The year 1860 also saw the signing of the Cobden–Chevalier treaty with France, which brought financial benefits, and was meant to assuage the fear of invasion that had been created in 1852 by the rise of the Second Empire under Napoleon III. (These fears of invasion are depicted allegorically in William Holman Hunt's *Our English Coasts, 1852*.) After much canvassing, and such patriotic outbursts as Tennyson's 'Riflemen Form!', a Rifle Volunteer Corps was finally founded in 1859, in the wake of the Orsini attempt on Louis-Napoleon's life (with a bomb supposedly made in Birmingham). The new movement drew tens of thousands of middle-class men into an amateur militia ready to defend Britain's shores from the French, and thrived in the 1860s. If the martial spirit of Britain's middle classes was praised by Tennyson, the treaty of 1860 did not go unmarked either: the drop in the price of champagne ushered in by the treaty produced such music-hall paeans to the good life as George Leybourne's 'Champagne Charlie' and 'Moet and Chandon'.[27]

The major international event of the early 1860s was, of course, the American Civil War, which dominated the news for four years and, as we shall see, also influenced the cultural sphere, from plantation melodrama to popular music. One reason why the American Civil War loomed so large in the English imaginary was its racial component: on the one hand, abolitionists saw Lincoln as a potential liberator of the slaves of the United States (and, of course, he became one, whatever his initial intentions may have been); on the other, the prospect of those same slaves mounting a 'servile insurrection' stirred up again the racial fears that were only just beginning to die down in the wake of the Indian Mutiny of 1857.[28] These fears were also, of course, refracted through Reform at home. The Civil War ended in April of 1865, but in October of that year racial conflict was again in the newspapers. The roots of the Morant Bay rebellion in Jamaica lay in a long history of exploitation, though in the end the trigger was a dispute over rent that resulted in a riot in which several people were killed. What caused Morant Bay to turn into a long-remembered bloodbath rather than a minor colonial incident was the way Governor Eyre restored order: executions, floggings and house-burning followed on a scale that dwarfed the original incidents His ferocious response led to a Commission of Inquiry, and the polarization of British public opinion for the rest of the decade and thereafter. Eyre's defenders included such prominent figures as Carlyle, Dickens and Tennyson; his critics included John Stuart Mill, T. H. Huxley and John Bright.[29] Closer to home, the Fenian Rising of 1867, and a series of attacks by Fenians in England itself, were a reminder that Irish disaffection had not gone away. At the end of the 1860s, attention turned again to France, this time because of the collapse of Napoleon III's Empire in the Franco-Prussian War of 1870–1; attention was also focused on the two-month reign of the Paris Commune in 1871, before its ruthless suppression.

Economically, the 1860s were relatively prosperous years in Britain. For ordinary workers there was a rise in real wages. The rise in the number of domestic servants suggests that there was an even more significant increase in middle-class prosperity: if no new great houses appeared, suburban villas proliferated.[30] Britain's industrial growth continued, and even British agriculture thrived, despite the repeal of the protectionist Corn Laws. Overseas investment, particularly in foreign railway projects, grew apace during the 1860s and 1870s: the £264 million invested overseas had grown to £1,058 milllion by the end of the 1870s. There were, nonetheless, local crises, such as the Lancashire cotton famine of 1862–5, attributed to the effects of the American Civil War, though probably also caused by a glut on the textiles market, that led to protests among the unemployed workers of Stalybridge and other cotton towns.[31] In London, the era of the joint-stock company had been ushered in through a series of limited liability acts from 1855 to 1862. An early crisis came in this 'age of paper', when the bill-brokers Overend and Gurney collapsed in 1866, and many of the weaker joint-stock companies went the same way.[32] (The rise of limited liability is one of the satirical targets of Dickens's *Our Mutual Friend*, and also underwrites a comic song of 1862, 'The Age of Paper'.[33]) Underlying the economic growth of this period were developments in technology and business methods, but also urbanization and population growth: by the 1860s the population of London alone was over two million, and by the end of the decade there were sixteen towns with a population of more than 100,000 (in 1801 there had been only one: London itself).[34] This new urban population would provide the audience for music hall, and would come to encroach on the leisure territory of the middle and upper classes, as Peter Bailey has shown. They would also increasingly demand a political voice in the nation whose prosperity they helped to provide.

The novel in the 1860s

By the 1860s the novel might truly be said to have risen, a dizzying ascent that was sometimes seen to have been achieved at the expense of such older modes as drama.[35] The novel's dominance in terms of the sheer numbers published was often remarked upon, and not always in favourable terms, but as a narrative mode it had attained a certain solid respectability by this time. While there had been pronounced opposition in the early years of the century among dissenters, who presumably agreed with the *Evangelical Magazine* of 1793, which had demonized novels as 'instruments of abomination and ruin', by the 1860s such views were relatively uncommon.[36] And while there were still those who bemoaned the novel's supposed superficiality, or its poetic or philosophical shortcomings, even they might accept the value of the complete works of Sir Walter Scott and Jane Austen. A work that remained in print for most of the nineteenth century, John Dunlop's *History of Fiction* could be pointed to as evidence of the highly respectable classical antecedents of the novel, and by 1859 the Professor of English Literature at University College, London, had published the first academic study of the English novel, *British Novelists and Their Styles: Being a Critical Sketch of the History of British Prose Fiction*.[37]

Nor did the genre lack for a more everyday source of self-consciousness, since there was no dearth of contemporary commentary upon it in the newspapers and magazines. It used to be a critical commonplace that the criticism of prose fiction only began in earnest in the 1880s with the appearance of Henry James's careful investigations of the art of the novel. But that is a view that has long since been corrected by the literary historical work of Richard Stang, David Skilton and others, who point out that although very few books of novel criticism appear in the mid-Victorian period, there existed a thriving critical industry in the periodicals. Nor were these all short ad hoc pieces on particular novels: as David Skilton notes, Victorian book reviewers were generally given plenty of scope, and some pieces could run to 30,000 words. If we have not always valued the critical contributions of such prolific reviewers as R. H. Hutton, G. H. Lewes and E. S. Dallas, or esteemed the views of the novelists themselves (with the exception, perhaps, of George Eliot), it has in part been because mid-Victorian novel criticism tends to be shot through with discourses that subsequent literary studies – until relatively recently – saw as extrinsic to it: politics, morality and social commentary. Now that cultural studies has come to reconsider the implication of literary discourse with others, and to take for granted the heteroglossic nature of the novel, mid-Victorian critical language may seem less alien.

What types of novels were being read at mid-century? In terms of numbers sold, the most successful authors were in fact those who aimed their work rather below the threshold of middle-class critical attention: G. W. M. Reynolds's serial stories, such as the *Mysteries of London* (1844) and the *Mysteries of the Court of London* (1849–56), both inspired by Eugène Sue's feuilleton *The Mysteries of Paris*, sold in the hundreds of thousands in penny or halfpenny numbers. Kate Flint points out that the first part of Dickens's novel of the mid-1860s, *Our Mutual Friend*, sold 30,000 copies in three days, but the first two numbers of Reynolds's *The Soldier's Wife* (1852–3) sold 60,000 each on the day of publication.[38] According to E. S. Dallas, the serial novels of J. F. Smith and Pierce Egan (the younger) were also enormously popular. By serializing fiction in his tuppenny weekly, *All the Year Round*, launched in April 1859, Dickens was attempting to appeal to at least some of that readership, notwithstanding Dallas's claim that *AYR* was 'addressed to a much higher class of readers than any which the penny journals would reach'.[39] At the height of its popularity, driven by the success of Wilkie Collins's sensation novels, sales of *AYR* reached 300,000, putting it into the same league, for a time at least, as such publications as the phenomenally successful *Lloyd's Weekly Newspaper*.[40] We should not think of British fiction as a hermetic entity. Quite a number of the successful novelists of mid-century were, in fact, Irish: for example, Charles Lever, Samuel Lover, Joseph Sheridan Le Fanu – even the Brontës are second-generation Irish, and were thought by their schoolfellows to have Irish accents. Moreover, the single most popular mid-Victorian novel was an American import, *Uncle Tom's Cabin* (1852), which is thought to have sold something in the region of 1.5 million copies in Britain and its colonies; the novels of Fenimore Cooper also enjoyed considerable popularity, the lack of copyright protection making them attractive prospects for British publishers.[41] At the other end of the scale, the educated classes probably read a good deal of French fiction (and when it came to the stage, the French drama was, of course, a rich source of inspiration – and plagiarism).

A more conventional literary history, one that is primarily concerned with what the middle-class reader read, tends to present the mid-nineteenth century as the heyday of the domestic realist novel. From a distance the Victorian realist novel appears as a formidable ideological ensemble, a medium in which local social and political antinomies could be solved symbolically, but also a medium for the production of powerful identification effects: the representation of centred, coherent realist characters; and the interpellation of the reader as a similarly stable and coherent self. In this light the realist novel resembles an interpellatory machine at least as effective as the classic Hollywood realist film. Of course, when looked at more closely, such monoliths tend to disaggregate into a less homogeneous set of cultural artefacts, as Linda Williams has argued in the case of the classic realist film.[42]

The purely realist novel is an equally difficult creature to find, the novel almost by definition being a heteroglossic form that entertains other modes besides the realistic; moreover, it is by no means to be taken for granted that realism is a more conservative form, ideologically speaking, than romance, or Gothic, or melodrama. Less abstractly, the 1840s and 1850s were marked by the publication of a set of politically engaged novels: *Sybil*, *Dombey and Son*, *Alton Locke*, *Hard Times*, *Bleak House*, *Mary Barton* and *North and South*. Even though these texts cannot all be incorporated easily into what Catherine Gallagher terms the 'industrial reformation of English fiction', they did all attempt to wrestle with 'the condition of England', to come to some assessment of the way in which life had been transformed by the industrial revolution, and by concomitant urbanization.[43] This is not to say that these novels radically depart from what is the really dominant subgenre of the nineteenth century – the domestic realist novel – but that in them the narrative devices of the domestic novel are harnessed to deal with the problems cast up by violent social transformation.

The 1860s, by contrast, are more usually associated with the eschewal of such directly political content and the turn to sensational and plot-driven material: tales of bigamy, adultery, mysterious disappearances, private mad-houses, theft and even murder. In short, these are considered to be the years of the sensation novel, a bracing cocktail of nouveau Gothic, Newgate novel and crime journalism.[44] Wilkie Collins is, perhaps, the best-known practitioner of the sensation novel, a label that was also affixed to the works of Mary Elizabeth Braddon, Mrs Henry Wood, Charles Reade, Joseph Sheridan Le Fanu and even Charles Dickens. Gallagher's account of the 1860s ignores the sensation novel: for her the significant transition is from the industrial novel to the subsequent realist triumphs of George Eliot, Thomas Hardy and Henry James, via the Arnoldian debate around culture. Critical accounts of the sensation novel, in turn, have with few exceptions tended to ignore the 'condition of England' novels and to focus on gender politics, noting in particular the sensation novel's disruption of domestic realism through its reworking of the female Gothic of the late eighteenth and early nineteenth century. Here, though, I want to suggest that it might be equally illuminating to link the novels of the 1860s to the condition of England debate and to the industrial novels, as well as to modernity more generally. In the sensation novel, social and political modernity are very much what is under consideration, but they appear there transmuted into problems of reader response, or attention engineering. In the *Woman in White*, as we shall see, Collins sets out not just to meditate on modernity, but to capture the mass audience who would be brought to power by Reform.

The theatre in the 1860s

The emergent entertainment industry of the 1860s had in large part been shaped by legislation, specifically the Theatre Regulation Act of 1843, that ended the stranglehold of the patent theatres on 'legitimate' drama, that is to say drama that depends primarily on the spoken word. The minor theatres had been able to circumvent the restrictions upon them in a variety of ways: temporary licences could be obtained from a magistrate; the addition of spectacle, or dumbshow, or music and song, could be used to dilute spoken drama so as to prevent prosecution. Melodrama, a mode that was well suited to such conditions because of the dominance within it of the visual over the verbal, was in part a French import, but the restrictions on the English stage shaped it in various ways, and made it the dominant theatrical mode. The 1843 Act allowed the minor theatres to stage Shakespeare, and indeed anything else that they wanted within the limits of the Lord Chamberlain's censorship, though it meant that they could no longer serve food and drink. But it also gave a defined role to the music halls, which were permitted to serve food and drink and provide entertainment, as long as that entertainment did not trample on the territory of the theatres. The Act did not create a theatrical boom, and no new theatres appeared until the end of the 1860s; the same period saw a veritable efflorescence of music halls, including such large venues as the Canterbury in 1852, the Alhambra in 1858, the Oxford in 1861, and a host of smaller venues.

A long-popular teleological narrative of theatre history sees the nineteenth century as a period in which modern drama gradually emerges at mid-century from the degradation of the early nineteenth century: beginning with the 'realistic' domestic comedies of Tom Robertson (e.g. *Caste*), the theatre starts to leave behind the spectacular and melodramatic excesses into which it had fallen; at the same time, a less rowdy and better-educated audience begins to return to the theatre; and the unified performance replaces a more careless, or at least laissez-faire, approach to production.[45] This narrative is not entirely inaccurate: it is possible to trace some of the later tendencies of English drama to the work of Robertson in the 1860s, insofar as in his work sophisticated and plausible dialogue-driven situations look forward to the plays of Arthur Wing Pinero, H. A. Jones and Shaw. At the Prince of Wales Theatre, where much of Robertson's work appeared, the Bancrofts set out deliberately to court a more middle-class audience, replacing some of the space devoted to the relatively cheap seats of the pit with the more expensive 'stalls'. In the same period, the appearance of the 'dress circle' can be seen as either the symptom or the cause of a more upper-middle-class audience.[46]

But there are also quite a few problems with this account. Spectacular melodrama did not disappear with the appearance of Robertson, nor with Shaw for that matter. The regular attendance of Queen Victoria is clear enough evidence that the 'better' classes were attending the theatre in the 1850s.[47] The seating innovations of the Bancrofts may be signs of increasing gentrification, but may also have been an attempt to carve out a niche for themselves, as well as to maximize profits, at a time when the theatres faced stiff competition for the pit audience, particularly from the music halls. Even the move towards a carefully directed unified performance can be seen to be characteristic of Charles Kean's elaborate, archaeological productions of Shakespeare in the 1850s. The real objection to the up-from-melodrama narrative, of course, is that it begs the question by assuming that the 'smaller' plays of Robertson and his successors are innately superior to melodrama. In the last few decades the status of melodrama has been radically revised, and there is now fairly widespread recognition that melodrama was not a crude form that appealed to the lowest common denominator, but a sophisticated form in its own right, and moreover one that in its visuality and use of musical effects resonates not just with cinema, but with some of the more innovative tendencies of late twentieth-century drama: it is easier to draw a line from the sensation melodrama of Boucicault than from Robertson to, say, Robert Wilson and Tom Waits's *Woyzeck* (2002).

This is not to say that the theatre of the 1860s was the happiest of all possible theatres. For one thing the flight of talent from the theatre to the novel instigated by the political censorship of the eighteenth century had left its mark. While the lifting of the restrictions on the 'minor' theatres by the Theatre Regulation Act of 1843 meant that it was easier to stage legitimate drama outside of the patent-holding theatres (Covent Garden, Drury Lane, the Haymarket during the summer), Michael Booth notes that up until the mid-1860s there had been something of a slump in the theatre business, with few new theatres being built in London, despite the enormous growth in population. In fact, it can be argued that the music halls had benefited more than the theatres from the relaxation of the licensing acts – certainly they had benefited from the growth of population. The managers of the 1860s were keenly aware of the challenge of the halls, as we shall see, and attempted on occasion to prevent by legal means what they saw as trespasses on their own artistic and commercial territory. Occasional pronouncements that the audience for theatre did not overlap with the audience for music hall were belied by such attempts to restrict the music halls, as well as by some of the testimony to the 1866 Select Committee on Theatrical Licences and Regulations.

In economic terms the theatre of the 1860s sees a number of important changes. One of the most striking of these was the transition from repertory to the long-run play. As Booth points out, the long-run play can only succeed when there is a large enough audience to make the initial investment in properties and personnel pay; this only happens when the population of London reaches a certain size (three million), and when the railway (and in the 1860s the underground) network is able to create a large suburban and provincial hinterland on which an urban theatre can draw. While there had been a few long-run successes before the 1860s, this decade sees the long run become a regular feature rather than an anomaly. *The Colleen Bawn* was one of the first of these long-run successes (231 performances, from 10 September 1861 to 13 July 1861); others included Tom Taylor's *Ticket-of-Leave Man* (407 nights), the same author's *Our American Cousin* (314 nights) and Fechter's 1861 production of *Hamlet* (115 nights). The long run of the *Colleen Bawn* encouraged Boucicault to pursue another innovation: payment of a percentage of the profits rather than a flat fee – a royalty payment, in other words. In the long term, the embrace of the royalty system (together with the reform of international copyright) would make writing for the stage a more attractive and lucrative proposition than it had been for much of the nineteenth century, and would do something to make intellectual property as valuable as the more established kinds. Boucicault also sent out touring productions of *The Colleen Bawn*, another innovation that would have considerable consequences for the provincial theatres.

What did audiences come to watch? 'Sensation dramas' like Boucicault's *Colleen Bawn* were hugely popular, as we shall see, but they did not have the field all to themselves. Shakespeare was, unsurprisingly, a draw, partly thanks to the revival instituted by Samuel Phelps at Sadler's Wells, and Edmund Kean at the Princess's Theatre. Charles Fechter built on their success, his *Hamlet* of 1861, as we have already noted, providing one of the great long runs of the decade. Among the successful comedies of the 1860s, *Our American Cousin* stands out, not for any innate qualities but for its extraordinary success. Its comic aristocrat, Lord Dundreary, took on a life of his own, largely owing to the improvisations of E. A. Sothern. Dundreary appeared in various 'sequels', such as H. J. Byron's farce, *Lord Dundreary Married and Done For* (Haymarket, 13 June 1864), as well as providing the inspiration for several popular tunes and songs of the 1860s ('Lord Dundreary's Galop', 'The Lord Dundreary Polka'), uncategorizable comic items like F. C. Burnand's *Bishop Colenso Utterly Refuted and Categorically Answered by Lord Dundreary* (1862), and a style of beard, Dundreary whiskers.[48] *Our American Cousin* was also, of course, a transatlantic hit, and the play that President Lincoln was attending when he was assassinated by the actor and Confederate sympathizer John Wilkes Booth on 14 April 1865. Also at the lighter end of the theatrical spectrum, burlesques, extravaganzas and pantomimes were extremely popular. Burlesque provided entertaining parodies of the literary and dramatic hits of the day, laced with tortuous puns and enlivened with popular songs and dance sequences. Fairy extravaganza provided sumptuous spectacle, including the use of elaborate and 'magical' transformation scenes, which audiences would already have been familiar with from large-scale dioramas of the kind perfected on stage by Louis Daguerre before he turned to photography, as well as from optical toys like *Spooner's Transformations* and *Spooner's Protean Views*.[49] J. R. Planché was an early exponent of this form; Boucicault's extraordinary effort in this direction in the early 1870s, *Babil and Bijou* (Covent Garden, 1872), on which Planché collaborated, might be regarded as the *ne plus ultra* of such theatrical spectacles. Backed by the wealthy Lord Londesborough, Boucicault spent £17,000 on stage properties in a production that featured 'every conceivable realm, from mid-air to the bowels of the earth', including 'a huge fantastic aquarium of pseudo-oysters, crabs, cockles, seals, periwinkles, sea-lions, sea-horses, sharks, alligators, sword-fish, devil-fish and lobsters'.[50] While a success, *Babil and Bijou* could never recover its costs, and Lord Londesborough was left £11,000 the poorer. Mid-Victorian pantomime can be difficult to distinguish from extravaganza, though it tended to draw more on familiar folk and fairy stories, as it still does today: *Dick Whittington*, *Aladdin* and *Cinderella* were endlessly reworked, and enjoyed considerable cross-class appeal.[51]

The Select Committee on Theatrical Licences and Regulations discovered that almost two thirds of the total seating capacity of the London theatres was outside the West End, and even this figure excludes the music halls and the penny gaffs of the East End. As Booth puts it, 'it is quite wrong to think of the audience experience of London theatre solely as a West End experience'. In Chapter 5 I will touch on music hall, but it is worth bearing in mind that the penny gaffs and other working-class theatres catered to large proportion of the theatre-going public, a public as 'unknown' to the middle-class critic as Wilkie Collins's 'Unknown Public' of penny-journal readers was to the critic of the novel. If *The Colleen Bawn* was seen by members of this public, they did not see it in the Adelphi but in sundry local adaptations that mushroomed in the wake of Boucicault's success.

The visual arts in the 1860s

The central institution of the art establishment that Whistler shocked with his sensation paintings and his aesthetic doctrines was the Royal Academy, then resident in Trafalgar Square in the same premises as the National

Gallery (it moved to Burlington House in Piccadilly in 1869). Rival centres of power existed, such as the Old Watercolour Society in Pall Mall and the New Society of Painters in Water Colours in Piccadilly, later known as the Institute of Painters in Water Colours. After 1865 the Dudley Gallery provided another outlet for more experimental work, including 'aesthetic' material. According to the tradition of academic painting shaped by Sir Joshua Reynolds, history painting – classical, religious and historical subjects treated in the grand manner – was considered the most prestigious; domestic scenes and portraiture came next; and on a somewhat lower tier lay landscape painting. The most respected art critic of the nineteenth century, Ruskin, entertained some notions on the relative value of the modes very different from Reynolds's, but his definition of great art in *Modern Painters* depends on a similar assumption that the highest forms of art deal with great themes:

I say that the art is greatest, which conveys to the mind of the spectator, by any means whatsoever, the greatest number of the greatest ideas, and I call an idea great in proportion as it is received by a higher faculty of the mind, and as it more fully occupies, and in occupying, exercises and exalts the faculty by which it is received.[52]

Nonetheless, Reynolds's academic hierarchy, never that firmly anchored in a country with no old masters of its own, was honoured more in the breach than the observance by the middle of the nineteenth century. The International Exhibition of 1862, which contained an extensive Fine Art section, gives us some idea of what was really valued by that period. The introduction to the official catalogue featured a survey essay by one 'F. T. P' [*sc.* the civil servant, art critic and anthologist Francis Turner Palgrave], 'The British School of Oil Painting', that illuminates the rationale under-lying the selections that had been made. The painters of the eighteenth century who had done most to carve a niche for a native English painting were taken to be Hogarth, Wilson, Reynolds and Gainsborough. Among the artists of the nineteenth century pre-eminence was given to Turner, who is represented as 'the Shakespeare of another and hardly less splendid kingdom' for his capacity to 'penetrate ... deeply into the soul of nature'.[53] With Turner, landscape painting had reached its apotheosis, delving into spiritual realms that might once have been the preserve of religious sub-jects. But perhaps the most interesting section of the short essay discusses the most powerful tendencies of the art of the present: the elevation of genre painting and of landscape. A minor figure of the late eighteenth cen-tury, Edward Bird, is singled out as a forerunner:

More decided steps onwards were made by Bird and Wilkie. The former (1772–1819), a painter little known, and not of conspicuous power, deserves notice as one of the very first who successfully worked in that style, which was destined, with landscape, to be the leading feature in modern art. Bird's subjects mark this aim: *The Saturday Night, The Will, The Country Auction, The Raffle* – incidents of common life, and each suggestive of some little tale, half humorous or half sentimental. It is by the introduction of the last elements, that this manner, with which from Wilkie onwards we are familiar, is distinguished from earlier attempts. Processions and ceremonies had been painted long before in Venice, courtly life in France, rustic in Holland; but the touch of the Tale is all but wanting in these works. (p. 5)

Palgrave is sufficiently struck by this English innovation, 'the touch of the Tale', to want to provide a historical explanation for it:

This style, and landscape – regarded no longer as the scene of some recorded human story, but as the representation either of nature embodying man's fortunes in her own features, or of nature in her solitary splendour – mark the art of this century not less distinctly than religious subjects mark that of the fourteenth. Hardly known to our great grandfathers, what could have rendered them so prominent now? In such inquiries the risk is great of considering as cause what is only itself an effect of some larger and, perhaps, undecipherable reason. Yet it is indisputable that the growth of the Incident style in painting runs parallel with the great outburst of novel writing from about 1790 onwards, with the social change which gave the patronage of art rather to the mercantile than to the educated classes, with that fusion of ranks and interests which (in another sphere) found expression in Burns, Scott, Crabbe, and Wordsworth (p. 5).

If the rise of 'domestic incident' parallels the rise of the novel, and indeed the rise of the novel-reading middle classes, the rise of landscape may be in part attributable to a different aspect of modernization, having 'appeared simultaneously with the love of traveling and the love of natural description'. 'These passions ... are due, no doubt, in part to simple increased opportunity; to recent wealth and peace, and multiplied facilities for journeying' (p. 7). But these new 'passions' might also be tied to the power of the mercantile classes: where once the grand tour was the exclusive province of the aristocracy, now the world had opened up to the middle classes, not least owing to the reticulation of railway lines around the country, and around Europe. The grand historical paintings that suited the habitus and scale of living of aristocratic patrons could not thrive in 'an age in which pictures are mainly desired for the adorning of private houses, and the subjects popular are domestic incident or landscape' (p. 6).

Palgrave's assumption that patronage had passed to the mercantile classes is, of course, correct. Nor was this patronage confined to the desire of the average prosperous bourgeois to have a few paintings in the house, since many of the great collectors of the nineteenth century were merchants rather than aristocrats: Lionel Lambourne lists the army contractor Robert Vernon; the wine merchants John Allnut and John James Ruskin (father of John Ruskin); the pill manufacturers Benjamin Godfrey Windus and Thomas Holloway; and the cloth manufacturer John Sheepshanks, who bequeathed his collection to the museum at South Kensington, now the Victorian and Albert Museum.[54] (One might add other names to this list, including that of shipping magnate F. R. Leyland, patron of Whistler until their dispute about the 'Peacock Room'.) Rather than simply compete with the aristocracy in the connoisseurship of old masters, these men were eager to pay for the work of living painters. This new source of patronage meant that there was more money to be made by artists, but it also to some extent delimited the kind of work that might be done. The Pre-Raphaelite Brotherhood, for all their genuine powers of innovation, were very fortunate, or very canny, in favouring subjects with a strong 'touch of the Tale', even if they chose literary sources over everyday sentimental scenes. When Whistler set himself against the traditions of the Academy, and the unofficial pressures of the market, with his *White Girl* (1862), better known now as *Symphony in White, No. 1: The White Girl*, he found the going could be very rough indeed. Neither the Academy nor his potential buyers were quite ready for a painting that combined aestheticism with shock value, and that refused narrative content as well as conventional notions of smooth, even composition.

For the majority of the population, of course, the visual arts were not encountered in the gallery, even when we take into account the hundreds of thousands who came to see W. P. Frith's *Derby Day* and *The Railway Station* when those show-stopping works went on tour. Reproductions in a variety of media would have been familiar to a wider section of the population. Engravings of well-known paintings appeared for purchase, but also came as 'free' components of various illustrated magazines. The latter included such middle-class publications as the *Illustrated London News*, but also penny journals: for example, in 1865 the temperance monthly, the *British Workman*, featured folio-sized reproductions of paintings by Frith (*The Crossing Sweeper*) and Frederick Tayler, as well as original illustrations by John Gilbert and Thomas Landseer, among others. Book illustration enjoyed something of a golden era in the 1860s, through the work of the group of artists (sometimes simply known as 'the Sixties') that included John Leech, George Du Maurier and others. (The lithographic artist whom we shall meet in Chapter 5, Alfred Concanen, remained outside this world, but nonetheless produced illustrations for a number of works in the 1860s and 1870s, including Wilkie Collins's *My Miscellanies*.) In terms of mechanical colour reproduction, aquatint had been a relatively expensive method more suited to the gentleman collector, but tinted lithography and later chromolithography proper opened up a much wider field for the reproduced image. As we shall see, chromolithography became a vibrant form that did not depend on the reproduction of Academic paintings for its subject matter. Through its association with music hall, it came to provide something like a vernacular art.

* * *

In this study I have tried to explore a range of responses by writers and artists to social and political modernity in the 1860s. Initially, I thought that these responses forked in a fairly straightforward way: the attention-engineering 'sensation school' sought to tackle the mass audience head on, by providing a series of spectacles that produced a visceral impact, aestheticism, by contrast, represented an attempt to escape the vulgar crowd by demanding that the viewer possess more cultural capital. I have over time come to see that this is a crude over-simplification. As we shall see in Chapters 1 and 2, the sensational 'effects' deployed by sensation novelists and dramatists represent a complex approach to issues of spectatorship and readership, one in which a physiological approach to audience response is in tension with other features: the deployment of the numinous, the evocation of utopian aspects of modernity. Conversely, as we shall see in Chapter 3, one of the first attempts by proto-aesthete James MacNeill Whistler to create a purportedly meaningless exercise in pure form, *Symphony in White No. 1: The White Girl*, can also be seen to be a conscious attempt to use sensational effects, to shock his audience into a near-physical response to the materiality of the image. For his one-time friend George Du Maurier, Whistler's techniques are excessively manipulative, a form of abuse of subject and viewer alike; when Du Maurier revisits the 1860s in his *roman-à-clef, Trilby* (1894), he transforms Whistler into the sinister hypnotist, Svengali. In the next chapter, the decade's concern with the shifting contours of class and power is related to another pressing issue of the period: race. Chapter 4 explores the way in which the responses to negro minstrelsy, to the American Civil War and to the 'Gorilla Sensation' of 1863 can all be read in the context of concerns about who exactly the British middle classes were, and doubts as to whether some crowds could ever be controlled (as *King Kong* would condense fears and longings around race and class in the 1930s, the figure of the gorilla seems to have done in the 1860s). Thus if the woman in white is one icon of the decade, we must imagine another figure, darker and more fleshly, as its foil: this body variously appears as the black slave, the gorilla, the simianized Fenian, and indeed the crowd itself.

In the last chapter of this book I take the discussion in a different direction by focusing on a cultural medium that represents a very different response to the anticipated collapse of the cordon sanitaire of class in the face of modernity and democracy. In the illustrated music of the 1860s, closely linked to the rise of music hall, we see, by and large, an enthusiastic response to the blurring of class boundaries through social and political modernization. Here we leave behind the imaginary of spectral women in white with their dark and menacing others, and pastoral fantasies of escape, for a vision of the modern city as a luminous place of fugitive but nonetheless real delight. Visual enchantment remains as a concern in this chapter, though what holds the viewer here is not the residue of the numinous but the brash tints of the street, relayed here in the eye-catching colours of chromolithography. In the work of Alfred Concanen, Thomas Packer, R. J. Hamerton and others, the unstable urban terrain of random encounters, consumer spectacle and sexual opportunity is presented in saturated colour as a resort of pleasure. The songs they illustrate tell cautionary tales of the consequences for those who stray away from domesticity to go on 'sprees' in the anonymous city, but there is far more investment in describing the pleasures of the spree than in the moral comeuppance. The illustrated covers are if anything even more celebratory, and suggest an alternative vision of modernity to that of either sensation or aestheticism. Here, if anywhere, we get a glimpse of how members of the crowd saw themselves in the run-up to the 1867 Reform Act – not as part of a threatening and engulfing mass, but as a loosely knit collectivity on the threshold of greater social, political and economic freedom.

CHAPTER I

The Woman in White *and the crowd*

A toast to Wilkie Collins
The painter's and the poet's fame
Shed their twinned lustre round his name

...

But on our artist's shadowy screen
A stranger miracle is seen
Than priest unveils or pilgrim seeks
The poem breathes, the picture speaks!
'A Toast to Wilkie Collins'[1]

'I saw something white, which had the appearance of a lady.'
Bernadette of Lourdes[2]

When in 1860 'sensation mania' first gripped the British public, one of its principal sources was a novel, *The Woman in White*, appearing in weekly parts in Charles Dickens's new flagship magazine, *All the Year Round*. Serialized from November 1859 to the following August, it immediately followed Dickens's own *A Tale of Two Cities*, and its author was, of course, Dickens's friend, employee and occasional literary collaborator, Wilkie Collins. As has often been recorded, *The Woman in White* was a huge success, helping to swell the sales of the magazine to the region of 100,000 copies a week.[3] Even without the figures we can measure the extent of its contemporary impact by browsing through the journals of the period, and noting the many references to its legitimate and illegitimate offspring, from such musical spin-offs as Charles Marriott's *The Woman in White Waltz* (1860) and J. E. Carpenter's *The Woman in White* (1860), to burlesques like Watts Phillips's *The Woman in Mauve* (1865), to say nothing of its more distant kin, such as the many Sensation Polkas, Sensation Quadrilles and Sensation Galops that appeared in the early 1860s.[4]

Now we generally identify it as the first of a whole new sub-genre, the sensation novel, a label generally attached to such tales as M. E. Braddon's

1. Illustrated cover for J. H. Stead's 'The Great Sensation Song', written
   by Frank Hall (1863). Chromolithograph by Concanen and Lee.

Lady Audley's Secret, Mrs Henry Wood's *East Lynne*, Charles Reade's *Hard Cash* and J. S. Le Fanu's *Uncle Silas*, as well as to Collins's own later work, notably *The Moonstone*.[5] These eventful narratives constituted not so much a rejection of the domestic novel as an aberrant strain within that genre, in which the darker aspects of courtship and family life – seduction, adultery, bigamy, and even murder – were foregrounded.[6] More arguably, *The Woman in White* can also be presented as the origin of other sensational forms: the journalism of the 1860s uses the term 'sensation' to describe everything from new songs, to sermons, to theatrical hits like *The Colleen Bawn*, to acrobatic performances by Leotard and Blondin.[7] While literary history tends to identify sensation fiction as a domesticated descendant of the Gothic novel, contemporary accounts often do not recognize sensation more generally as a British phenomenon at all, seeing it as an American import, sometimes crediting Boucicault with its introduction.[8] Whatever its immediate origins, the contours appear in the 1860s of a culture of sensation that revolves around suspense, shock and the production of a physical response in the reader or viewer, but that also depends on publicity, and innovative commodity experiences. Polymorphous and polygenetic, 'sensation', as we saw in the introduction, also appears at a time when debates about culture are inflected by the issue of Reform.

The Woman in White itself places politics off-stage, or rather overseas, in Italy (Italian politics kept the idea of violent political change very much in focus in these years).[9] Centre-stage is a case of identity theft, specifically a plot by the impecunious Sir Percival Glyde and his Italian friend, Count Fosco, to fake the death of Sir Percival's wife, Lady Laura Glyde, so that her substantial estate falls into their hands, and rendering harmless her supposed knowledge of Sir Percival's family secret. To this end, her lookalike, a physically and mentally frail young woman called Anne Catherick, is substituted for Laura, while the latter is incarcerated under Catherick's name in a private asylum for the insane. The novel is told in the first person by a series of narrators who tell their own part in the story, the principal of these narrators being Walter Hartright, a young drawing master who falls in love with Laura, and eventually frustrates the plot against her, uncovering in the process Sir Percival's great secret. In the novel's most famous episode, Walter is returning on foot to London from a visit to his mother and sister in Hampstead when he has a startling midnight encounter with an 'apparition' (p. 15), in the form of 'a solitary woman dressed from head to foot in white garments' (p. 15), later revealed to be Anne Catherick, who, clearly in some distress, asks him for directions to London. He walks with her and helps her to get a cab, but no sooner has this apparition 'melted into the dark shadows on the road' (p. 21) than a chaise appears with two men, who tell a passing policeman that they are on the track of 'a woman in white' (p. 22), an escaped lunatic. The episode acquires an additional uncanniness some days later when Walter, having arrived at his new position in Cumberland, first meets Laura

Fairlie, the niece of his employer, and realizes that she is the mirror image of the mysterious woman in white.

According to the son of John Everett Millais, the episode, and thus the novel as a whole, had its origins in Collins's own private life, in his first meeting with Caroline Graves, the woman who would become his wife in all but name for some thirty years. It is a story that has been repeated many times: according to his son's biography, Millais was walking home with Wilkie and his brother, Charles Allston Collins, from a party at the Collinses' house in Hanover Terrace when they heard a scream from the garden of a villa they were passing. The gate opened, and:

From it came the figure of a young and very beautiful woman dressed in flowing white robes that shone in the moonlight. She seemed to float rather than to run in their direction, and on coming up to the three young men, she paused for a moment in an attitude of supplication and terror. Then, seeming to recollect herself, she suddenly moved on and vanished in the shadows cast upon the road.

'What a lovely woman!' was all Millais could say. 'I must see who she is, and what's the matter,' said Wilkie Collins as, without another word, he dashed off after her ... They [subsequently] gathered from him ... that he had come up with the lovely fugitive and had heard from her own lips the history of her life and the cause of her sudden flight. She was a young lady of good birth and position, who had accidentally fallen into the hands of a man living in a villa in Regent's Park. There for many months he kept her prisoner under threats and mesmeric influences of so alarming a character that she dared not attempt to escape, until, in sheer desperation, she fled from the brute, who with a poker in his hand, threatened to dash her brains out.[10]

As Collins's most recent biographer, Catherine Peters, points out, it is not a very convincing account of Collins's first meeting with Graves, and it is one that appears only after the death of all the principals (Charles Collins in 1873, Wilkie in 1889, Graves in 1895, Millais in 1896). Moreover, its details seem just a little too artistic: the description of the young woman recalls Frederick Walker's famous poster for the stage version of *The Woman in White*; and the detail of the villain using his mesmeric powers to subdue his female victim smacks too much of George Du Maurier's novel *Trilby* (1894), the stage version of which was doing great business in 1899.[11] Vivid though it is, it seems we cannot take it at face value as shedding any light on the origins of *The Woman in White*.

But Millais's tale does tell us a few important things, I think: for one, that Hartright's fateful moonlit meeting with a white figure lingers in the memory when other details of the novel are forgotten ('Don't forget: a woman in white' the men in the chaise enjoin the policeman (p. 22), and, at one remove, us – and we do not). Anne Catherick's sudden appearance out of the darkness comes to be iconic of the novel as a whole, as Walker's poster, and other visual artefacts, such as illustrated sheet-music covers, testify. Moreover, however apocryphal it may be, the anecdote gives us a useful indication of the cultural milieu to which Wilkie Collins belonged. We might think of Collins as part of Dickens's circle, but Collins's family and original set of friends were more artistic than literary or dramatic. Millais, one of the most successful painters of his time, subsequently Sir John Everett Millais, Chairman of the Royal Academy, was a close friend, as were a number of other artists, including Henry C. Brandling, Augustus Egg, William Holman Hunt and Edward Matthew Ward.[12]

Nor was it only Wilkie's friends who linked him to the art world. Charles Allston Collins, his brother, was a painter, closely associated with the Pre-Raphaelite Brotherhood, and although he was never considered a full member of the group, his work appeared with theirs at the Royal Academy in 1850 and 1851; his work was praised by Ruskin in his *Pre-Raphaelitism*, and he was attacked along with the others by critics who could find no merit in the new school.[13] (*Convent Thoughts* [1851], perhaps his most frequently reproduced painting, is very much in the Pre-Raphaelite mode.) He felt in the end that his work had lost its individual qualities: in 1858 (the year in which this midnight encounter is supposed to have taken place), worried that his work drew too heavily on that of John Everett Millais, Charles stopped work on his painting of modern technology, *The Electric Telegraph*, and turned to writing.[14] In this he followed the example of his brother: Wilkie himself had also given up the brush for the pen, having exhibited a painting entitled *The Smuggler's Retreat* at the 1849 Royal Academy Exhibition. 'Skyed' in the Octagon Room, it failed to attract much attention from visitors to the exhibition, and never found a buyer. But if the twenty-four-year-old Wilkie's work did not attract critical or commercial interest, its very appearance at the Royal Academy must still have been a source of some satisfaction to him, coming as he did from a family that was so much a part of the art world. (As a result of his literary success, he was invited to the Academy's annual Exhibition dinner in 1864, to his evident satisfaction.) His grandfather, the County Wicklow-born William Collins, was a picture dealer, and the author of, inter alia, a poem, *The Slave Trade* (1788), and a memoir-cum-novel about the art world, *Memoirs of a Picture* (1805).[15] Wilkie and Charles's father, also William Collins, was a successful artist, and a member of the Royal Academy, and when in 1848 Wilkie published his first book, it was not a novel but a biography of his father, *Memoirs of the Life of William Collins, Esq., R. A.* Wilkie grew up surrounded by artists, and he was named for one of them, his godfather, Sir David Wilkie, RA, a pioneering figure in

British genre painting. It was not only the men of the family who were gifted in the visual arts, since Wilkie's maternal aunt, Margaret Sarah Carpenter, née Geddes, was a successful portrait and genre painter who exhibited 156 works at the Royal Academy between 1814 and 1866 (as a woman she was ineligible for membership of the Royal Academy, though there was a movement to change the rules in her favour); three of her children, William, Percy and Henrietta, also became painters.

We might assume, in short, that whatever his evident flair for narrative, Collins's *habitus* would have predisposed him to be sensitive to the power of images, to issues of colour, line, composition and spectatorship; we might further guess that the modality of the visual is important within the novel, and that his use of white as the novel's signature colour is significant.[16] (We might also note that by becoming a popular novelist Collins was courting a wider and more variegated audience than that aimed at by his family and friends.) That the visual has a peculiar importance in the narrative is given internal support by the fact that its central character and principal narrator is a second-generation drawing master who later earns money more anonymously by producing pictures for the illustrated newspapers. In this chapter, then, I want to try to do something rather obvious with a novel that might be thought to have already received its fair share of critical attention: to consider what whiteness might mean in *The Woman in White*. This is not something, I believe, that can be explained purely in terms of Collins's personal history: even if Millais's story were true, it would be a great coincidence if a single episode out of Collins's complicated private life struck such a chord with readers in 1859–60. Nor can we entirely understand the significance of white in terms of the narrative's own internal logic. Instead I want to argue that the novel's colour scheme – and its success – owed more to its resonance with the broader historical currents of these years. Whiteness, I will argue, is closely tied in the novel to the idea of mystery, but it is also aligned with modernity, with the distracted consciousness of the modern subject, and with the use of the sensational and spectacular to secure the attention of that subject.

Elsewhere I have argued that the sensation novel in general, with its deployment of suspense and invocation of nervous states, takes part in something resembling the temporal training of its readers for their part in industrial society; that these are novels for the railway age.[17] Here I want to foreground a different aspect of this fiction, examining how it relates to the shifting class relations of the 1860s, as much as to the history of modernization I was attempting in my earlier work. *The Woman in White* does indeed deploy suspense and invoke nervous states, but the narrative also represents the distracted consciousness of the urban crowd while simultaneously developing new techniques to capture its attention.[18] Crucially, the issue of attention links the sphere of aesthetics to the realm of mass politics; Collins's self-conscious preoccupation with the power of spectacle suggests a mission for the artist in the age of crowds, and connects his literary project to conservative reactions to the nascent power of the masses. But I will also suggest that the power of Collins's novel owes something to what might at first glance seem to be the very opposite of the modern age: the woman in white who appeared to Bernadette Soubirous at Massabielle Grotto, outside Lourdes, in February 1858.

* * *

It is tempting to assume that *The Woman in White*'s colour-coding is quasi-allegorical, the equivalent of a sort of moral chiaroscuro. We might, that is, assume that there is a contrast between the characters on the side of vulnerable but pure feminine goodness, Laura and Anne, half-sisters who both like to wear white, and the agents of darkness, notably Count Fosco, whose name means 'dark' or 'gloomy' in Italian, and Sir Percival Glyde, who resides at the dreary Blackwater Park. But this melodramatic opposition collapses almost at once: it fails to account for the good but swarthy Marian Halcombe, for example, but it also glosses over a more all-pervasive use of whiteness. Whiteness – like nervousness, as critics have noted – is everywhere in the novel, and not just among the good characters: Sir Percival, for example, turns 'of an awful whiteness all over' (p. 356), as the plot to confine his wife to an asylum nears its crisis. Count Fosco keeps a family of white mice about his person: 'They crawl all over him, popping in and out of his waistcoat, and sitting in couples, white as snow on his capacious shoulders' (p. 206); he terms them his 'forlorn white children' (p. 207). In a more traditional symbolic register, Marian associates the colour white with death. When she has her dream-vision of Walter's expedition in Central America, it is as a white mist that she imagines the fever that kills his fellow explorers: 'White exhalations twisted and curled up stealthily from the ground; approached the men in wreaths, like smoke; touched them; and stretched them out dead, one by one, in the places where they lay' (p. 248). Elsewhere, the white motif reappears in the form of the tombstone supposedly marking Laura Glyde's grave, and the scraps of paper on which Fosco scribbles his confession, until he has 'snowed himself up in paper' (p. 552).

Indeed, as critics have noted, at the heart of the novel's plot is not so much a woman in white as a piece of blank paper.[19] Walter finally uncovers the nature of the Secret so jealously guarded by Sir Percival Glyde when he walks from Old Welmingham to Knowlesbury to inspect the copy of the church register kept by the vestry clerk, the late M. Wansborough, and now maintained by his son. In one of the novel's many self-conscious passages, Walter approaches the pages of the Marriage Register with the same suppressed excitement that Collins's readers might be expected to derive from his novel: 'My hands were trembling – my head was burning hot – I felt the necessity of concealing my agitation as well as I could from the persons about me in the room' (p. 470). He has already seen the record of the marriage of Sir Percival Glyde's parents in the Register at Old Welmingham, but when he turns to that same page in the copy a shock awaits him:

I turned to the month of September, eighteen hundred and three. I found the marriage of the man whose Christian name was the same as mine. I found the double register of the marriages of the two brothers. And between those entries at the bottom of the page – ?

Nothing! Not a vestige of the entry which recorded the marriage of Sir Felix Glyde and Cecilia Jane Elster, in the register of the church!

My heart gave great bound, and throbbed as if it would stifle me. I looked again – I was afraid to believe the evidence of my own eyes ... The last entry on one page recorded the marriage of the man with my Christian name. Below it, there was a blank space – a space evidently left because it was too narrow to contain the entry of the marriages of the two brothers ... That space told the whole story! (pp. 470–1)

The blank space tells the whole story to the extent that all mystery stories, as Tzvetan Todorov showed many years ago, are built around an absence, a hole in the story: to narrate a mystery is to suppress information for the precise purpose of revealing it later. Wilkie Collins, writing an early version of what would come to be one of the dominant genres of modernity, recognized this essential fact of composition, and places a *mise en abyme* memorial to it within the text by ensuring that his amateur detective, unwinding the skein of the plot against his beloved Laura, finds at its very centre a literal blank. Anne Catherick, the woman in white, prefigures this blankness at the heart of the mystery novel, an empty space that must be introduced so that it can be 'filled in' later. In this light, she begins to look less like a real character and more a figure for mystery itself, a cipher.

But literally, at the level of the novel's plot, that white space in the register also reveals the whole story: that the entry in the original Marriage Register at the Old Welmingham church has been forged; that Sir Percival's awful Secret is that he is not in fact Sir Percival Glyde, Baronet, at all – his parents were unmarried, and as an illegitimate son he has no claim to his father's estate. His persecution of Anne Catherick has been driven by his fear of her knowledge of this secret, and his willingness to be involved in the plot to steal his wife's identity has been underwritten by a similar dread. Thus the long concatenation of events that seems to begin with Walter's midnight encounter with Anne Catherick on the road to London actually begins here, with the secret of illegitimacy.

The topos of the illegitimate usurpation of aristocratic power – sometimes appearing as the topos of the aristocratic secret – ties Collins's novel to the Gothic tales of the eighteenth century, a lineage that is often claimed more generally for the sensation novel (sensation, it can be argued, is updated Gothic, with castles in the Apennines replaced by more domestic landscapes: in Henry James's much-reproduced words, 'To Mr Collins belongs the credit for having introduced into fiction those most mysterious of mysteries, the mysteries which are at our own doors ... What are the Apennines to us, or we to the Apennines?').[20] Horace Walpole's genre-shaping *Castle of Otranto* (1764) depends on the extravagant treatment of the theme of usurpation, and appropriated power, legitimacy of title and concealed aristocratic crime appear as the themes of many subsequent Gothic novels, as well as of William Godwin's proto-detective novel, *Caleb Williams* (1794). But Sir Percival Glyde is no Manfred, and one might think that the spectre of *ancien régime* corruption and illegitimacy had much less purchase in the England of the 1860s than it had in Godwin's day (though it might still be considered a significant context for J. S. Le Fanu's sensation-cum-Gothic novel of 1868, *Uncle Silas*, which derives from an Irish rather than an English political background).

More importantly, the fact that Sir Percival's identity is founded on a blank scarcely distinguishes him from the other characters in this novel, in which loss of identity, or suppression of identity, is more or less the norm: Laura's is stolen, as is that of Anne Catherick (and she, like Sir Percival, is illegitimate); Marian, Laura and Walter are forced to live anonymously in the poorer parts of London to escape the surveillance of Sir Percival and Count Fosco; Pesca, like the Count, has to conceal the mark of the Brotherhood that reveals his former political allegiances; Mr and Mrs Rubelle are spies – like their employer, the Count – living under, one assumes, false names (of course to the extent that Walter claims to have changed the names of the actors in his account, they all come before us under false names). Although there are superficial resemblances, then, between Sir Percival and the tormented aristocratic villains of the Gothic novels (as there are between Count Fosco and the swarthy foreign villains of those narratives), his painful anxieties about his identity suggest his resemblance to other characters as much as they mark him as a man apart.

This is not to say that *The Woman in White* is a very early example of post-structuralist unease over identity. On the contrary, I want to argue that its all-pervasive concern with questions of the instability of identity mark it very much as a novel of its time. Whiteness in Collins's novel is not just the emblem of mystery but also the mark of this pervasive instability, and the difficulties of self-possession. The ultimate spectre of this instability is madness; the novel's most awful location is not Blackwater House but the private asylum for the insane, which for a time, at least, makes Laura into Anne.

Even later in the novel, when we are momentarily sidetracked from the plot's main drive and allowed to witness an episode of domestic intimacy, the status of the self seems peculiarly precarious, and we see Walter reduced to a state of simultaneous blankness and hypersensitivity. At the beginning of Part the Third, the three have left their Fulham refuge for a short holiday in 'a quiet town on the south coast' (p. 519), and it is there that Walter feels that he will be able to declare his love again to Laura, now almost restored to her former self. This time Marian does not oppose them, and even takes a hand in bringing them together. When she leaves Walter for a moment to bring in Laura, Walter goes into a reverie:

> I sat down at the window, to wait through the crisis of my life. My mind, in that breathless interval, felt like a total blank. I was conscious of nothing but a painful intensity of all familiar perceptions. The sun grew blinding bright; the white sea birds chasing each other far beyond me, seemed to be flitting before my face; the mellow murmur of the waves on the beach was like thunder in my ears. (p. 522)

Motifs that might be thought to represent future happiness – the coast as pastoral and restorative space, romantic love as transcendence, a window offering a vista of the future – offer in fact no respite from a blankness and hypersensitivity that threatens to collapse the distinction between self and world. The white theme reappears here as the seagulls who chase each other, suggestive in the collapse of perspective they bring of some disturbing sexual annunciation rather than soaring Romantic transcendence. (Curious though it may seem, we are not too far here from similar deployments in twentieth-century Modernism, from Yeats's rapacious swan, to Hemingway's 'white bird flown'; and those waves perform a similar function in the visual vocabulary of popular cinema – *From Here to Eternity* (1953) is a familiar example.) Even at this point in the novel, when the nightmare of the private asylum is behind them, Walter's nerves are stretched to the pitch of mental collapse, to an extent that seems out of all proportion to the tension of the moment.[21] Identity, then, is something precarious in this novel, and ordinary consciousness threatens to drift into reverie and even madness; people are blank cards who can be shuffled and rendered indistinguishable; and whiteness seems everywhere connected to these aspects of the novel. Why should this be?

To historicize the recurrence of whiteness/blankness and loss of self within *The Woman in White*, it is instructive to see how it is at once like and not like the novel that preceded it in serialization in *All the Year Round*, another tale of confused identities and induced madness: Charles Dickens's own *A Tale of Two Cities* (1859). Although Dickens's novel is at first glance more about the past than the present, it is actually a far more obviously political novel than that of Collins. Specifically, it uses the French Revolution to meditate upon the nature of historical change in the present. As any reader of the novel will remember, although it gives space to the crimes of the *ancien régime*, it evokes far more vividly the spectre of mob rule: the novel's wicked and selfish blue-blood autocrats never appear quite as terrifying as the many-headed hydra of the revolutionary crowd, with its capacity to overrun and absorb individuals. Nor is the revolutionary state in any sense an improvement on its predecessor: the Bastille, the apparent symbol of the oppressive power of the old state in *A Tale*'s opening chapters, reappears later as a symbol of Jacobin misrule, which has replaced a cruel order with a cruel chaos.

Dickens's target is, of course, Britain at the end of the 1850s rather than France in the 1790s. The decline of Chartism and the resounding success of the 1851 Great Exhibition at the Crystal Palace had done something to assuage the establishment's fear of the working class en masse, while also suggesting a way in which culture, broadly understood, could be used as an instrument of social management . But in the years leading up to the 1867 Reform Bill, it was clear that the fear of the masses had not gone away. Sometimes it surfaced in relatively displaced forms, as with the London garrotting panic of 1862, or the response to events at Morant Bay in 1865.[22] But fear of the crowd could also be triggered by more obvious factors: the demonstrations in Hyde Park in 1862, which featured clashes between pro- and anti-Garibaldi crowds, the latter containing many Irish Catholics (these were also the years of Fenianism, which represented a direct threat to the British state); and the Reform demonstrations in Hyde Park in 1866.[23]

In Dickens's novel, fear of the populace is made all the more vivid by its projection into a different time and place. Set during the French Revolution, the plot turns on the accidental resemblance between a dissolute London barrister, Sydney Carton, and a French aristocrat, Charles

Darnay (really Charles Evrémonde). Although he has renounced his title and estate, Darnay is imprisoned when he returns to France during the early months of the Revolution, and seems destined for the guillotine, despite the intervention of his father-in-law, Dr Manette. Manette has himself been a prisoner in the Bastille under the *ancien régime*, reduced to near madness by his lengthy incarceration there until he is 'returned to life' in the novel's opening chapters. Carton, who has all along loved Manette's daughter, Lucie, who becomes Darnay's wife, takes his double's place in the Bastille, allowing Darnay and his family to flee to England.[24]

But if the plot turns on the idea that, as in *The Woman in White*, two individuals can be interchangeable, the novel's most brilliantly realized moments dramatize the annihilation of all subjectivity in the revolutionary crowd, which appears in nightmarish form as a hysterical mob, crazed by blood (if white can be considered to be the signature colour in Collins's novel, in Dickens's it is red). Here the mob perform the Revolution's famous dance, the Carmagnole, around Lucie Darnay, who has ventured into the Place de la Bastille to allow her imprisoned husband to see her from his cell window:

There could not be fewer than five hundred people, and they were dancing like five thousand demons. There was no other music than their own singing. They danced to the popular Revolution song, keeping a ferocious time that was like a gnashing of teeth in unison. Men and women danced together, women danced together, men danced together, as hazard had brought them together. At first, they were a mere storm of coarse red caps and coarse woollen rags; but, as they filled the place, and stopped to dance about Lucie, some ghastly apparition of a dance-figure gone raving mad arose among them. They advanced, retreated, struck at one another's hands, clutched at one another's heads, spun round alone, caught one another and spun round in pairs, until many of them dropped. While those were down, the rest linked hand in hand, and all spun round together: then the ring broke, and in separate rings of two and four they turned and turned until they all stopped at once, began again, struck, clutched, and tore, and then reversed the spin, and all spun round another way. Suddenly they stopped again, paused, struck out the time afresh, formed into lines the width of the public way, and, with their heads low down and their hands high up, swooped screaming off. No fight could have been half so terrible as this dance. It was so emphatically a fallen sport – a something, once innocent, delivered over to all devilry – a healthy pastime changed into a means of angering the blood, bewildering the senses, and steeling the heart. Such grace as was visible in it, made it the uglier, showing how warped and perverted all things good by nature were become. The maidenly bosom bared to this, the pretty almost-child's head thus distracted, the delicate foot mincing in this slough of blood and dirt, were types of the disjointed time ... This was the Carmagnole. (pp. 307–8)

This is a nightmare vision of the absorption of individual identity and even individual physical agency into an unthinking mass. Dickens presents the crowd variously as a natural phenomenon ('a mere storm of coarse red caps and coarse woollen rags'), something with a fierce group consciousness ('keeping a ferocious time that was like a gnashing of teeth in unison'), and something mechanical with its own cyclical routines ('then the ring broke, and in separate rings of two and four they turned and turned until they all stopped at once ... and then reversed the spin').

The mob is simultaneously animated and brought into a species of temporary repose by sensational spectacle, and this the Revolution has provided in the form of the mass executions of aristocrats and other enemies of the state. At the centre of the new Paris stands a gleaming machine, the guillotine.

Above all, one hideous figure grew familiar as if it had been before the general gaze from the foundations of the world – the figure of the sharp female called La Guillotine ... It was the popular theme for jests; it was the best cure for headache, it infallibly prevented the hair from turning grey, it imparted a peculiar delicacy to the complexion, it was the National Razor which shaved close: who kissed La Guillotine, looked through the little window and sneezed into the sack. It was the sign of the regeneration of the human race. It superseded the Cross. Models of it were worn on breasts from which the Cross was discarded, and it was bowed down to and believed in where the Cross was denied. (p. 302)

The spectacle of public execution not only produces its own rituals: it has produced nothing short of a national religion, one that has as its iconic image a parody of the crucifixion, in which the instrument of death rather than its victim is the object of veneration; and this religion has even produced its own material culture, as if the revolutionaries could not get close enough to the killing machine ('models of it were worn on breasts'). Lest his readers too readily assume that such bloodthirsty mobs are to be found only among the French, Dickens has earlier shown us the almost equally ferocious audience at London's Old Bailey (Book 2, Chapters 2 and 3) and, albeit in comic mode, a London street mob, which makes a charivari of the (supposed) funeral of Roger Cly, a police spy (Book 2, Chapter 14). (Cly later turns up in Paris, again acting as a spy, this time for the revolutionary state, suggesting perhaps that the flipside of the annihilation of the self in the crowd is the surveillance of resistant individuals.) If the Great Exhibition and the museum movement suggested that the populace could be trained into new habits of improving recreation through the judicious use of material culture, Dickens's novel would seem to suggest that only the most violent of spectacles can hold the attention of the crowd, and that such spectacles always run the risk of further enflaming the mass they are meant to captivate.[25]

There are many parallels between *A Tale of Two Cities* and *The Woman in White*, so many that it is possible to see Collins's novel as a revision – or double – of that of Dickens. The theme of doubles is itself the most obvious resemblance between the two novels, the Carton/Darnay dyad reappearing as Anne/Laura. That theme shades into another, loss of identity, which appears in its strongest form in *A Tale* as Dr Manette's Bastille ordeal as a guiltless and nameless prisoner, and in Collins as Laura's (and indeed Anne's) experience of the private asylum, that favourite nightmare space of the sensation novel.[26] Manette all but loses his wits, becoming obsessed with his shoemaking; Laura loses her memory, and much of her vitality. Nor is the asylum/prison the only site for the control of others: spying, surveillance and secret societies recur in both novels, most obviously in the characters of Cly and Fosco, but also more pervasively, as with the minions employed by Sir Percival Glyde to watch Walter. (There are some more throwaway parallels between the two novels: for example, one might, without being too fanciful, see a nod to Madame Defarge and the knitting women of the revolution in the constant needlework of Countess Fosco.)

But there is a further link, and one that I think is essential to an understanding of Collins's work: like Dickens's novel, *The Woman in White* is also a tale of those two great nineteenth-century cities, Paris and London, though the former appears only in a cameo role. At the narrative's commencement Walter has his blood frozen by his moonlit meeting with Anne Catherick outside London; just before its end he is equally arrested by the sight of his old enemy, Count Fosco, laid out in the Paris Morgue. That Fosco's body has been removed from the Seine counterpoints, of course, another crucial episode from the novel's opening chapters: Walter's rescue of his friend Pesca from drowning at Brighton – attracted by the flailing of his 'two little white arms' (p. 4). It is this heroic deed that secures Pesca's devoted friendship, leads him to recommend Walter for a job as a drawing master at Limmeridge House (teaching, appropriately enough, watercolours), and ultimately ensures his willingness to betray his oath to the Brotherhood. But this English seaside episode too may have a Parisian origin, since it seems to parodically recall the opening of *A Tale of Two Cities*: just as Dr Manette is 'recalled to life', Pesca comically states that Walter 'found [him] dead at the bottom of the sea [through Cramp]' (pp. 6–7).

In literal terms, *The Woman in White*'s origins are also Parisian, since Collins borrowed the story from a collection of old French trials – he described it as 'a sort of French Newgate Calendar', which he found at a bookstall during a visit to Paris with Charles Dickens in 1856.[27] This is usually identified as Maurice Méjan's twenty-one-volume work *Recueil des Causes Célèbres et des arrêts qui les ont décidées*, published as a series of volumes between 1808 and 1814. Volume 3 contains the 'Affaire de Madame de Douhault', which describes how in 1787 a French widow – wearing a white dress as it happens – was drugged and confined to the Salpetrière under a different name by her relatives, who hoped to inherit her property by faking her death.

But the novel's origins are French in another and more important sense: it is a novel that both draws its energies from and thematizes those forces of modernization that Walter Benjamin sees most vividly present in nineteenth-century Paris, the city he places at the heart of his Arcades project. Here, I want to argue, we can locate a significant point of divergence between the two novelists. Where Dickens's Paris is primarily a city of political modernization, a double for London in the present, for Benjamin, and I want to argue for Collins, the French capital also appears to stand for more intimate forms of modernization: the modernization of the self, linked in complex ways to the transformation of the fabric of the city and of its consumer economy. One symptom of this divergence is that what Dickens presents as the political mob out for blood appears in Collins as the crowd out for entertainment, an entity that comes to stand for Collin's understanding of his own readership. Walter Benjamin's account of nineteenth-century Paris in 'Capital of the Nineteenth Century' is some help here. In this essay, or rather précis, the city is the site not just of the Ur-forms of capitalist modernity in the Arcades and the other flotsam and jetsam of an emergent consumer culture, but also the site of the transformation of subjectivity itself, which involves the retraining of the subject for life in an urban habitat, one characterized by the shocks of the street, and by the anonymity of the crowd, but also by a kaleidoscope of spectacle-based leisure. Two of the key figures in Benjamin's analysis of Parisian life are the crowd and the *flâneur*, the lone dandy-cum-artist who, for a brief period longer, experiences the city and the crowd aesthetically, before being ultimately absorbed into them. He is not the sinister 'Man of the Crowd' of Edgar Allan Poe's enigmatic short story of urban life; for Benjamin, following Baudelaire, he is the convalescent narrator who observes the man of the crowd from a café window, treating the street as a landscape. But this is also to say that the relationship between the *flâneur* and the crowd figures that between the individual and the masses, or that between the artist or writer in the marketplace and his increasingly unknown and unknowable public. It is not that the author of 'The Unknown Public' is not interested in the rise of Demos, but in his work such matters appear in a different form, refracted into issues of audience and attention. Further, he is as much attracted by the energy of the crowd as repelled by it – there is something of Baudelaire in *The Woman in White* as well as something of Dickens.

Collins knew the Paris described by Benjamin at first hand: a lifelong Francophile, he made frequent visits to Paris, where he delighted in the art galleries, the theatres, the shops (struck by the low prices compared to London, he buys boots and opera glasses, among other things), the cafés and restaurants, the sights of the city, and perhaps most of all the relative freedom he enjoyed there. He writes of the crowds of Paris as an essential part of the experience: 'Paris is twice as full as it was last year. The Palais Royal is … more crammed with [a] heterogeneous crowd of people every evening than even I saw it before … in short Paris flourishes its "flesh pots of Egypt" and nourishes "the old man Adam" with the serious industry and perseverance of former days.'[28] He saw at first hand the Haussmanization that Benjamin describes, the carving of the modern structure of boulevards out of the more chaotic fabric of the medieval streets. In 1853, for example, he finds the Tuileries 'altered … past all recognition by the commencement of a magnificent new street, running from the Orlace to the Hotel de Ville. Old houses were being demolished, new houses were [springing] up, over nearly a mile of space in the heart of Paris. The street will be the broadest, longest, and grandest in the world, when it is finished.'[29] The modern city Collins encountered on these trips was characterized not by its high polish, but by its inchoateness and unevenness. Crumbling, mean medieval streets still co-existed with the classical grandeur of the new boulevards; *grand magasins* competed for customers not only with older shops, but with street vendors.

In letters written during two earlier visits he highlights the less savoury, if no less spectacular, aspect of the city, and in these we glimpse the understanding of the crowd that will later appear in the novel. In Paris in September 1844, he writes to his mother to describe a 'a glorious subject for Charlie [*sc.* Charles Collins] – a dead soldier laid out naked at the Morgue; like an unsaleable codfish all by himself upon the slab. He was a fine muscular fellow who had popped into the water in the night and was exposed to be recognized by his friends.'[30] The following year, on his way back from the Musée des Beaux Arts, he visits the Morgue again:

A body of a young girl had just been fished out of the river. Her bosom was black and blue. I suppose she had been beaten into a state of insensibility and then flung into the Seine. The spectators of this wretched sight were, for the most part, women and children.[31]

In this city of flux Collins notes that high-cultural consumption (he sees Rachel in *Les Horaces* at the Theatre Français, he visits the Louvre and the Historical Exhibition at the Musée des Beaux Arts, and lingers for a long period of contemplation before Vernet's *Taking of the Smalah* at Versailles) competes with more democratic pleasures: the Morgue, the cafés, the shops and the boulevards themselves.

Where *A Tale of Two Cities* seems to identify the urban crowd as a monster to be feared and avoided, Collins recognizes that it also represents a source of vitality. In this light we might consider Baudelaire's comments in 'The Painter of Modern Life', his homage to Constantin Guys (published in 1863, but written, like *The Woman in White*, in 1859–60), that the artist, like Poe's convalescent observer in 'The Man of the Crowd', can find his inspiration in the street life of the modern city more than in classical forms, and that he 'moves into the crowd as though into an enormous reservoir of electricity'.[32] This same tapping of the energy of the street, this same willingness to find artistic material in the present, characterizes Collins's work from *Basil* (1852) on (his earlier, and now largely unread, novels, are historical romances), and might be thought of as a significant aspect of sensation culture more generally, with its 'newspaper novels'. Like Guys, who worked for the *Illustrated London News* and *Punch*, among other publications, or indeed like Baudelaire himself, Collins's raw material was 'modernity ... the transient, the fleeting, the contingent; [which] is one half of art, the other being the eternal and the immovable'.[33]

While much of Collins's experience of Paris as the capital of nineteenth-century modernity undergoes a sea change to become the stuff of fiction, some of it reappears almost whole. He reworks his memories of the Paris Morgue to create one of the novel's crucial scenes, Hartright's sight of the dead Count Fosco in Paris (where Hartright has gone at the behest of the illustrated newspaper for which he works, in order to examine a new technique in engraving). On a sightseeing visit to Notre Dame, his attention is caught by the crowd:

Approaching Notre Dame by the river-side, I passed on my way the terrible dead-house of Paris – the Morgue. A great crowd clamoured and heaved round the door. There was evidently something inside which excited the popular curiosity, and fed the popular appetite for horror ... I should have walked on to the church if the conversation of two men and a woman on the outskirts of the crowd had not caught my ear. They had just come out from seeing the sight in the Morgue, and the account they were giving of the dead body to their neighbours described it as the corpse of a man – a man of immense size, with a strange mark on his left arm ... The moment those words reached me I stopped and took my place with the crowd going in ... Other vengeance than mine had followed that fated man from the theatre to his own door – from his own door to his refuge in Paris. Other vengeance than mine had called him to the day of reckoning, and had exacted from him the penalty of his life ... Slowly, inch by inch, I pressed in with the crowd, moving nearer and nearer to the great glass screen that parts the dead from the living at the Morgue – nearer and nearer, till I was close behind the front row of spectators, and could look in ... There he lay, unowned, unknown, exposed to the flippant curiosity of a French mob! There was the dreadful end of that long life of degraded ability and heartless crime! Hushed in the sublime repose of death, the broad, firm, massive face and head fronted us so grandly that the chattering Frenchwomen about me lifted their hands in admiration, and cried in shrill chorus, 'Ah, what a handsome man!' The wound that had killed him had been struck with a knife or dagger exactly over his heart. No other traces of violence appeared about the body except on the left arm, and there, exactly in the place where I had seen the brand on Pesca's arm, were two deep cuts in the shape of the letter T, which entirely obliterated the mark of the Brotherhood. His clothes, hung above him, showed that he had been himself conscious of his danger – they were clothes that had disguised him as a French artisan. For a few moments, but not for longer, I forced myself to see these things through the glass screen. I can write of them at no greater length, for I saw no more. (pp. 580–1)

It is a scene with multiple significance in the novel, performing structural, narrative and thematic functions. In terms of the novel's structure, this shocking encounter is the long-delayed echo of the encounter with the Woman in White at the narrative's opening; the sudden appearance of the ethereal Anne Catherick is now brought into implicit contrast with the bulky dead flesh of the Count.[34] (It is not the only time that the novel implicitly links them, of course: at Blackwater Park, Marian is startled by the sudden appearance on the road of the Count, who stands before her as if he had 'sprung up out of the earth' (p. 245), the phrase that Walter earlier uses to describe Anne Catherick's first appearance (p. 1).) In terms of the novel's revenge narrative, this is a sensational scene that has been long anticipated, since we already know that the Count is a member of the mysterious Brotherhood, the revolutionary society of which Pesca is also a member. Walter has told us that even he knows how such secret societies hunt down their renegade members with ruthless efficiency, so we should know Fosco will be found in the end:

Considering the subject only as a reader of newspapers, cases recurred to my memory, both in London and in Paris, of foreigners found stabbed in the streets, whose assassins could never be traced – of bodies and parts of bodies thrown into the Thames and the Seine, by hands that could never be discovered – of deaths by secret violence which could only be accounted for in one way. (pp. 540–1)

In thematic terms, this Gothicized version of Foucauldian surveillance has its own importance, especially in the way the historical event that provides the context for the novel's latter half, the 1851 Crystal Palace Exhibition, is described as having brought such surveillance (and counter-surveillance) into Britain:

The year of which I am now writing was the year of the famous Crystal Palace Exhibition in Hyde Park. Foreigners in unusually large numbers had arrived already, and were still arriving in England. Men were among us by hundreds whom the ceaseless distrustfulness of their governments had followed privately, by means of appointed agents, to our shores. (p. 525)

The scene at the Paris Morgue might be considered to be the culmination of this visuality, in which the penetrating glance yields to more literal penetration, and surveillance turns to murder.

But it also takes us into a different modality of the visible: spectacle. What I want to foreground here is not the object of this secret surveillance, now turned into a public spectacle, but that public itself, the crowd that gathers to gape through the glass at Fosco's body, and Hartright's presence within that mass.[35] It is one of the scenes in which the novel is at its most self-reflexive: we, Collins's eager readers, are captivated by the sight of Fosco's body, laid out 'like an unsaleable codfish all by himself upon the slab', as Collins had earlier described the dead soldier he himself saw in Paris; but we are also brought to contemplate our own activity through our alignment with the Parisian crowd of gawkers. To be a page-turning reader of sensation fiction is to merge with that sensation-hungry crowd. This is not quite Dickens's vision of the bloodthirsty mob that envelops Lucie Darnay, dancing its macabre Carmagnole around her, nor is it the well-behaved artisan crowd at the Crystal Palace, whose benign conduct helped to assuage ruling-class fears. It is at once less dangerous and less definite, less knowable. But in it, I think we see the ultimate source of the novel's concern with unstable identity, precarious consciousness and blankness.

Consider the novel's 'official' villains, Sir Percival Glyde and Count Fosco. The former is a reduced, papier maché version of the aristocratic Gothic villains of the past, just as Blackwater Park is a domesticated version of the castle in the Apennines. The latter character, to be sure, is one of the great creations of Victorian fiction. However, it is very difficult to see what political force Fosco might be seen to represent. A one-time member of the revolutionary Brotherhood turned counter-revolutionary Royalist government agent, his principal political cause nonetheless appears to be himself; in this respect his chameleon nature suggests that he is at least in part Collins's reworking of Dickens's turncoat spy, Roger Cly. Fosco's final recourse is to try to blend into the crowd, to disguise himself as 'a French artisan'. The great individualist becomes a man of the crowd, only to later be turned into an object of their slack-jawed interest. In this absorption by the crowd, of course, he follows the example of Walter, Marian and Laura, who find lodgings 'of the humblest kind' over a newsagent's shop 'in a populous and poor neighbourhood' of London, where they live under an assumed name (p. 379). Indeed, long before this Walter has already been represented as having being swallowed up by the crowd. The lawyer, Gilmore, describes a happenstance London street encounter with a much-changed Walter:

As I came out into Holborn a gentleman walking by rapidly stopped and spoke to me. It was Mr. Walter Hartright ... If he had not been the first to greet me I should certainly have passed him. He was so changed that I hardly knew him again. His face looked pale and haggard – his manner was hurried and uncertain – and his dress, which I remembered as neat and gentleman-like when I saw him at Limmeridge, was so slovenly now that I should really have been ashamed of the appearance of it on one of my own clerks. (pp. 138–9)

Having emerged from the masses on the pavement, Walter questions Gilmore about Laura before vanishing back into its anonymity: 'He took my hand, pressed it hard, and disappeared among the crowd without saying another word' (p. 140). (It is also to be borne in mind that this is a novel of which the most famous scene, that midnight encounter on the London road, is itself a stylized version of an ordinary street encounter, from which the crowd has been removed, as it were, to focus the action.)

But what is this crowd that is both a refuge and a threat? It is not Dickens's crowd, the mob, a phobic version of mass democracy, that haunts Collins's pages. Jonathan Loesberg astutely suggested some years ago that the sensation novel encodes the 'fear of a general loss of social identity from the merging of the classes – a fear that was commonly expressed in the debate over social and parliamentary reform in the late 1850s and 1860s'.[36] But Collins is not simply registering the fears of his own class; his novel is at once an experiment in capturing the attention of the masses, and a meditation on the place of the artist under the new dispensation. It is the crowd of gawkers, or *badauds*, outside the Paris Morgue as much as potential Hyde Park demonstrators who underwrite the anxieties about selfhood in his work. The gawkers who come to admire Fosco are a very thinly disguised figure for his own readership, the better-off section of the unknown public who dramatically increased the circulation of *AYR*. It is not, then, the despotic aristocratic past that simultaneously threatens and animates in *The Woman in White*: it is the future – and not only the political future of the 1867 franchise reform, but a more general age of the masses.

To recognize the importance of the crowd in the novel might help us to read it in a new way. Ann Cvetkovich peruasively argues that what *The Woman in White* does is to distract us from Walter's upward mobility through the sensation plot itself.[37] I want to suggest that it is not so much Walter's upward mobility that is dissimulated as his reassignment to a different sector of the cultural market: he begins the novel as a drawing master, whose principal clients are the gentry and those sections of the upper-middle classes who strive to emulate them, and by the novel's end he is presumably saved from the need to work through the prospect of his son's inheritance of Limmeridge. But by then he has learned to earn his bread a different way, by working for the illustrated papers, and it is in fact while working in this capacity that he travels to Paris and happens upon Fosco's bloated corpse at the Morgue. Walter initially appears before us as dependent on the patronage of the upper class, and by the novel's end we might assume that he has entered that class by the side door, as it were, but for much of the narrative he takes his place in the popular marketplace (again there are curious echoes here of the life of Constantin Guys, who worked as a tutor of French and drawing for an English family, the Girtins, before finding employment with the illustrated papers).[38]

It is not difficult, I hope, to see that this particular career trajectory is only a slightly disguised version of that of Collins himself. The son of a member of the Royal Academy, as we have seen he for a period must have had some hopes of following in his father's footsteps, or so the submission to the RA Exhibition of 1849 of *The Smuggler's Retreat* indicates (his father had died two years earlier, so this was not simply a gesture to please him). If his fine-art ambitions had succeeded, this would have placed him in a situation not dissimilar to Walter's: dependent on the patronage of the wealthy minority, the landed aristocracy, as well as the newly important captains of industry and merchant princes. Of course, this is not what happened, and Collins ended up working in a different mode, the verbal rather than the visual, but also courting a much broader section of the market. His new audience was not just the novel-reading public, but readers of Dickens's *All the Year Round*, a tuppeny weekly magazine that very deliberately set out to capture a larger share of the market than that of the new shilling weeklies, let alone the more austere monthly magazines.[39]

Despite strong competition *AYR* succeeded in securing a wide readership, with an estimated circulation of 100,000, rising to up to 300,000 for the Christmas issues, and it achieved this position in a short space of time not least through the enormous success of Collins's novel. If this is not the mass market as we now understand it, it is so by the standards of mid-Victorian Britain. Collins's *habitus* equipped him to deal with the market for high culture; whether by choice or not he found himself in quite a different marketplace, on the cusp on an emergent mass market for fiction.[40] The writer of 'The Unknown Public' increasingly wanted to capture that public: by 1867, angry at the poor sales of *Armadale*, he writes to his mother of his plans to pitch his work directly at the penny journals, to see what a new public will think of him.[41] Two days later he returns to the same idea, showing a keen sense of the potential of what Norman Feltes terms the 'commodity text': 'we shall see one of these days, what the books will do in another form, and at another price'.[42] The success of *The Moonstone* in 1868 may in part have diverted him from this plan, but he returned to it in later years, writing for the syndicate Tillotson's, and thus reaching a public much wider than that of Mudie's circulating library, that arbiter of middle-class literary taste.

Collins's trajectory indicates one of the things that 'sensation' stands for in the 1860s: it registers, albeit somewhat obliquely, a reconstitution of the market for cultural goods. On the one hand Britain in the 1860s no longer seemed to face quite so desperate a struggle between workers and rulers, or between labour and capital, and culture became increasingly recognized as a way of securing hegemony over the working class. The gradual erosion of the 'taxes on knowledge' (*sc.* stamp duty, abolished in 1855, and paper tax in 1861) was one aspect of this détente.[43] But this in turn facilitated the expansion of a more profit-driven form of culture, of which the many new literary magazines were a part: the Arnoldian moment of culture as a substitute religion, with a small number of high priests, and the rapid expansion of commercial publishing that seems its opposite, were, in fact, hard to separate. This transformation of the culture industry was not confined to the sphere of letters, of course: as Richard Altick suggests, the old 'shows of London' began to be replaced by new commercial fare by the middle of the nineteenth century; and as Peter Bailey has shown, the lineaments of the modern culture industry began to be visible.[44]

That 'sensation' encodes a transformation of the cultural marketplace returns us to the Paris Morgue, and the spectacles provided by both Fosco's body and the body of the crowd itself. Walter had gone to Paris to investigate a new technique in illustration, seemingly a new form of engraving. Whether he finds the new technique useful or not we never discover, but we might surmise that what he does learn is one technique for capturing the minds of

a mass audience: sensationalism, the means to 'stagger the public into attention', as Collins puts it in a letter to W. H. Wills, enclosing the first number
of *The Woman in White* for serialization in *All the Year Round*.[45] What was
needed, that is, was to create an 'effect', to use the contemporary term that
circulated between the criticism of the visual arts and that of the novel, and
that implied an essentially materialist conception of aesthetics, and the possibility of managing response, as Martin Meisel has shown.[46] That Fosco's
body holds the crowd reveals to us Collins's self-awareness as a creator of
sensation. But there is something else at stake here with the confrontation
of gaping crowd and Fosco-as-spectacle. Fosco has all along been the most
magnetic character in the narrative for the other characters. His cheerful
ebullience, his considerable intellect, and not least his almost mesmeric powers over others make him not just a formidable criminal, but also a vivid
character. Review after review of the novel singles out Fosco for praise as the
novel's greatest success in characterization, as the most lifelike of Collins's
creatures. For the *Times* reviewer he is 'very vividly portrayed, and is the one
interesting character of the work'; for the *Spectator* 'the delineation of Count
Fosco was a far higher artistic effort than constructing the plot'; for Mrs
Oliphant in *Blackwood*'s, 'no villain of the century, so far as we are aware,
comes within a hundred miles of him'; even the hostile writer of the *Saturday
Review* was prepared to concede that Fosco was 'drawn with much more
animation than the rest'.[47] Thus even those reviewers who are most critical
to what they see as Collins's sacrifice of characterization to plot are prepared
to see in Fosco an exception. For Fosco to be reduced to don an artisan's
clothes, and then to be further reduced to the level of a popular amusement,
may seem a particularly harsh brand of poetic justice. But it also suggests
that the form of subjectivity that Count Fosco represents – that of the Great
Man – is doomed in the age of crowds. The larger-than-life individual, the
self-styled man of destiny, is in the end overrun by the masses. (He will, of
course, come to exert a powerful attraction for Collins's descendants among
the writers of popular fiction: such characters as Dr Nikola, Dr Fu Manchu
and Professor Moriarty all owe him a debt.)

What replaces Fosco is the crowd itself, with its drifting and unfocused
consciousness, the logical opposite of Fosco's astonishing powers of focus
and concentration. But that drifting consciousness, which we might
assume to be that of Collins's anonymous readers as much as his Parisian
gawkers, is also imagined by Collins to be susceptible of unification, of
capture through moments of local sensation or through the relentless
deployment of the hermeneutic code, the Secret. I am assuming here a
continuity between types of spectatorship (that of characters, readers) that

may seem merely fanciful, and ahistorical at that. But in fact a similar collapse of levels is imagined by a number of Collins's contemporary reviewers. Here is one of the more hostile (possibly E. S. Dallas) writing in the *Saturday Review*, criticizing Collins's subordination of his characters to the needs of the plot:

None of his characters are to be seen looking about them. They are not occupied in by-play. They are not staring at the spectators, or, if they are, they are staring listlessly and vacantly, like witnesses who are waiting to be called before the court, and have nothing to do until their turn arrives. *There they stand, most of them, like ourselves, in rapt attention*, on the stretch to take their share in the action of the central group – their eyes bent in one direction – their movement converging upon one centre – half-painted, sketchy figures, grouped with sole relation to the unknown mystery in the middle. The link of interest that binds them is that they are all interested in the great secret. By the time the secret is disclosed, the bond of unity will have been broken – the action of the drama in which they figure will have been finished – and they will go on their own ways, in twos and threes, and never meet again.[48] (my emphasis)

It is a striking passage in many respects, not least for the way it seems to generate a vividly imagined landscape out of an account of Collins's handling of his minor characters. But what is of interest to us here is that it quietly equates the subordination of the novel's minor characters to considerations of plot with a similar subordination of the novel's readers, and it imagines both as a crowd detained by some striking incident, that is to say very like the crowd in Collins's Morgue scene, 'their eyes bent in one direction – their movement converging upon one centre – half-painted, sketchy figures, grouped with sole relation to the unknown mystery in the middle'. This equation of characters and readers is not by any means unique to *The Spectator*'s reviewer: Mrs Oliphant's much-cited review claims that 'the reader's nerves are affected like the hero's' by the resemblance of the Woman in White and Laura Fairlie; 'he feels the thrill of the untoward resemblance, an ominous painful mystery. He, too, is chilled by a confused and unexplainable alarm.'[49]

Collins's original readers felt that they were physically gripped by the novels, and to a lesser or greater extent this same effect was associated with his rivals and imitators. As a poem in the *Comic News* of 30 July 1864 puts it:

> When Man upon these pages looks,
> How spell-bound he remains!
> His eyes, his heart, his mind, his soul;
> Fixed like the 'Man in Chains'.[50]

The estimates of Collins's achievements as a novelist that came in the 1880s consistently comment on this quality of his narratives. Here is the art critic of *The Times*, Harry Quilter, in an 1888 appreciation of Collins's oeuvre:

However intricate the plot may be, however numerous the people, we feel more and more certain, with every page we read, that every detail and every action, nay, even every speech, is helping on the development of some purpose, which we cannot guess, but dimly foreshadow. The conviction that this is so, holds the interest as in a vice, and excites an attention to the less obvious parts of the story, which is proportionately intensified in its more exciting portions.[51]

The following year, in an unsigned obituary article, M. W. Townsend isolated this same forceful quality: 'the interest goes on accumulating till the looker-on – the reader is always placed in that attitude – is rapt out of himself by strained attention'.[52]

The novel contains its own self-conscious commentary on the creation of such vice-like effects in a passage, which brings us back to where we began, Collins's painterly tendencies. As I noted earlier, the plot of the novel hinges on a blank, the blank space in the copy of the parish register that makes Walter realize that Sir Percival is in fact illegitimate, and thus not Sir Percival at all. The false Sir Percival, whose wealth and power has been based on a forgery, is shortly after this quite literally expunged from the narrative by the fire at the old church at Welmingham, burnt alive in the same flames that destroy his forgery in the original register. In one of the novel's many ironic touches, it is Walter who is asked to put a name to the blackened remains. Collins strives for vividness of effect in this nocturne, one of two such scenes in the novel where a crowd gathers around a dead body:

I was standing inside a circle of men. Three of them, opposite to me, were holding lanterns low down to the ground. Their eyes, and the eyes of all the rest, were fixed silently and expectantly on my face. I knew what was at my feet – I knew why they were holding the lanterns so low to the ground.

'Can you identify him, sir?

My eyes dropped slowly. At first I saw nothing under them but a *coarse canvas cloth*. The dripping of the rain on it was audible in the dreadful silence. I looked up, along the cloth; and there at the end, stark and grim and black, in the yellow light – there was his dead face. (my emphasis, p. 481)

It is a meticuously worked piece, designed for narrative as well as visual impact, with its carefully delayed climax, sound effects, multiple points of view and Gothic lighting. The lookers-on here, like the reader, have indeed been rapt out of themselves by a particularly grisly spectacle. The site of this spectacle is not incidental: we have been carefully told that the church is very old, 'an ancient weather-beaten building, with heavy but-tresses at its sides, and a clumsy square tower in front' (p. 457). It contains ancient (presumably pre-Reformation) wood-carvings, 'portraits of the twelve apostles in wood – and not a whole nose among 'em. All broken and wormeaten, and crumbling to dust at the edges – as brittle as crockery … and as old as the church, if not older' (p. 460). The descendants of the same people who might once have been brought together by the religious icons of the medieval church are now gathered around a secular object of wonder – a local sensation (it is perhaps a deliberate echo of Dickens's use of the guillotine-crucifix as that which holds the attention of the Parisian mob). As with the crowd who gather around Fosco in the morgue, we can easily read this as a self-conscious commentary on the sort of effects that the modern author can – or must – use to secure the wandering attention of his distracted readership. But we might also note that Collins winks at us here, as it were, to tell us that he, the second-generation artist, the son of William Collins, RA, brother of Charles Allston Collins, and one-time RA exhibitor himself, knows exactly what he is doing, even if his painting must be done on that 'coarse canvas cloth' for an unknown and possibly unknowable audience. For some readers, at least, the novel is holding out the possibility of a more intellectual relation to the all-absorbing text.

The Woman in White, a novel that was seen by some reviewers as embodying a bad new modernity, can be characterized more accurately as a novel about the age of crowds, and about the place of the artist in that age. Perhaps sensitized by his experience of the consumer's paradise of Paris, Collins recognized a new dynamic of distracted spectatorship, and the first great sensation novel records one aspect of that new dynamic in the scattered consciousness and lost wits of his characters, as well as in the fragmentary form of the narrative. But he also deploys and represents the 'fixing' of attention, the way in which the crowd – and the reader – can be held spellbound by sufficiently strong material.[53] The whiteness of the woman in white is at once the blankness of modern distracted conscious-ness and the representation of the dazzling (if temporary) cure for that dis-traction in sensation and spectacle.

* * *

The spellbound faces drawn to the drowned body of Fosco laid out on a slab in the Paris Morgue, and to the scorched body of Sir Percival, offer us two of Collins's self-aware representations of the relationship between spectacle and attention, of an aesthetics of shock in an era of emergent mass literacy. But what, finally, of the first appearance of the Woman in

White herself, an episode that is somewhat different from that of the subsequent spectacular scenes involving Fosco and Glyde? Where does that
apparition come from? As I suggested at the beginning of this chapter,
it is not from Collins's meeting with Caroline Graves. It may be simply
a painterly night-piece that also draws on the long oral tradition of solitary travellers and supernatural encounters, such as the White Ladies
or Dames Blanches of French folklore. But what kind of supernatural is
this? In a recent article Susan M. Griffin suggests that Collins draws on
contemporary anti-Catholic discourse for his sermons to the nerves: tales
of the horrors of convent life (e.g. *The Awful Disclosures of Maria Monk*
(1836)) and the abuse of the confessional by Svengali-like Catholic priests
provided him with an example of how to combine mystery and shock, but
also with a narrative mode (the evidentiary narrative), plot materials (tales
of escaped nuns), characters (the Jesuitical Fosco), and not least iconography (the nun-like woman in white, who has escaped from an asylum
rather than a convent).[54]

However, it is also possible that, consciously or not, Collins is drawing
upon a rather different religious source, a famous encounter with a woman
in white that stands in a curious relationship to modern spectacular culture. On 11 February 1858 the fourteen-year-old Bernadette Soubirous experienced the first of her Marian visions outside the town of Lourdes. At first
she described it as 'something white', or as a white lady; later, she claimed, it
represented itself to her as 'the Immaculate Conception', or the Virgin Mary.
Soubirous's experiences soon attracted crowds of fascinated spectators, who
looked on as she appeared to go into a trance or reverie. It also, of course,
drew the attention of the authorities, local and later national, and eventually
of the Vatican.[55] The London *Times* soon picked up the story, not least, perhaps, because it pleased them to see that, for all the splendour of Napoleon's
III's Paris, France still laboured under a 'strange mixture of irreligion and
superstition'.[56] That the apparition seemed to resemble a similar occurrence
in 1846 at La Salette, near Grenoble, suggested to *The Times* a predisposition
on the part of the French for such dubious religious tendencies. (With the
benefit of hindsight we might speculate that it was the very pace of modernization rather than some primitive survival that gave people an appetite for
Marian apparitions.[57]) The period from the 1830s to the 1870s sees a flurry of
Marian apparitions in France. Other such apparitions were to follow, including those at Knock, in Ireland, in 1879, and Fatima in Portugal in 1917, in
counterpoint to the spread of modern technologies of the image.[58]

By September, irritated by the way the Parisian papers had begun to
use the events to political (and anti-British) ends, *The Times* was wrathful

enough to devote a leader to the French apparitions, condemning the 'formalism' that led France to a repetition with variations of any phenomenon that excited interest, in this case the

perpetual repetition of a portentous miracle: This is the Virgin, who is supposed to show herself here or there in a field, at a mountain cave, or some other out of the way place, to a peasant girl, or some children, or anybody not very capable of testing the value of the apparition.[59]

Continuing in the same vein, it poked fun at 'the monthly appearance of the Virgin, sometimes in a stage costume, sometimes in a ball dress of white muslin'. Where the miracles of the New Testament were meaningful, the newspaper could see little meaning in the appearance of the Virgin Mary 'in the capricious character of a pixie, or a White Lady of Avenel'.[60] Some of the hostility of these reports derives from traditional Anglo-French rivalry, as well from actual fears of invasion by the new Empire during these years. But we might also speculate that Lourdes acted as an unwelcome reminder of the susceptibility of crowds: such primitive popular enthusiasm might also appear at home. The France of 1858, in other words, like the France of 1789–93 in Dickens's *Tale*, provides a screen on which to project domestic fears.

What binds the world of Marian apparitions in white muslin to the world of Marian Halcombe and Laura Fairlie? The ghostly apparition of Anne Catherick is the most obvious connection, but it is worth recalling that Collins's novel is also marked by dream visions, premonitions, and the heavy hand of destiny guiding Walter along on his journey. Dickens, as we have seen, represented the modern spectacle of the guillotine as a grotesque and secularized form of an older form of religious experience. While Collins's view of the crowd differs from that of his friend, he may have felt that his special effects, if they were to hold successfully the unknown public, would have to draw on the otherworldly, to give us a frisson as much as a shock, to make us doubt our senses, and to hold us somewhere between belief and the fear of illusion. The secular spectacle of the Paris Morgue would have to be supplemented by the spiritual power of something like the Massabielle Grotto; where *The Times* saw signs of dangerous French enthusiasm, Collins saw a potentially useful effect. The whiteness of the woman in white may also, then, be his way of 'staggering us into attention' with a carefully judged dose of the numinous. In 1867–8, Matthew Arnold in *Culture and Anarchy* would present culture as something like a substitute for religion for a mass society; in 1859, Collins seems to have imagined a different set of relationships among religion, culture and the masses: religious experience could be shorn of its theological and spiritual aspects and reduced to a pleasurable shiver, a commodity experience like any other, a ride on a ghost train, or a trip to see 'Pepper's Ghost', the sensation of 1863.[61] In the next chapter we shall see that Dion Boucicault shared this insight: the first of the sensation dramas, *The Colleen Bawn*, gave its audiences shock and suspense, but also offered a glimpse into another world, with its own adaptation of the grotto of apparitions, the Water Cave in which an Irish peasant, Myles-na-Coppaleen, witnesses 'something white'.

CHAPTER 2

The many lives of the Colleen Bawn: pastoral spectacle

What's this? It's a woman – there's something white there.

The Colleen Bawn, II.vi

Over the course of the 1860s, the 'sensation novel' solidified as a new narrative form, and it is still a readily understood term to the literary historian. But the novel does not have sensation all to itself, and indeed when the term 'sensation' first came into widespread use in the early 1860s to describe cultural goods, it was more often identified with the theatre than with fiction.[1] As in the case of the novel, the term 'sensation drama' often denoted a concern on the part of middle-class commentators that the taste of consumers of their own caste, the theatre-goers of London's West End, was being corrupted by the cheap and nasty cultural food of another class. There is a similar perception that social class and taste are not properly aligned, and again such perceptions tend to cohere around the 'effects' that the theatre was striving for, in this case the kind of spectacle associated with the lower-middle-class and working-class 'transpontine' theatres.[2] For veteran playgoer Henry Morley, lamenting what he sees as the decline of the stage in the early 1860s, part of the problem was 'the temptation ... to meet debility [with] stimulants'.[3] And stimulants there were. Where Collins and his followers describe sensational moments, in the theatre these moments are brought to life: athletic performances, lighting, realistic sets, atmospheric music and mechanical devices of various kinds, including elaborate trapdoors and optical illusions of the 'Pepper's Ghost' variety, were all deployed to create 'sensation scenes' that would not only draw the crowds, but hold them in rapt attention. Last-minute rescues, exploding river boats and burning buildings were only some of the set pieces that appeared, tilting the balance of drama away from dialogue and towards pure spectacle. As with the sensation novel, contemporary settings helped to close the distance between audience and spectacle, and create a sense of dramatic immediacy.

But curiously, when sensation drama first arrives, it comes not as a tale of the times, like *The Woman in White* and its many imitators, but as a costume drama, complete with a red-cloaked peasant heroine and a wicked hunchback. On 1 October 1860, the theatre advertisements in *The Times* contained a notice for the New Adelphi Theatre announcing the 'continued success of the new and original drama of *The Colleen Bawn*'. Citing approving reviews from the *Morning Chronicle*, the *Daily News*, and the *Morning Post*, inter alia, the ad claimed that 'the London public at last has been roused by a real theatrical "sensation"'.[4] We might allow for a certain degree of advertiser's exaggeration here, and certainly the critical response was more mixed than the ad suggests, but other sources indicate that the public had indeed been stirred to no small extent, securing what the *Illustrated London News* termed a 'triumph' for the Adelphi while other theatres enjoyed mixed fortunes.[5] *Punch*'s 'roving correspondent', 'Jack Easel', described his own visit to see the popular play:

Of course I went to see the *Colleen Bawn*. I couldn't help myself. Everyone was bothering me about it. 'Have you seen the Colleen?', says one. 'What d'ye think of the Bawn? ... (between ourselves I've not the wildest notion what either of those words mean).[6]

The 'Bawn' that drew the crowds to Benjamin Webster's theatre in the Strand, a venue already well known for its melodrama, was Dion Boucicault's *The Colleen Bawn, or The Brides of Garryowen*, a romantic mortgage melodrama adapted from Gerald Griffin's *The Collegians* (1829). The action unfolds in rural Ireland towards the end of the eighteenth century, and centres on the financially beleaguered Cregan family, country gentry who face ruin and the loss of their Killarney estate to the counter-jumping moneylender, Corrigan.[7] The villain also hopes to obtain the hand of the extremely reluctant Mrs Cregan, who sees a chance of saving herself and the estate by marrying off her son, Hardress, to Anne Chute, an heiress (also known as the Colleen Ruadh, or red-haired girl). Unfortunately there are impediments to this marriage: a minor one, in the shape of Anne's attraction to Hardress's friend, Kyrle Daly; and a major one in the form of Hardress's existing clandestine marriage to a local ropemaker's daughter, Eily O'Connor.

Eily is the Colleen Bawn, translated in the play by Anne Chute as 'the pretty girl' (II.iii), though a more literal translation of the Irish *cailín bán* would be the white, or fair, or fair-haired girl. Eily is, in other words, not so much a woman in white as a white woman: whiteness is presumably associated less with her dress, and more with her own fair-skinned person (her hair seems to be dark in Boucicault's play, and in the opera version).[8] For despite her low origins, there is nothing earthy about Eily – she is, as the title of the later operatic version of the play (*The Lily of Killarney*) makes clear, a Lily (a mere letter away from Eily), a pale and delicate flower, and thus eminently suited to the 'virtue in distress' formula of melodrama. In the *Melodramatic Imagination* Peter Brooks describes melodrama as a secularized drama of good and evil, in which the absolutes of a religious moral universe fight it out in more quotidian forms.[9] Eily's whiteness is in this light the physical mark of her moral goodness, the visible correlative of her virtue, as well as a badge of her Irish ethnicity.

Hardress secretly visits his pale beauty every night, rowed across the lake to her cottage by Danny Mann, a hunchbacked servant, who is fiercely loyal to his master and foster-brother, although it was the latter who was responsible years earlier for the injury to his back. Through a series of misunderstandings Danny comes to believe that his master wants him to murder Eily. He takes her out on the lake in his boat and attempts to drown her in a water cave, known variously as Pool a Dhiol (*sc.* Ir. *Poll an Dhiabhail*, the devil's cave or hole) and O'Donoghue's Stables, but is prevented in the nick of time by Myles-na-Coppaleen (*sc.* Ir. *Myles na gca-paillín*, Myles of the ponies), a local poacher, poteen-maker and general scapegrace, who is also in love with Eily, and who has come to visit the illicit still he maintains in the same cave.[10] In one of the play's more ludicrous contrivances, Myles mistakes Danny for an otter and shoots him, but not before the hunchback has pushed Eily into the water, having already persuaded her out of the boat and onto a rock. Myles then swings across to the rock and, seeing 'something white' in the water (perhaps her petticoats, but it may also be her lily-white skin), saves the drowning girl by making a daring dive, or 'header', into the lake in the play's famous sensation scene:

DANNY: ... Take your marriage lines wid ye to the bottom of the lake. (He throws her from rock backwards into the water with a cry; she reappears, clinging to rock.)

EILY: No! save me. Don't kill me. Don't Danny, I'll do anything, only let me live.

DANNY: He wants ye dead. (Pushes her off.)

EILY: Oh! Heaven help me. Danny – Danny – Dan – (Sinks.)

DANNY: (looking down). I've done it. She's gone. (Shot is fired; he falls – rolls from the rock into the water.)

(Myles appears with gun on rock.)

MYLES: I hit one of them bastes that time. I could see well, though it was so dark. But there was somethin'moving on that stone. (Swings across.) Divil a sign of him. Stop! (Looks down.) What's this? It's a woman – there's something white there. (Figure rises near rock – kneels down; tries to take the hand of figure.) Ah! That dress; it's Eily. My own darlin' Eily. (Pulls off waistcoat – jumps off rock. Eily rises – then Myles and Eily rise up – he turns, and seizes rock – Eily across left arm.) (II.vi)[11]

This is pure melodrama: virtue is endangered and then saved, and we are given a tableau of virtue triumphant. Night after night, these 'Adelphi effects' were greeted by enthusiastic applause, and the moonlit tableau of Myles supporting the Colleen Bawn, her trademark red peasant's cloak trailing in the water, comes to be the play's most iconic image, appearing in a number of the illustrations to the music inspired by the *Colleen*: for example, T. Browne's 'Colleen Bawn Galop' (1861) and Willam Forde's 'Colleen Bawn Quadrille' (1861).[12] The chromolithographs to these pieces strongly resemble the *Illustrated London News*'s picture of the scene, which suggests that the images are closely based on the actual staging. We can see how elaborate the water-cave set actually was, with its detailed rec-reation of the Killarney picturesque; lighting was cleverly used to create the effect of moonlight, with gauze to suggest the reflective waters of the lake.

After this show-stopping rescue, Myles conceals the heroine at his cot-tage, but the moneylender, Corrigan, has heard Danny's deathbed con-fession, and arrives at Castle Chute with the militia to arrest Hardress for Eily's murder on the day set for his marriage to Anne Chute. At the last minute, Myles and Eily appear and all is resolved: Eily is restored to Hardress and Anne to Kyrle Daly; and offstage Corrigan is ducked in the nearest horsepond, as if in a curious comic re-enactment of Eily's ordeal.

The crowds came for months to see Dion Boucicault and his wife, Agnes Robertson, in the starring roles, to see scenic Killarney evoked in the elaborate sets, and to see Dion, as Myles, make that thrilling dive into a lake of gauze to rescue the drowning heroine. Among the play's most fervent admirers was Queen Victoria, who went three times in February and March of 1861, and recorded in her journal that 'D. Boucicault and his wife (former Miss Robertson whom I remember some years ago at the Princess's) acted admirably as the ragged Irish peasant and the Colleen Bawn. The scenery was very pretty and the whole piece characteristic and thrilling.'[13] To her daughter Vicky she wrote that 'People are wild about it – and the scene when the poor Colleen is thrown into the water and all but drowned is wonderfully done.'[14] She enjoyed the play enough to commission a number of paintings based on it.[15] The more general popu-larity of the play was at the time seen as almost unprecedented: it ran for

2. Illustrated cover for C. H. R. Marriott, 'The Colleen Bawn Waltz' (1861).
Chromolithograph by John Brandard.

231 performances, or a total of some ten months in its original run at the Adelphi, one of the longest ever runs at the time. Over the next few years it clocked up many more nights at Drury Lane and elsewhere, while also inspiring an array of imitations and spin-offs.[16] These included such burlesques as the anonymous *Oily Collins*, H. J. Byron's *Miss Eily O'Connor*, Martin Dutnall's *The Coolean Bawn*; Andrew Halliday's *The Colleen Bawn, Settled at Last*; non-parodic versions, presumably intended to evade

3. Illustrated cover for William Forde, 'The Colleen Bawn Quadrille' (1861).
Chromolithograph by Concanen and Lee.

copyright, like the anonymous *The Colleen Bawn: or The Collegians Wife* and *Cushla Ma Chree*; and even a French translation, *Le Lac du Glenaston*, by Adolphe D'Ennery (some small recompense for the number of theatrical properties that Boucicault had borrowed from France over the years).[17] Nor were these the play's only offspring. Edmund Falconer, whose performance as Danny Mann attracted enthusiastic reviews, put on another

Irish drama, *Peep O'Day, or Savourneen Deelish*, which contained a very similar rescue scene to that in the *Colleen*, with Falconer acrobatically swinging down from the branch of a tree to rescue Kathleen, the heroine, from the clutches of the villainous Black Mullins. According to Henry Morley, who disapproved of the sensational turn in the London theatres, the eminent 'intellectual' actor Charles Fechter had been inspired to add a similar 'sensation scene' to *The Duke's Motto* (Lyceum, January 1863), where he 'haul[ed] himself up a rope, hand over hand, with a baby in his arms', and to *Bel Demonio* (Lyceum, November 1863), in which he 'tumble[d] down a rock into a torrent, because since the successful header in *The Colleen Bawn*, melodrama has bidden for favour by the introduction of gymnastics'.[18] Thus even Fechter, whose performances in Shakespearean roles were widely seen to be bringing the Victorian theatre to new levels of sophistication, was perceived by Morley to be caught in the wake of Boucicault, whom he credits with introducing the term 'sensation', a 'popular Americanism', to Britain.[19] And these were only the most directly theatrical manifestations of the *The Colleen*'s success, which also impacted in more concrete ways upon the practice of everyday London life: as with *The Woman in White*, the public rushed to buy sheet music – Colleen Bawn galops, quadrilles, polkas and waltzes – that they could play at home on the piano; they wore red 'Colleen-Bawn cloaks' inspired by Eily's costume; and they got stuck in the traffic jams generated by hundreds of 'Colleen cabs' lined up in the Strand.[20] In short, like Collins's sensation novel, this 'sensation drama' was rapidly assimilated into the bloodstream of the city.

In this chapter I want to track the play's phenomenal popularity and consider its antecedents, before suggesting some of the reasons for its impact. Its success can be attributed to the more general rise of 'sensation', and the deployment of attention-engineering effects analogous to the ones that Collins uses and theorizes in *The Woman in White*. Just as Collins wanted to 'stagger the public into attention', Boucicault wished to 'hit the public between the eyes' (Fawkes, p. 148). However, I will also argue that the *Colleen*'s peculiar appeal lies in its pastoral dimension: sensational modernity arrives here dressed as the pre-modern, and cross-class conflict is replaced by an almost feudal set of mutual bonds. Recent discussions of sensation melodrama have considered it as a mode that mediates modernity, and this is my own position, but here I want to suggest that this did not always involve, as one might expect, the staging of modern city life, as in *Les Bohémiens de Paris* (1843) or *Under the Gaslight* (1867), or Boucicault's own London-set urban melodrama, *After Dark* (1868). The key to the *Colleen* in this respect is the water-cave 'sensation scene', in

which the heroine's ordeal and rescue is combined with an elaborate pictorial set piece, though also crucial here is the more general deployment of
eighteenth-century Ireland as a colourful and romantic heterotopia. (Even
the hostile account of the play in the *St. James's Magazine*, possibly written
by Mrs S. C. Hall, admits that it is 'the most picturesque representation of
Irish life, from an Irishman's point of view, ever seen in a theatre'.[21]) But if
part of the play's popular drawing power lay in its evocation of a past that
was not really the past, in the second part of this chapter I want to suggest that, as with *The Woman in White*, the play's peculiar resonance also
owes something to its deployment of the numinous. In this case echoes
of the events at Lourdes overlap with the real history that the play both
preserves and distorts, specifically the 1819 murder that Boucicault turns
into the stuff of last-minute rescues and happy endings. Like the Grotto of
Massabielle, the water cave of *The Colleen Bawn* suggests the existence
of worlds beyond the merely visible.

* * *

In attempting to analyse the play's success and the significance of the
water-cave sensation scene we are rehearsing one major strand of the many
contemporary responses to Bouciault's work. Many of these responses
indicate a degree of puzzlement at the play's power. *Punch* in particular
seems to have been fascinated by the phenomenon of the *Colleen*, and we
can track the play's continuing success through the satirical magazine's
often barbed references to it. In April, the Easter break in the play's long
run prompted the 'Dramatic Correspondent' to consider the extent to
which the *Colleen* had become part of London life:

How it used to make me shiver during the cold weather to see daily side by side
with first leader in *The Times*, the stereotyped account of how the dauntless Mr
Boucicault was nightly taking his 'tremendous header' in the lake ... No fewer
than 167 times did the daring Miles-na-Coppaleen [*sic*] take his daring plunge,
and come up nightly covered with cold water and applause and judging by the
unabated rush to see him, the chances are that when his Dublin trip is over, he
will have to take in London as many headers more.[22]

On 4 May he returned to this topic:

Before this letter sees the light the gallant Miles-na-Coppaleen will have begun
again to take his 'tremendous header' nightly in the lake at the Adelphi, which
(the house, not the water) I suppose will be crammed nightly to see the daring
plunge. However high-flown critics may have carped at the *Colleen*, and sneered
at its defects in writing and construction, which I see no good in attempting to
defend, there is clearly no denying it has been a great success, and the cause of its

so being it is worth to inquire into … Of course the 'header' aforesaid has been to some eyes the attraction, and the business of the cave scene is so cleverly contrived that I am not disposed to wonder at the plaudits it calls forth. Still I can't believe that the Strand would have ever been blocked up with Colleen cabs as it has been, or that by wish of the police the doors need have been opened sooner than their wont, merely on account of this one aquatic feat.[23]

It is clear that the 'Correspondent' is at a loss to explain the play's theatrical force. He is unwilling to see the special effects of the water-cave spectacle as the source of its peculiar magic, but his own explanation – that the audience was drawn by the degree of care with the details – scarcely convinces.

Punch continued to worry like a Jack Russell at the *Colleen* phenomenon. In a comic dialogue, a 'Mild Youth' foolishly asks a 'Horrid Girl' if she has seen the *Colleen Bawn*. She replies 'with extreme velocity':

Seen the *Colleen Bawn*! Dear, Dear! Yes, of course. Saw it last October! And I've been to the Crystal Palace [*sc.* presumably to see the high-wire artist, Blondin], and I've read the Gorilla Book [*sc.* Paul Du Chaillu's *Explorations and Adventures in Equatorial Africa* (1861)].[24]

This dialogue suggests that for *Punch* at least Boucicault's play was beginning to be understood less as a phenomenon in its own right than as part of a more general cultural trend, that of audiences passing uncritically – and with extreme velocity – from one form of commodified novelty to another. It was a symptom, then, of what was seen as the new cult of sensation.[25] Subsequent references to the *Colleen* confirm the association of the success of the play and the rise of sensation. In a poem of July 1861, 'sense v. Sensation', *Punch* laments that a term coined to suit the fast-paced social world of America, 'where all's in the high-pressure way', was now spreading from New England to 'Old England'. 'This pois'nous exotic "sensation"' has now come to infiltrate the advertising vocabulary of England:

> When an acrobat ventures his neck
> In the feats of the flying trapeze
> Or some nigger minstrel would deck
> His wool-wig with extra green bays;
> *If a drama can boast of a run,*
> *By dint of a strong situation,*
> *The posters e'en now have begun*
> *To puff the thing up as 'sensation'.*[26] (my emphasis)

The play with the long run and strong situation was clearly *The Colleen Bawn*, the *Times* advertisements for which were using the term 'sensation' as early as October of 1860, as we have seen. *Punch* regrets the 'vulgar excitement' the term brings, but also anticipates that England will follow the US in growing numbed by sensation culture: 'by dint of Sensation at last / There's nothing excites a "sensation"'.

When the play was about to end its long run on Saturday, 13 July – because of the exhaustion of the Boucicaults rather than that of the play-going public – comic poems appear in *Punch* to mark the occasion. One of them, 'The Strand Lament', highlights the macabre repetition of the *Colleen*:

> How that pretty piece was made to draw, dear,
> And that pretty star was made to shine –
> And a pretty lot of times you've drowned dear –
> Last time it made 229!
> That wicked Webster here is snarling –
> He takes your loss to heart, d'ye see
> Could he drown you oftener, Colleen darling,
> Why then transported he would be![27]

Notwithstanding the earlier musings of the 'Dramatic Correspondent', it is now Eily's ordeal, the 'strong situation' in the water-cave scene, that is seen as the play's peculiar draw.

The comic coterie at *Punch* were not the only source of ironic commentary on the play: burlesque versions, as I have mentioned, also made fun of the play while simultaneously testifying to its impact. H. J. Byron, who had already burlesqued the Sensation phenomenon in *Esmeralda, or the Sensation Goat*, turned his hand to Boucicault with *Miss Eily O'Connor*, which opened at the Theatre Royal, Drury Lane, on 25 November 1861.[28] Byron's piece largely uses the plot of *The Colleen Bawn*, though as with most burlesques many of the female roles are played by men, and vice versa; the dialogue is in rhyming verse; and the action is frequently interrupted for song-and-dance sequences. Much of the fun comes from the atrociously laboured puns and the frequent use of topical allusions, and from the high levels of dramatic self-reflexivity. The centrepiece of the burlesque, though, is again the water-cave scene:

DANNY: Gracious, it's over without any din,
How very smoothly the poor gal went in;
To make a pun, which would be groaned at vilely,
She slipped in smoothly, p'raps because she's iley [*sc.* oily]. (scene iv)[29]

But just as he is saying, 'I didn't think at all that she'd give in so', she pops back up. Danny pushes her down again, but she rises to complain (in nasal tones): 'There's such a cold a cubbing in my head.' And so the slapstick fun continues:

> DANNY (wildly): Away! (pushes her off again into the water)
> I am the wretchedest of men;
> EILY (rising – provokingly, in the manner of a clown): Here we are again! (scene v).

At this point in the action the two begin to bob up and down while singing a duet adapted from J. H. Stead's popular music-hall hit *The Perfect Cure*, which Stead famously sang while performing a seemingly endless series of jumps, like some kind of wind-up toy.[30] Byron, perhaps following *Punch*, puts his finger on something interesting: the success of the rescue scene also testifies to the public's willingness to see the fair Colleen drown over and over again, a rather grisly version of the kind of mechanical repetition that Stead used for comic purposes. As the *Dublin University Magazine*'s 'Sensation! A Satire' puts it, ''tis not wit or nature draws the town / They wait to see the luckless maiden drown'.[31] The scene in which this particular woman in white has her greatest impact, that is, is the one in which she is (almost) murdered. (The whole point of the play for the *St. James's Magazine*, its real source of sensation, was its ability to 'convey a life-like picture of a woman being drowned in a lake by design and saved by accident as she is making her last struggle for existence'.[32]) As Byron notes, Eily's unsinkability mimicked that of the play itself and its derivatives: Corrigan greets the reappearance of the Colleen Bawn with the line: 'Well this is a most wonderful revival', a pun on the fact that this burlesque version, like the play itself, ended in one theatre only to be revived at another, the burlesque reappearing at the Strand theatre after a run at Drury Lane.[33]

Byron pokes fun at the conventions and popularity of the *Colleen*, but it also offers, of course, the flattery of imitation, and it is unlikely that Boucicault was greatly troubled by jokes that continued to reflect light back on his own creation. If he had any doubts about the merits of his play, they must have been considerably assuaged early the following year when the *Colleen* received the compliment of more serious musical treatment. In February, a critic in the *Athenaeum* announced that *The Colleen Bawn* had now been transformed into an opera, Julius Benedict's *Lily of Killarney*. Summing up the fortunes of the play so far, he concluded that the popular melodrama had 'come to the honours of burlesque, of equestrian spectacle, and now of opera – there remains but ballet to crown its glory'.[34]

* * *

If such trans-generic success was the *Colleen*'s destiny, what of its origins, and of its author? Dion Boucicault himself was far from being a novelty in 1860: he had won his first great London success almost twenty years before, with *London Assurance*, and had achieved further stage success in the 1850s with such plays as such *The Corsican Brothers* (1852) and *The Vampire* (1852), plays in which he also acted. (*The Corsican Brothers*, another favourite of Queen Victoria, with its famous ghost scene, looks forward to the idea of the sensation drama.) From the early 1850s he had concentrated on writing and translating, leaving the acting to his wife, Agnes Robertson. In the late 1850s, based in the US, he started another winning streak with *The Poor of New York*, adapted from Edouard Brisebarre and Eugène Nus's *Les Pauvres de Paris* (1856). The success of this piece showed him the potential for the combination of present-day *mise en scène*, topical content, and the use of 'sensation' scenes (not named as such at this point) deploying spectacular special effects. This formula was also to underwrite the success of *Jessie Brown* (1858) and *The Octoroon* (1859), both of which combined recent and contemporary issues with exotic spectacle and timely rescues.

Boucicault himself did not confine his powers of invention to the stage, and he appears to have given no little thought to shaping his own public persona. Born Dion Boursiquot at 28 Middle Gardiner Street in Dublin in 1820, at various times he styled himself Boursicault, Bourçicault, Lee Moreton (his first stage name), Belvedere Dion Boucicault, the Vicomte de Boucicault (after his marriage to a French woman, Anne Guiot, in 1845) and Dion de P. Boucicault. Yet he never seems to have altogether lost his Irish accent, or 'brogue' as it is usually styled in the contemporary reviews, and his greatest successes as an actor were in Irish parts. At times he would put his Irishness more to the fore, as in his much-cited performances of *The Shaughraun* to raise money for Fenian prisoners. The Irishness that Boucicault created on stage can be seen neither as a straightforward performance of his own identity, nor as a purely traditional stage role. Rather it appears to be something formed in a complicated relation to the international audiences before which it appeared: the metropolitan audiences of London, but also, crucially, those of New York and other US cities. Boucicault, that is, played a significant role in shaping modern international popular culture in his creation of a picturesque and tuneful stage Ireland, populated not just by the stock heroes, heroines and villains of melodrama, but also by mischievous but good-hearted rascals like Myles-na-Coppaleen and the Shaughraun.

For the *Colleen*, he put his knowledge of Ireland to work. The play's origin story exists in various versions.[35] In the winter of 1859–60 the Boucicaults were in New York in need of a new play for Laura Keene, and in the most romantic version, that given in *Leaves from a Dramatist's Diary*, Boucicault found inspiration on a cold night on Broadway when he saw a copy of Gerald Griffin's 1829 novel *The Collegians* in a cellar store near the theatre:

The following morning Miss Keene received this letter: 'My dear Laura: I have it! I send you seven steel engravings of scenes around Killarney. Get your scene-painter to work on them at once. I also send a book of Irish melodies, with those marked I desire Baker to score for the orchestra. I shall read act one of my new Irish play on Friday; we rehearse that while I am writing the second ... We can get the play out within a fortnight'. (Fawkes, p. 114)

Agnes Roberson in later years gave a slightly different account of Boucicault's 'discovery' of the *Collegians*, claiming that in fact they had been together that night in the bookstore, and that she initially refused his offer to buy Griffin's novel for her, as she had read it before. She changed her mind, however, re-read it, and suggested that they produce an Irish drama based on it, as they had just done a successful 'Scotch play', *Jeanie Deans*, based on Scott's *The Heart of Mid-Lothian*. He readily agreed, and wrote the play in nine days.[36] This also may be a somewhat embellished account, of course, and it contradicts yet another version, in which Boucicault had in fact been working on the play for some time for the husband and wife team of Barney Williams and Maria Pray, who were less than amused when they saw their play performed at Laura Keene's.[37]

Griffin's *Collegians* is a pastoral tragedy rather than pastoral melodrama. The central episode of the novel is a thinly disguised version of an actual murder that had occurred when Griffin was growing up in Limerick, and behind Eily O'Connor stands the real figure of Ellen Hanley. In 1819 a young County Limerick gentleman, John Scanlan, was arrested for the murder of the fifteen-year-old Hanley, daughter of a small farmer, and a local beauty. The two had eloped, but when Scanlan tired of her he employed his boatman, Stephen Sullivan, to kill her; the latter took her out in his boat, clubbed her to death with his musket, bound her and threw her overboard.[38] Scanlan was unsuccessfully defended at his trial by the Irish parliamentarian and champion of Catholic Emancipation Daniel O'Connell, then one of the country's leading barristers.[39] He was hanged at Gallows Green in Limerick, on 16 March 1820.[40]

Based on this dark episode, *The Collegians* was a very successful novel in its day, earning for its author some £800, and it seems unlikely that Boucicault's first knowledge of it came in 1859. Even if he had missed the novel, there had been at least one stage version, *Eily O'Connor* (1831), and Boucicault had a prodigious grasp of stage history.[41] It is a good deal more probable that his recent success with another 'mortgage melodrama',

The Octoroon (1859), had triggered memories of the central events of *The Collegians*. *The Octoroon*, loosely based on Irish-born Thomas Mayne Reid's novel, *The Quadroon; or, A Lover's Adventures in Louisiana* (1856), deals with the doomed romance between the hero of the piece, George Peyton, and the 'octoroon' of the title, Zoe, who appears to be white, but is of mixed race. If the hero can bring himself to marry a local heiress, Dora Sunnyside, he can save the family plantation, just as Hardress Cregan could save his family's estate by marrying Anne Chute – if he were not already married to the Colleen Bawn. Where racial difference leads to the suicide of Zoe in *The Octoroon*, barriers of class and wealth lead to the murder of Eily O'Connor in *The Collegians* – a grim conclusion that Boucicault avoids, of course.[42]

In March 1860, Boucicault presented the play as his first ever Irish play, acknowledging that it was based on the events that inspired *The Collegians*.[43] The *Colleen* was a hit in New York, where it played at Laura Keene's Theatre from the end of March until July, with Laura Keene herself taking the part of Anne Chute, the Colleen Ruadh, and with the Boucicaults taking the main roles, as they would in London that September. In a detailed review in the *New York Saturday Press*, Ada Clare praised the play, rejoicing that 'An Irish play has been produced without a single Shillalah [*sic*] in the cast, with no hideous dancing, no fighting, no ragged coats [and] no howling unclean family driven from their tenement.' She felt that the strong characters and 'a quick succession of startling events, together with striking scenic display, ever keeps the mind from losing its vivid and eager interest'.[44] The *New York Times* also welcomed the play as a departure from an older style of Irish drama, in which the shillelagh had played too large a part. By adapting Gerald Griffin's novel, *The Times* felt Boucicault had 'opened new ground ... and a rich harvest may be anticipated from his initial effort'.[45] It deplored some of the awkwardness in construction, such as the use of eavesdropping and letters falling into the wrong hands to forward the plot, and regretted that the haste with which the play had been put together had detracted from Boucicault's usual 'closesness of construction'. Nonetheless, it saw the play as 'the most intense drama of the season'. A subsequent report testifies that the play has done well so far 'without any unusual degree of excitement', but 'Mr Boucicault's countrymen will undoubtedly pay homage to a work of such startling originality, and beyond this its striking merits as a sensational drama will ensure for it a steady run to the end of the season'.[46]

* * *

What, though, was the source of the 'intensity' of *The Colleen Bawn*? Undoubtedly part of the play's appeal in New York lay in Boucicault's creation of a certain kind of stage Ireland, a place of whiskey-drinking priests, rakish squireens, pale and virtuous beauties in distress, and loveable and resourceful rogues, that appealed to an Irish-American audience happy to sentimentalize their country of origin. Perhaps too some of that audience could identify with a heroine with an incurable brogue, one whose murderous 'voyage' is explicitly linked to that of Ireland's emigrant masses by Danny's offer to Hardress to remove her if his master will 'pay her passage out to Quaybec, and put her aboord a three-master widout sayin' a word. Lave it to me' (II.i).

But this would hardly explain why the play was an even greater hit on the other side of the Atlantic, where it 'achieved a success to which there had been few, if any, precedents in the theatrical chronicles of London', as *The Times* noted some years later.[47] The 'sensation scene' is, of course, crucial to the play's success, but let us consider also the particular kind of 'sensation play' that the *Colleen* is. What is immediately obvious is that it does not follow the formula that Boucicault had earlier perfected in such plays as his 1857 success *The Poor of New York*, where sensational incident and topical content are married to a more or less contemporary and urban setting. Rather, he follows Gerald Griffin in setting the play's events in the eighteenth century. To this extent the *Colleen Bawn* combines the ingredients of his contemporary-setting sensation plays (*The Poor of New York*, *The Octoroon*) and great costume successes like *The Corsican Brothers* (1852; set in the 1840s, but contrasting contemporary Paris with the colourful and 'primitive' life of Corsica) and *The Vampire* (1852; featuring a variety of historical periods, including the near future).

The play's title is the first hint that this is a story from an exotic place – as *Punch*'s commentator suggests, few who were unfamiliar with *The Collegians* would know what the play's title meant. This linguistic gap is reproduced in miniature within the play, where there is a divide between the peasant characters, including the Colleen herself, who use Irish-language phrases, and the more anglicized characters, who largely do not. Thus Eily's letter to Hardress is a patchwork of English and Irish:

Come to your own Eily, that has not seen you for two long days. Come, acushla, agrah machree [Ir. *a chuisle, a ghrá mo chroí*: pulse, love of my heart]. I have forgotten how much you love me – Shule, shule, agrah [Ir. *Siúl, siúl, a ghrá*: walk, walk, my love]. (I.i)

This linguistic exoticism is not the play's only tactic for conjuring up an Ireland that is picturesquely different from the life of the metropolis, a romantic heterotopia. In visual terms the play deploys elaborately constructed sets to represent 'picturesque' Killarney (already a cliché in the travelogues of this period), and colourful historical costumes – the vogue of the red Colleen Bawn cloak suggests that even the peasant garb of the heroine possessed an exotic appeal. The everyday codes of this pastoral world are also different from those of metropolitan London: this is a society of priests, poteen and poaching, but also one of almost feudal, or even tribal, loyalty, as displayed by Danny Mann's actions on behalf of the man who is not just his employer but also his foster-brother – this is not, in other words, a society dominated by the cash nexus, or by class hostilities. The villain, Corrigan, as is often the case with Victorian melodrama, is perhaps the only one in the play who is clearly marked as a modern type, a man for whom custom, kin and caste mean far less than pounds, shillings and pence.

This stage Ireland is also a place of happy endings. The greatest change that Boucicault made to Griffin's novel was to turn a tragic tale of violent death into one of romantic cross-class reconciliation: Eily, the beautiful young peasant, is saved, and her clandestine marriage to the gentry-class Hardress is openly endorsed by his family. This does not seem to be so much the play's 'political unconscious' as an explicit allegory of cross-class harmony, at a time when the class structures of Victorian England were under threat. That the representative of the lower classes is a delicate female beauty, and that audiences came repeatedly to see her almost drown, complicates that fantasy in various ways. It suggests for one thing the wish-fulfilling substitution of a docile, female peasant for a less manageable, urban male working class; at same time it indicates a high level of barely disguised hostility to even that attenuated version of an upwardly mobile lower class.

But interesting though this allegorical aspect of the play is, it is not, I would argue, the *Colleen*'s most powerful attraction for its London audience. Let us look again at the sensation scene, which, after all, presents quite a complex image of the pastoral. Boucicault transforms Griffin's narrative by placing not a murder, but a rescue, at the heart of the play, and the great heroic act of the play, which riveted the audience's attention night after night, was Myles's great 'header' to save the drowning Eily. If Myles dives a moment too late, the fair Eily will be dragged down into the cold waters of the lake. And this means that into the pastoral world of the play enters the same kind of split-second timing that characterizes not just other rescue dramas, but also industrial modernity. Peter Brooks showed some years ago that melodrama is a theatrical mode that arises alongside the advent of the political modernity of the French revolution, and subsequent critics have refined and adapted that theory in a number of ways, suggesting, for example, that it is the social modernity of the city that melodrama captures and perhaps even assimilates, or that it provides a form of public sphere for an emergent consumer culture.[48] In rescue melodramas it is clearly also the spatio-temporal world of industrial modernity that is important, the modernized time and space described by Wolfgang Schivelbusch in *The Railway Journey*.[49] That the suspense of the last-minute rescue encodes the triumph of the heroic individual over the systems of the modern, industrial world is made much clearer in such urban human v. locomotive spectaculars as Augustin Daly's *Under the Gaslight* (1867), or Boucicault's London-set adaptation of it, *After Dark* (1868), where the Myles-like-figure, Old Tom, bravely plucks his friend out of the path of a train on the London underground line.[50] There we can see more directly that the enjoyment of theatrical spectacle also aligns the audience with industrial time: the machine is defeated, though in the process the audience is trained in a new kind of temporal consciousness.

But the split-second events of the water-cave rescue depend on just the same sense of industrialized time, for all that the action is displaced into the pastoral realm: this is a thoroughly modern rescue, depending not just on timing, but also on all of the illusive resources of the stage: lighting to imitate moonlight, trapdoors and a small army of stage hands to facilitate the disappearance and reappearance of Myles and Eily from beneath the 'waves', and not least those gauzy waves. The special effects and the temporal framework of this rescue are no different from those of the more obviously urban and industrial-age rescues of *The Poor of New York* or *After Dark*. Far from coming to enjoy an escapist evening in the 'timeless' Irish landscape, then, audiences were coming to be thrilled by what we might think of as industrial pastoral, a pastoral-modern hybrid. The question to ask, I think, is why did London audiences find this anachronism so riveting? At some level they appear to have preferred to experience the time–space of the sensational industrial rescue in a pastoral disguise rather than face it head on. Several years before they were willing to be thrilled by the railway rescues of the late 1860s, they were able to derive very similar pleasures from emotional investment (however conflicted) in the drowning peasant girl, Eily, and her equally markedly non-modern rescuer, Myles-na-Coppaleen.

Such disguises were a crucial part of Victorian modernity, which elsewhere created Gothic railway stations, and factories. Walter Benjamin long ago pointed to this curious process by which modernity decks itself in the trappings of other eras: 'Corresponding in the collective consciousness to the means of production ... are images in which the new is intermingled with the old.'[51] As Susan Buck-Morss describes, the new technologies themselves provide the clearest examples of the 'thirst for the past' that characterizes the nineteenth century, and which Benjamin began to trace in his incomplete Arcades project:

Early photography mimicked painting. The first railroad cars were designed like stage coaches, and the first electric light bulbs were shaped like gas flames. Newly processed iron was used for ornament rather than structural supports, shaped into leaves, or made to resemble wood. Industrially produced utensils were decorated to resemble flowers, fauna, seashells, and Greek and Renaissance antiques.[52]

For Benjamin, this mimicry does not attest to a form of mystification of historical change, but rather bespeaks, as through a form of dreamwork, the utopian longing unleashed by new forces of production. The water rescue, then, joins a whole series of such dialectical images. Benjamin suggests that this form of imaginative flight skips over the proximate past to a classless prehistory, and 'intimations of this, deposited in the unconscious of the collective, mingle with the new to produced the utopia that has left its traces in thousands of configurations of life, from permanent buildings to fleeting fashions'.[53]

In the case of the *Colleen*, though, modernity arrives cloaked in a version of pastoral rather than prehistory, perhaps because for metropolitan audiences eighteenth-century Ireland already seemed an age away from their own world. Moreover, it is political as much as industrial change that is being reworked here: stage Ireland offers a comforting image of an organic society, though not a classless one. *The Colleen Bawn*, appearances to the contrary notwithstanding, is then a play that captures the utopian desire of the Victorian present, not a simple evocation of the Irish past. What the play offers is not a purely escapist fantasy but a way of living modernity, social and political, through a fantasy of the pre-modern, *Gesellschaft* imagining itself as *Gemeinschaft*.[54] It is very unlikely that the middle-class women who wore red Colleen Bawn cloaks, or the couples who danced the 'Colleen Bawn Waltz', wished to *be* Irish peasants, but they may have wanted to inhabit a modern world that displayed the colour, intensity and close-knittedness of Boucicault's pastoral heterotopia.[55] This retrofitted pastoral idyll must have seemed all the more attractive at a time when the spirit of reform threatened the relative stability of their own world. We might also note that the sensation scene, by creating moments of nail-biting suspense over the fate of its lily-white heroine, forged a form of temporary close-knit community in its audience, albeit one quite different from the version represented on stage.

* * *

And yet there are elements of the water-cave scene that are not accounted for by reading it as industrialized pastoral for the years of Reform. Boucicault may or may not have been aware of the recent events at the grotto of Massabielle, and he carefully keeps religion out of his play (with the exception of the bibulous priest), but Ireland would have been seen by his audience to be a superstitious, Catholic country to an even greater extent than France. It seems more than a coincidence that he makes his heroine a colleen bawn, and his cave a conduit into other realms, a place more supernatural than pastoral – indeed, a place where miracles happen.

Gerald Griffin's *Collegians* places the murder off-stage, and the body is washed up on the shores of the Shannon: where, then, did the play's most famous scene come from? To create the strong pictorial quality of his mythic cave scene it is possible that Boucicault and his technical staff dusted off an already extant Romantic image of Ireland as timeless and mythical space, Daniel Maclise's allegorical *Origin of the Harp* (1842).[56] But there is something else going on here, a conjuring with the sort of mythic locations that Gaston Bachelard theorizes in his *Poetics of Space*, spaces that allow the irrational or numinous to emerge.[57] If Boucicault was not deliberately invoking the Lourdes apparition, he evidently thought of the water cave as a portal to other worlds, heavenly or infernal. Its Irish name suggests fairly clearly what the water cave represents in the play: Poul a Dhiol (Ir. *Poll an Dhiabhail*) literally means the devil's hole, or cave, or pool (cf. actual Irish placenames, such as Poulaphouca). This may seem merely a colourful local appellation in a play in which Mrs Cregan is described as being 'proud as Lady Beelzebub' (I.i), and in which expressions like 'Divil an address is on it' (I.i) are not uncommon. But that last phrase is spoken by Danny, and it is he too who tries to assuage his master's anger with the phrase 'divil burn me if I meant any harm' (II.i), and who – seemingly already suffering the pangs of hell – dies roaring for 'wather' at the end of act III, scene i, having earlier needed large quantities of fiery spirits to screw his courage to the grim task he thinks he has been assigned by Hardress via Mrs Cregan. He is prevented from his purpose only by Myles, who thinks Danny is an otter he has seen earlier ('ow! ye divil! if I had my gun I'd give ye a leaden supper' (II.vi)). It is difficult not to conclude from this string of diabolical reference that in fact the Colleen Bawn is not simply being drowned – she is being consigned to a species of underworld, a Hades for which Danny the boatman acts as a hunchbacked Charon. In these terms Eily is brought back from the dead by Myles: as he puts it himself, 'I am her mother; sure I brought her into the world a second time' (III.iii). (It is also to be borne in mind that Danny's aptness for the role of agent of death is related to the fact that he was not always a hunchbacked killer. While now he provides a beastly foil to Eily's beauty, he was once himself his mother's 'white-haired darlin'' (II.vi) before Hardress crippled him.)

That the cave is a passage to another realm is treated jokily by Myles, who after all is able to illegally distill spirits in its Stygian darkness (his spiritual guide, Father Tom, is one of his best customers) because of the reputation that O'Donoghue's Stables/Pool a Dhiol has for being haunted:

Now I'll go down to my whiskey-still. It is under my feet this minute, bein'in a hole in the rocks they call O'Donoghue's Stables, a sort of water cave; the people around here think that the cave is haunted with bad spirits, and they say that of a dark stormy night strange unearthly noises is heard comin'out of it – it is me singing 'The Night before Larry was stretched'. Now I'll go down to that cave, and wid a sod of live turf under a kettle of worty, I'll invoke them spirits – and what's more they'll come. (Exit Myles singing). (II.v)

The curious placename O'Donoghue's Stables at first seems less troubling than Pool a Dhiol, and Myles's consistent use of it in keeping with his comic persona. But this is not quite the full picture, as O'Donoghue's Stables is just as redolent of the spirit world as the Devil's Cave, though in another register, that of Irish folklore in which the Christian thematics of good and evil, Heaven and Hell, rub shoulders with a very different conception of life after death. Rather than returning us to some timeless folkloric world, though, the name O'Donoghue introduces into the play some distinctly historical resonances. Boucicault presumably found this place name, like many others in the play, in a Killarney guide book, or from a travelogue such as *Hall's Ireland*, the account given by Anna Maria and Samuel Carter Hall of their 1840 tour of the island. Here is an excerpt from their account of Killarney and its environs:

The name of O'Donoghue is closely associated with Killarney ... The legends all agree ... that the men and women who then peopled this lovely valley did not perish when it was flooded, but continue to exist beneath the lake, where O'Donoghue continues to lord it over his people, living in his gorgeous palace, surrounded by faithful friends and devoted followers, and enjoying the delights of feasting, dancing, and music ... And annually, since his death – or rather disappearance – he is said to revisit the pleasant places among which he lived. Every

May morning he may be seen gliding over the lakes mounted on a richly capari-
soned white steed ...[58]

The Halls are determined to read these tales of revenants from underwater
kingdoms as quaint, as picturesque local colour as well as indications of
the superstitious nature of the natives, who mistake some natural phenomenon for a supernatural one. Nor were they alone in this. As Luke
Gibbons points out, eighteenth- and nineteenth-century descriptions
of Killarney 'returned monotonously to the question of O'Donoghue's
ghostly apparition, endeavouring to explain it as a trick of light, a mir-
age, the "Fata Morgana", and so on'.[59] The ghostly O'Donoghue, though,
derives not from some antediluvian quasi-historical figure, but recalls the
actual O'Donoghue family, the Gaelic lords whose power was broken during the Cromwellian conquest of the seventeenth century. In this light
Gibbons argues that the ghostly apparition that appears on May Day has
to be understood in relation to the close association of May Day with
ongoing agrarian insurgency (by the Whiteboys, Ribbonmen and others
across the eighteenth and nineteenth centuries), but also as part of the
more general emphasis within the popular imagination on 'the "undead"
and ... narratives of recurrence and return' (p. 38) that can be understood
as a mode of imaginative resistance to the colonial project, conjuring up
the re-emergence of a pre-colonial order.

Twenty years after the Halls' tour, in the aftermath of the famine of the
1840s, the idea of an Irish landscape that conceals a lost people also has a
rather different significance, perhaps, and it is tempting to read the play as
a whole, with its colourful evocation of a vanished eighteenth-century rural
Ireland as, among other things, a memorial to the decimated peasant class.[60]
But without discounting this possibility, I think the images of a drowned
world and a return from beneath the waves have a more precise significance
for this play. It is worth examining the dissonance between Myles's comic
tone and the grisly events that are just about to unfold in the water cave.
Eily rapidly grasps that her boat trip is not going to end anywhere pleasant:

EILY: I don't like this place – it's like a tomb. (II.vi)

And for her it very nearly is, when the music changes, and her heart-
rending pleas to Danny – 'Don't kill me. Don't Danny, I'll do anything,
only let me live' (II.vi) – avail her nothing. But then just when we appear
to be entering the emotional depths, we veer away from tragedy and back
to melodrama with the bathetic shooting of Danny as an otter ('I hit one
of them bastes that time ... Divil a sign of him'(II.vi)), and of course the
great header and curtain.

With this awkward modulation in tone – from Myles's prattle to Eily's terror and back again – we are getting closer to the sources of the play's peculiar resonance. If Danny cannot drown Hardress's inconvenient past in Poul a Dhiol, nor can Boucicault entirely immerse his recalcitrant source material; for of course Boucicault's painted water cave is indeed haunted with spirits, just as the locals suspect. The infernal aspect of the water cave, that awkward shift in tone and those all-too-credible lines bind the melodramatic energies of the *Colleen Bawn* to the actual events of July 1819. That the audience went to see Eily almost drown as well as to see Myles save her was not lost on *Punch*, as we have seen in its 'Strand Lament' of July 1861: 'And a pretty lot of times you've drowned dear – Last time it made 229!' Byron's burlesque highlights this same aspect of the play by exploiting the comic possibilities of Eily's bobbing back up over and over again. What they both bring into focus in their comic treatment of the play's centrepiece is that it is hard work to turn the savage beating and drowning of a fifteen-year-old girl into light entertainment, even using the powerful mode of melodrama, and that the repetition of the scene night after night as light entertainment is macabre – more grisly ritual than drama.

If the murder of Ellen Hanley was both remembered and forgotten in Boucicault's treatment, a story of cross-class as well as cross-gender violence transformed into a story of providential rescue and cross-class reconciliation, we might consider what other kinds of memories of the events of 1819 were in circulation in the 1860s. The *Freeman's Journal* review of the play's Dublin debut in April 1861 notes that the story of the Colleen is 'well known by tradition in the South of Ireland'.[61] For a metropolitan audience, though, we might assume there was no such continuity of memory, though some might be expected to remember the story from *The Collegians* (certainly a number of the reviewers show familiarity with the novel) or perhaps from an earlier stage version like the 1831 *Eily O'Connor*, and a much smaller number might even have had some vague sense that the story was based on real events (cf. the perennial popularity of the *Murder in the Red Barn*). And yet the memory of the bloody original events *does* seem to have survived, whether from broadside sources or, for want of a better term, urban tradition. Consider the version of the play that is reprinted in *Purkess's Penny Pictorial Plays, The Colleen Bawn, or The Collegian's Wife, A Popular Melodrama in 3 Acts, As Performed at the London Theatres*, which in fact departs to a considerable extent from Boucicault's play, and contains a different treatment of the central episode:

Act II, scene iii: The Waterfall at Macgillicuddy. Bright Moonlight.
. . .

DANNY: Fear not Colleen, we are near the end of our voyage. It will be over sooner than you expect.

EILY: What do you mean? Surely you do not intend foul play? Hardress would never have trusted you unless he could depend on you, yet I dread your looks. Heaven help me! Here alone with no one but you near me, and –

[while she speaks Danny *raises the gun from the boat: with the butt end he hits her a blow on the head*. She falls senseless with a shriek. A storm rises. Danny raises her body and throws it into the water, and then makes off with the boat, and at the same time Myles rushes on again.

MYLES: I thought I heard a death cry (looks around) – no all is still. [The moon rises and shows a part of the body of Eily rising to the surface.] . . . Let me try to save the unhappy creature. [He dashes into the water, and as he raises the head of Eily he utters a wild cry of horror.]

MYLES: Great God! 'Tis Eily O'Connor. [Tableau, Curtain][62] (my emphasis)

Here we are actually much closer to the events of 1819. The gun in particular is a detail that does not feature in *The Collegians* or Boucicault's *Colleen Bawn*, and must ultimately derive from Stephen Sullivan's confession:

When the boat was about the centre of the river, he stood up and took a musket in his hand, with which he made a blow at her head, but having missed her, struck her on the arm, which was broken. He then beat her with the gun till she was quite dead, and afterwards tied her right leg to her neck, to which a large stone was attached, and flung the body in the river, which sunk immediately.[63]

Its appearance in this version of the play suggests that Ellen Hanley's story continued to circulate independently of the Griffin and Boucicault treatments. *The Colleen Bawn* might be an example of a modernizing urban *Gesellschaft* imagining itself to be, if only for a West End evening, a *Gemeinschaft*, but even a *Gesellschaft* can have a version of popular memory, it would appear.

*   *   *

The Colleen Bawn is not the last stage in the remembering/forgetting of the murder of Ellen Hanley, of course. On 10 February 1862 the public flocked to Covent Garden to see *The Lily of Killarney*, Julius Benedict's operatic treatment of the play, with a libretto by John Oxenford and Boucicault himself. (Covent Garden audiences had recently had their appetites whetted for operatic tales of love triumphing over water by William Vincent Wallace's *Lurline* (Covent Garden, 23 February 1860), an adaptation of the Lorelei legend that also features an impecunious young gentleman and an unsuitable match.) While Boucicault lamented the way in which his 'lamb was butchered into a marketable shape', *The Times* reported a 'brilliant reception' to this latest avatar of the play, musing that 'it would seem we are never to see the last of the Colleen Bawn'.[64] The shape of the drama had been changed, with much of the original disappearing, including the entire Kyrle Daly/Anne Chute subplot, while other elements appeared for distinctly operatic purposes (e.g. the Hunting Chorus in act II). Nonetheless, the choicest cut of Boucicault's 'lamb' remained: the water-cave scene, in which the Adelphi staging was carefully imitated. The opera in fact clarifies and heightens the symbolic aspect of that episode. For example, Danny now refers to 'the Divil's Island' (II, no. 14) rather than the less transparent Pool a Dhiol.[65]

The most significant way in which the opera heightens the effect of Boucicault's play is with the addition of a Chorus of Boatmen in act II, whose song leads into and overlaps with the water-cave scene. Myles's reference to O'Donoghue's Stables must have been lost on many who saw the play at the Adelphi, but the Chorus spells out the significance of the cave's name:

> A friend to the friendless the good king appears,
> The humbled he raises, the mourners he cheers,
> And oft by him wonderful stories are told,
> About our green isle and her glories of old,
> Yes, gladly we'll welcome the brave Donohue,
> To the sons of poor Erin a friend, a friend, a friend ever true!
> (II, no. 16, Finale)

At this point Eily speaks (rather than sings): 'What place is this you have brought me to, Danny? It is like a tomb' (II), echoing her lines in the play. Clearly, then, we are meant to think of Myles's heroic intervention to save Eily from drowning as a parallel act to the magical interventions of 'the brave Donohue' ('the humbled he raises'), though we can also see the brave king on his white steed as a double for Eily, who reappears from beneath the waters night after night in the play, and who dramatically comes back from the dead, as it were, in the last scene. But it is just as easy to trace the resemblance between the legendary Donohue and the real Ellen Hanley, who has also been preserved from the hand of history, not by magic, but by Boucicault's melodrama. The mutilated corpse and semi-decomposed body washed up on the beach at Moneypoint has been transformed into something rich and strange, the figure of the Colleen Bawn.

CONCLUSION

The audiences who came to see *The Colleen Bawn* were thrilled by a modern sensation that by deploying suspense, coupled with the full gallery of

mid-Victorian special effects, held their attention in a carefully manufactured spectacular vice; this was attention-engineering of at least the same
intensity as Collins's page turner. But the crowds who queued to see *The
Colleen Bawn Settled at Last* or *The Lily of Killarney*, who wore Colleen
Bawn cloaks around town, or who played Colleen Bawn Galops and
Quadrilles on their pianos, were also taking part in a distinctively modern
practice in which the present is welcomed in the clothes of the past. If the
play manipulated its audience by creating a collective consciousness held
together primarily by sensation, it also allowed them to imagine their own
social world transformed into something more utopian.

The historical past, though, uneasily co-exists in the play with this pastoral fantasy of the present-as-past. Audiences were held by a pleasurable
commodity-experience of industrial pastoral, but they were also invited
to take part in a very complex act of simultaneous remembering and for-
getting, something closer to ritual than representation. If, as we noted at
the beginning, melodrama provides a secularized drama of good and evil
in a fallen world, the melodrama of *The Colleen Bawn* threatens at times
to turn back into religious experience, and Eily O'Connor to become an
apparition.[66] Some found this aspect of the play more problematic than
others. Agnes Robertson played the part of Eily many hundreds of times:
at Laura Keene's, at the Adelphi, at Drury Lane and in many subsequent
revivals – a suitable term in this context. Looking back on her long stage
career in 1899, she claims that if she ever writes her autobiography she

shall have much to say about [the *Colleen*] … with which my fortunes and indeed
my personality have been so intimately bound up. Gerald Griffin founded his
novel … upon tragic incidents in real life, and the whole trial scene is rather a
transcript of reality than mere romance. I may mention that I possess among my
papers the whole of the notes taken during the trial by the judge who tried the
case.[67]

Unfortunately she never did write such an account of her life, and all we
have is this brief reference to suggest that in the end she came to be troubled by the act of surrogation by which she came to take the place of Ellen
Hanley, and to act over and over again a happy ending to the dead girl's
short and unhappy life. That she ended up owning 'real' artefacts from the
1819 case suggests an attempt to get some purchase on a piece of history, as
well as on a role that had come to possess her. As an actress she presumably
understood that the absolute line between the living and the dead that is
often assumed to be characteristic of modernity is something as alien to
the practices of the theatre as it is to religious ritual.[68]

When Eily reappears alive at the end of the Purkess's edition of the *Colleen*, Hardress begs her forgiveness, Kyrle and Anne pair off, and the ensemble cheer Eily:

Loud cheers from all: Long life to Eily O'Connor.

In some ways it is an apt enough ending, since the many reincarnations and revivals of *The Colleen Bawn* did give a strange kind of life after death to Ellen Hanley. Perhaps in a way this is a tribute to rather than a criticism of Boucicault's play, in which the whole never completely subordinates its historical ingredients. In our next chapter we move from the theatre to the gallery, and to a much more determined aesthetic programme, one that, like the *Colleen*, wants to spellbind its audience, but one that also hopes to turn its fair-skinned Irish subject into pure form.

CHAPTER 3

The White Girl: *aestheticism as mesmerism*

The early 1860s are, as we have seen, white years. The arrival of 'sensation' as a byword for the breathlessly modern in these years seems curiously wedded to that colour, and is ushered in by a series of female figures identified with it, just as a new wave of counter-modern Marian devotion is announced by the appearance of a woman in white outside Lourdes in 1858.

Whiteness was also finding its way into the fine-art galleries, notably the Berners Street Gallery, off Oxford Street, where a painting by James Abbott McNeill Whistler, *The Woman in White*, was exhibited in the summer of 1862. Better known now as *Symphony in White No. 1: The White Girl*, or simply *The White Girl* (and this is the title that I will use here), this was the first of his attempts at a new type of 'painterly' painting. The girl was the young Joanna ('Jo') Hiffernan (sometimes Heffernan), Whistler's Irish model and mistress, who appears in many of his other works of the 1860s: *Wapping* (1861); (probably) *The Lange Leizen of the 6 Marks* (1864); *Symphony in White No. 2: The Little White Girl* (1864); *Symphony in White No. 3* (1865–7); the incomplete *Artist's Studio* (1865), *Whistler in his Studio* (1865) and *White Note* (1861–2); and the dry-point sketch *Weary* (1863).[1] In *The White Girl* Hiffernan, wearing a simple white muslin dress, stands on a wolfskin before a white curtain, her long, loose red hair providing a brilliant contrast to her pale surroundings.

Rejected by the Royal Academy earlier in the year, the painting caused a sensation when it appeared in June at Matthew Morgan's new gallery. In 1863 it appeared in the *Salon des Refusés* at the Palais de l'Industrie in Paris, where together with Manet's *Le Bain*, later retitled *Déjeuner sur l'herbe*, it again created a sensation.

With *The White Girl*, Whistler wished to break with the classical conception of paintings with 'content': a picture should have nothing to do with fictional or historical sources outside itself; nor should it have any narrative content of its own. As the later title, *Symphony in White, No. 1*, suggests, the aim was to subordinate content to form; we are to approach the

4. James McNeill Whistler, *Symphony in White No. 1: The White Girl* (1862).

painting not as a representation of a particular young woman, be it the fictional Anne Catherick as the original title seemed to indicate, or the real Jo Hiffernan, or even as a figure for all young women, but as an artistic composition true to its own internal formal principles. Whistler adopted this new musical title from a review in the *Gazette Des Beaux Arts* by the French critic Paul Mantz, who had described the painting as a 'symphonie du blanc'. He may also have been thinking of the principles of colouruse proposed by Michel-Eugène Chevreul, the first English translation of whose work appeared in 1854 as *The Principles of Harmony and Contrast of Colours*, though theories that linked complementary colours with harmony in music had been around since Isaac Newton's *Opticks*.[2] There may be another meaning to the later title, of course: *Symphony in White, No. 1* also suggests a symphony in 'White No. 1', that is, a commercially available painter's pigment.[3] This pun further emphasizes the painterly aspect of the piece, drawing our attention to its actual physical nature as paint on canvas. In any case, the later title makes clear that the subject of the painting is not the 'girl', but colour, whiteness itself, the choice of white over some other colour perhaps signalling an ambition to work with the least contrastive of tints (cf. the term 'white work' used in embroidery). Imbued with such a will to bravura minimalism, Whistler's work may appear to us less a symphony than a five-finger exercise; one thinks of Gustave Courbet's claim that he learned to paint by drawing a white vase on a white serviette.

How, then, can we link Whistler's *White Girl* with those other White Women of the 1860s without foundering on the rocks of self-referentiality? Insofar as *The White Girl* has a context at all, surely it is not such stuff as sensation drama or sensation novels, but art itself: synchronically the mid-Victorian narrative painting that Whistler rejected – William Powell Frith's enormously successful *Railway Station*, for instance, then on view in the Haymarket, admission one shilling – or diachronically, by affiliation, the bold handling of figures that Whistler admired in the portraits of Velasquez. I will attempt to show otherwise. In the first section of this chapter I will argue that *The White Girl* is very much of the sensation era, and moreover that it depends for its success on the same shock effects that sustained the sensation novel and drama. In short, I will be suggesting that aestheticism and sensation are formed in the same cultural matrix; *The White Girl* is as much a secular apparition as her sensational sisters.

But what about the girl in Whistler's *White Girl*? To use the language of the Russian Formalists, does she simply motivate the device through which the painting achieves its particular effects? Or to use the language of Alfred Hitchcock, is she a McGuffin? What does it mean to turn Jo Hiffernan, a real person, into an icon, or a symphony? Put another way, what is the status of the represented within aestheticism? To approach these questions I want to turn in the second part of this chapter to George Du Maurier's enormously successful 1894 reanimation of the sensation novel, *Trilby*. Marrying a nostalgic evocation of Bohemian life in the Paris of the late 1850s to a sensational plot involving occult mesmeric powers, it captivated readers on both sides of the Atlantic when it appeared in *Harper's Magazine*, and generated a wave of Trilbymania, a

passionate popular interest in anything even remotely connected to the
novel. Du Maurier met Whistler in Paris in the 1850s, and they moved
in the same circles in London in the early 1860s. As is well known, the
painter forced his one-time room-mate to remove from *Trilby* the character of Joe Sibley, 'the idle apprentice', a talented but feckless Bohemian,
who was quite clearly based on Whistler. I want to argue, though, that
the novel returns us to their shared past more directly still, and that
Trilby offers us not just an insight into Du Maurier's mixed feelings about
his Bohemian youth and hostility to the aesthetic movement, but also a
Gothicized narrative of the relationships among Whistler, his model-mis-
tress and the artwork. By evoking a very different painting of the 1860s,
Gustave Courbet's infamous 'secret' painting *L'Origine du monde*, *Trilby*
offers a sceptical account of Whistler's formalist ambitions, suggesting
that, like the numinous, sex can be used to engineer attention.

WHITE GIRLS

Like *The Woman in White*, *The White Girl* is a product of London and
Paris, though its creator's origins are more complex still. Whistler was
born in the industrial town of Lowell, Massachusetts, and educated in
St Petersburg (where his father worked as a railway engineer) and at the
United States Military Academy at West Point, New York, before decid-
ing to pursue a career in art. He spent his apprentice years in Paris, where
he sometimes worked at the studio of Charles Gleyre (Monet, Renoir,
Bazille and Sisley would also study there). There he became friendly with
a number of British artists, including the Anglo-French Du Maurier,
the two of them being frequent visitors at the studio apartment of
Thomas Armstrong, Thomas Lamont and Edward Poynter in the Rue
Notre Dame des Champs, later the model for the studio in *Trilby*. In
1859 Whistler came to live and work in London, where his sister lived –
while maintaining strong ties to Paris – renting a studio-cum-flat at 70
Newman Street in Chelsea, which he later sublet to Du Maurier, while
continuing to use it himself at times. He seems to have been attracted by
two types of modern English subjects in these years: bourgeois interiors,
such as *At the Piano* (1859), and paintings and etchings of the 'low life' of
the Rotherhithe docks, such as *Wapping* (1861). The impressionistic interior *At the Piano* was accepted at the Royal Academy exhibition in 1860,
as was a portrait, *La Mère Gérard*, in 1861.[4] Whistler's 'Tamise' work
is very different in subject, though not in treatment. In a letter to his
mother, Du Maurier describes Whistler at work on *Wapping* in October

of 1860: 'I see less of him now, for he is working hard and in secret down in Rotherhithe, among a beastly set of cads and every possible annoyance and misery, doing one of the greatest *chefs d'oeuvres* – no difficulty discourages him.'[5] *Wapping* depicts a scene in a tavern overlooking the busy Thames in which a red-haired young woman (Hiffernan), perhaps meant to be a prostitute, sits at a table with two men, the human commerce in the foreground doubling the scenes of maritime commerce in the background. Patricia de Montfort suggests that its risqué theme marks it as a 'sensation painting', a piece meant to shock the sensibilities of its original viewers.[6] Yet despite some mixed reviews, the painting was hung, and was sold. In 1862 his etchings were considered good enough to be part of the British section at the International Exhibition then taking place in London, and were favourably reviewed. In terms of Whistler's general reception in London, then, the rejection of *The White Girl* was a decided anomaly.

Though first exhibited in London, *The White Girl* was actually painted in Paris in the winter of 1861, in a studio on the Boulevard des Batignolles. In a letter of February 1862 to Tom Armstrong, Du Maurier relates Whistler's account of the painting and the effect he was aiming at:

'Besides this [Breton painting] he is painting the woman in white – Red-haired party, life size, in a beautiful white cambric dress, standing against a window which filters the light through a transparent white muslin curtain – but the figure receives a strong light from the right and therefore the picture barring the red hair is one gorgeous mass of brilliant white. My notion is that it must be a marvellously brilliant thing – you can fancy how he described it' (*L*, pp. 104–8, p. 105).

The first to succumb to the painting's brilliant composition was Whistler himself, according to Du Maurier in a letter to Armstrong of March 1862: 'The woman in white is nearly finished – Jim working at it all the winter from 8 in the morning; got painter's colic very severely, but worked pluckily through it all' (*L*, pp. 117–22, p. 118). Painter's colic, or lead poisoning, was the natural result of Whistler's exposure to the massive quantities of lead white, essentially lead carbonate hydroxide, $2PbCO_3.Pb(OH)_2$, that he was using to achieve his spectacular effects (it would be some years before painters fully adopted the less dangerous zinc white).[7] Soon, the painting's intoxicating effect was felt by others. 'Sensation' is the term Hiffernan herself uses to capture the reaction to it in a letter of 16 June 1862 to Whistler's American friend, George Lucas:

'the White Girl has made a fresh sensation – for and against. Some stupid painters don't understand it, while Millais [John Everett Millais, friend of Wilkie and Charles Collins, and founding member of the Pre-Raphaelite Brotherhood] for instance thinks it splendid, more like Titian ... but Jim says that for all that perhaps the old duffers [*sc.* the hanging committee of the Royal Academy] may refuse it altogether.'[8]

Why did Whistler so clearly anticipate a negative reaction, when the 'old duffers' had not shown themselves to be altogether inimical to his earlier work? While *At the Piano* had been accepted though, and was far from being a sensation painting, it was probably already rather on the fringe of what the art establishment considered to be good and interesting art. It is useful to consider for a moment Whistler's choice of mode: genre painting. In traditional terms, classical, religious and historical painting were considered the most prestigious, with landscape and portraiture on a somewhat lower tier, and genre painting – the painting of everyday life – on a lower rung again. But this traditional hierarchy was not as stable as it once was, and genre painting, like landscape, enjoyed considerable popularity in the mid-Victorian period, even at the Royal Academy. This elevation of the ordinary is sometimes attributed to the rise of the commercial classes as purchasers of art. But the painting of everyday life was best received when it had a topical theme or narrative component, like Frith's *Derby Day* (1856–8) and *Railway Station* (1862); Augustus Egg's *Past and Present* (1858); or Abraham Solomon's *Waiting for the Verdict* (1857). The introduction to the Official Catalogue of the 1862 International Exhibition claimed that, with landscape, the 'the leading feature in modern art' was the 'Incident style', which focused on 'incidents of common life, and each suggestive of some little tale, half humorous or half sentimental'.[9] Whistler himself later gave a comic account of the inimical art culture of the 1860s within which he tried to create a niche for his own work:

It was the era of the subject. And, at last, on Varnishing Day, there was the subject in all its glory – wonderful. The British subject! Like a flash the inspiration came – the Inventor! And in the Academy there you saw him: the familiar model – the soldier or the Italian – and there he sat, hands on knees, head bent, brows knit, eyes staring; in a corner, angels and cogwheels and things; close to him his wife, cold, ragged, the baby in her arms; he had failed! The story was told; it was as clear as day – amazing! The British subject! What.[10]

At the Piano could just about be accommodated within this world; *The White Girl* could not, and the 'duffers' of the Royal Academy did refuse his subject-less painting. Whistler avenged himself in a minor way by describing it in the catalogue as 'Rejected at the Academy' when he exhibited it at the Berners Street Gallery, part of his effort to '[wage] open war with the academy'.[11] What repulsed the art establishment was not so much its theme – the sexually suggestive *Wapping* would be accepted by the Academy in 1864 – but its apparent lack of one, and scarcely better, its impressionistic treatment.

Although any viewers at the Berners Street gallery who had seen the *Times* advertisement ('Now on VIEW, at the Gallery, 14 Berners Street, Oxford Street, WHISTLER'S extraordinary PICTURE of the WOMAN IN WHITE. Admission 1s, including the gallery of 150 paintings'), or the similar sandwich-board ads, must have been expecting something unusual, they seem to have been no more willing than the Academy to accept readily a painting without a subject, and they were equally perplexed by the painting's lack of 'finish'.[12] Here is the reviewer of the *Athenaeum*:

The most prominent [painting] is a striking but incomplete picture by Mr James Whistler … Able as this bizarre production shows Mr Whistler to be, we are certain that in a few years he will recognize the reasons for its rejection [by the Academy]. It is one of the most incomplete paintings we have ever met with. A woman in a quaint morning dress of white, with her hair about her shoulders, stands alone in the background of nothing in particular. But for the rich vigour of the textures, we might conceive this to be some old portrait by Zucchero, or a pupil of his, practising in a provincial town.[13]

In 1862 Whistler's attempt to modernize painting was interpreted not as modern, but as unfinished, or as the work of some kind of curious throwback. As for the subject, viewers supplied their own narrative context, assuming that Whistler's startling exercise in colour was really an attempt to illustrate Wilkie Collins's *The Woman in White*: the *Athenaeum* reviewer continued, 'the face is well done, but it is not that of Mr. Wilkie Collins's Woman in White'.

This assumption that Collins's novel was Whistler's real 'subject' was, to be fair, quite understandable, since the painting had been hung with the title *The Woman in White*, and advertised as such. As we have seen, the midnight appearance of the fey Anne Catherick, 'dressed from head to foot in white garments', is the novel's iconic moment.[14] Moreover, as we also saw, Collins's novel was such a luminous success in the early 1860s that it is easy to imagine how visitors to the gallery might see the painting in its afterglow even without the prodding of publicity: in 1862 an unofficial stage version of the novel was packing them in at the Surrey Theatre, and there was a Woman in White perfume, two dances (the Fosco Galop and the Woman in White Waltz), and various other spin-offs and parodies to kept the novel fresh in the public mind. So wide were the ripples that emanated from the novel that Whistler's friend and sublessee, Du Maurier, illustrated one of these parodies, F. C. Burnand's *Mokeanna, Or the White Witness*, which appeared in *Punch* in 1863.[15]

5. George Du Maurier, illustration for *Punch*'s parodic sensation narrative, 'Mokeanna, or The White Witness' (1863).

If Whistler wished to free painting from narrative, and from the tyranny of the subject, he had made a very curious choice: in 1862 it would have been hard to keep a painting of any white-clad female figure out of the powerful orbit of Collins's novel. Though he was presumably quite happy with the free publicity generated by the associations made between his narrative-free painting and the novel, he affected otherwise, and began what would be a long career of writing letters to the press by informing the *Athenaeum* that the gallery had added the title without his 'sanction': 'I had no intention whatever of illustrating Mr Wilkie Collins's novel; it so happens, indeed, that I have never read it. My painting simply represents a girl dressed in white, standing in front of a white curtain.'[16] This seems somewhat disingenuous, since Du Maurier refers to the painting as the 'woman in white' as early as February 1862, which suggests that Whistler had in fact at some point used that title, even if he had not read Collins's novel. And whether or not he had read the book, he could hardly have failed to notice its many spin-offs, and indeed the more general pervasiveness of the 'sensation' phenomenon. Years later, in his 'Ten O'Clock' lecture of 1885, he would pour scorn on those art critics who treat pictures like novels, and always try to find out the plot; and yet in this picture he seems to be teasing us to find just such a novelistic connection.

The painting created just as much of a stir when it reappeared in Paris the following year at the *Salon des Refusés*, the alternative exhibition ordered by Napoleon III to accommodate the many works that had been rejected by the committee for that year's official Salon. (The extra Salon can be seen to be part of the bread and circuses laid on by the monarch to shore up popular docility in the face of his autocratic rule, an aspect of that mid-century consumer's paradise in which Walter Benjamin read the shape of things to come.[17]) According to some reports, Whistler's work was more a *succès pour rire* than *succès de scandale*, generating ridicule as much as shock (the reaction of the Parisian crowd is described in Zola's *L'Oeuvre* (1886)). English critic and artist Philip Hamerton describes how each group who passed the painting 'stopped instantly, struck with amazement … then they always looked at each other and laughed'.[18] Some were more deeply impressed, though. Paul Mantz commented on the painting's strange charm in the *Gazette des Beaux-Arts*, and coined the term 'Symphonie du Blanc'. Fernand Desnoyers, in his pamphlet on the Salon, described Whistler as 'le plus spirite des peintres' and the painting as a portrait of a spirit, a medium.[19] Whistler's friend Henri Fantin-Latour wrote to say that 'Baudelaire finds it charming … Legros, Manet, Bracquemond, de Balleroy and myself; we all think it's admirable.' Gustave Courbet, reported Fantin, was also struck by the work's spiritual quality: '[he] calls your picture an apparition, with a spiritual content (this annoys him); he says it's good' (*WB*, p. 86). (Again, it is hard not to see echoes of Lourdes here.)

What was so unusual about this genre painting of a young woman in a white dress that caused viewers in England and France to be baffled by it, to attack it, to take refuge in laughter, but also in some cases to see it as strangely powerful? As I have suggested, it was not the sort of painting that the Royal Academy favoured, but the depth of the reaction to it suggests that there were other factors at work in its reception. In fact, although the viewers of 1862 may have been wrong in seeing Whistler's *White Girl* as an *illustration* of *The Woman in White*, I think they were onto something. *The White Girl* is not so much an illustration of Collins's sensation novel as its analogue: it is a sensation painting, though not quite in the sense that *Wapping* is.

As we have seen, in the case of the drama and the novel, the term 'sensation' testified to a common awareness that there was something qualitatively different about these forms, that they were connected to the blurring of the boundaries of middle-class taste as well as to the modern, and to the industrialization of everyday life. One element of this constellation of associations was that 'Sensation' mimicked the tastes of the working class because it produced a physical rather than a mental response. Sensation drama placed the audience within a permanent present: not just through setting, but also through the techniques of suspense, the audience was radically interpolated into the drama rather than invited to view it aesthetically. The sensation novel worked along similar lines, producing an essentially somatic effect on its readers, what H. L. Mansel memorably called 'preaching to the nerves'.[20] The exemplary instances of this effect were the 'sensation scenes' shared by novel and play alike, where the audience or reader's attention is focused on a spectacular set piece, often a last-minute rescue, or the sudden appearance of a figure who is supposed to be dead: the rescue of Eily O'Connor from drowning in *The Colleen Bawn*; the burning river-boat in Boucicault's *The Octoroon*; Laura Fairlie's appearance at her own graveside in *The Woman in White*; the railway rescue in Augustin Daly's *Under the Gaslight*, Boucicault's *After Dark*, and many others. For many contemporary critics of drama these scenes meant the upstaging of actors by stage carpentry, and the usurpation of the play as a whole by its spectacular scenes; for critics of the novel the effect of the sensational scene was to replace all nuance with what Mrs Oliphant called a 'simple physical effect'.[21]

This same species of immediately immersive intensity, this 'simple physical effect', was deployed by Whistler. His deliberate eschewal of the procedures of the Academy meant that the viewer was forced to come to terms with this particular painting at this particular moment – there could be no easy recourse to narrative, symbology, or classical or historical sources. Like the sensation scene, it immersed its audience in a thrilling commodity experience – in this respect Eily's literal immersion in *The Colleen Bawn* is self-reflexive of the genre as a whole, as is the title of a popular play of 1862, *A Moment of Terror*.[22] Whistler, of course, was not simply trying to give his audience a frisson. There was a serious artistic purpose to his shock techniques: he wished to jolt the viewer out of a comfortable and contemplative relation to the work, and to confront him or her with both its hereness and nowness, and its material medium specificity, its nature as paint on canvas.

If one effect of the sensation novel and the sensation drama was to capture the reader or viewer's attention, another was the pleasurable acclimatization of their consumers to the speeded-up, stimulus-saturated world of Victorian urban modernity; they provided a species of temporal training, a form of shock-lite that inoculated the subject against hyperstimulus.[23] 'Sensation' at this level plays its part in that modernization of the subject described by Benjamin as taking place on the streets of Paris, more recently identified by Wolfgang Schivelbusch in the railway carriages of Europe, and by Jonathan Crary in the fine art of the last quarter of the nineteenth century. But as we have seen, in the sensation novel normal consciousness is always in danger of tipping over into some altered state, where self-presence is extremely precarious. Laura Fairlie comes to resemble the feeble-minded Anne Catherick in *The Woman in White*; the hero of *The Moonstone* turns out to have committed the crime himself in a trance-like state; Lady Audley in *Lady Audley's Secret* ends her days in a private asylum – her real secret is that she is mad. A similar preoccupation with liminal mental states, if not with actual madness, is evident in the fine art of the period, and Crary shows how a number of artists thematize and critique the new discourse of attention/distraction in their work from the 1860s on. But in the case of *The White Girl* this thematics, in the form of Jo Hiffernan's distracted, vacant stare, goes hand in hand with an attempt to solicit attention, to retrain the viewer, not as a subject capable of dealing with urban, industrial capitalist society, but as an aesthete who can respond to balanced masses of colour, to niceties in shades of white on white, without recourse to explanatory narratives or external interpretive schemes. Whistler, that is, may be trying to engineer the attention of the crowd, but it seems even more likely that he is attempting to shape an elite audience for modern painting. Obviously he cannot recreate the effects of the theatre, where a collectivity is tutored in the temporality of modernity; nor can he feed his audience on a diet of suspense and shock over a period of months, as the serial novelist could do. Instead, the artwork galvanizes the audience into a close encounter with the material artwork; not some Paterian idealist encounter, but a more material and abrasive one.

If the effect aimed at by Whistler was the retraining of his audience for a new orientation to the artwork, some commentators at least could register this even while resisting. Here is the reaction of an American critic who saw *The White Girl* at the French Universal Exhibition in 1867:

> [it shows] a powerful female with red hair, and a vacant stare in her soulless eyes. She is standing on a wolfskin hearthrug, for what reason is unrecorded. The picture evidently means vastly more than it expresses – albeit expressing too much. Notwithstanding an obvious want of purpose, there is some boldness in the handling, and singularity in the glare of the colours which cannot fail to divert the eye and weary it.[24]

What the critic glosses as 'want of purpose' is not some Kantian non-purposiveness so much as a powerful *effect* aimed at the eye of the viewer without the usual rationale of subject matter – a more concentrated and less motivated form of the 'sensation scene'. The eye is captured, and has to adjust not just to the 'glare', but also to the minimal contrast of white on white. The reference to the 'weary[ing]' effect of this on the eye is not just a throwaway remark, since in terms of nineteenth-century colour theory the painting would indeed exhaust the eye. According to such theories the presence of any of the primary colours (red, blue and yellow) required the use of the product of the other two to provide 'rest' for the eye.[25] But here the eye has to travel from the dazzling red hair across whole swathes of bright white to encounter the complementary product in the green flowers, though blue and yellow (of a sort) are present in the rug and in the wolfskin. The theories of Chevreul and others are being harnessed here to create nervous strain rather than harmony: for the viewers of the 1860s this was a very discordant colour symphony. (In this respect the painting provides a negative anticipation of the use of 'soothing' interior design schemes in hospitals to provide an antidote to shell-shock and nervous cases, following the colour theories of H. Kemp Prossor.[26])

That this attempt to fix the viewer's gaze was a violent one is evident: perhaps inspired by his friendship with the Fenian leader John O'Leary, Whistler was prepared to use drastic methods to launch his artistic revolution.[27] As it happens, in 1867 Whistler also began to acquire a reputation for less figurative violence. In Paris he appeared in court for taking part in two street brawls: the first time for assaulting a workman who had dripped plaster on him as he passed in the street below, the second for shoving his brother-in-law, Seymour Haden, through a plate-glass window (he was let off on the first occasion; on the second the Judge recognized him as a previous offender and fined him). An earlier story of his assaulting a black fellow passenger while en route back to London from Valparaiso also began to circulate. Even his Bohemian friends did not approve, D. G. Rossetti penning a rather barbed limerick:

> There's a combative artist named Whistler
> Who is, like his own hog-hairs, a bristler;
> A tube of white lead
> And a punch in the head
> Offer varied attractions of Whistler.[28]

Rossetti evidently grasped that Whistler's use of white lead was intended as a punch in the eye, as a visual assault on the viewer. And of course not everyone wanted such vigorous treatment: Whistler's career, like that of many proto-modernists, testifies to the difficulties of creating an audience for unfamiliar material.

Of course the extent to which the painting really does break with precedent, and even with Academy practice, is worth questioning. There are eighteenth-century paintings by Jean-Antoine Watteau that *The White Girl* appears to cite, and even at the time Paul Mantz linked it to Jean-Baptiste Oudry's Salon painting of 1753, *The White Duck*.[29] Closer in time, Gustave Courbet's *The Diligence in the Snow* (1860), originally entitled *Naufrage dans la Neige*, might have provided an example of the effects achievable through the use of whiteness on a grand scale (137 cm × 199 cm): the coach is all but invisible, the composition dominated by a sea of snow. Nor is Whistler's painting empty of all symbolic resonance: if the painting refuses us the sort of lofty 'subject' much favoured by the mid-Victorian art establishment, it is scarcely a non-representational exercise in pure colour, and at least some of its content seems to at once offer and withhold meaning. Some viewers, like Courbet, saw it as an 'apparition, with a spiritual content', presumably reminded of the Lourdes apparition, rather than the more mischievous 'dames blanches' of French folklore. As with the figures of the Colleen Bawn and the Woman in White, the painting also puts into play a long iconographic tradition of representing female innocence and chastity as white: this is the virginal white of wedding dresses. That Whistler deliberately activated at least some of these connotations is indicated by the fact that Hiffernan is holding a broken lily, while other flowers lie scattered on the floor before her. We are being invited to think of bridal bouquets, as well of the association of young women and flowers, and of course of young women and deflowering. And yet the fact that this young woman is standing on a wolfskin might suggest that she is not so vulnerable, that she can keep predators – wolves and perhaps even wolf-Whistlers – under her heel. This is to address only the more obvious symbolism of the painting. In 1862 we might imagine a range of other meanings at work. The loose white dress invokes its opposite: the fashionable aniline-dyed corseted dress. This, with her loose red hair, links the White Girl to the female icons of the Pre-Raphaelites, and their studied anti-modernity.[30] The whiteness of Hiffernan's skin evokes the science of race that increasingly defined white European identity against a variety of others, while white femininity summons up the racial stakes of the American Civil War, in which the spectre of servile insurrectionists menacing white women and children was used by both sides. (The war, which had been under way since April 1861, was unlikely to have been too far from Whistler's mind, since his brother was an officer in the Confederate army, and the artist himself, a former cadet at West Point, seems to have been rather ashamed at missing his chance for action.) Nor is black/white the only opposition in play here. Hiffernan's fair skin and red hair announces an English/Irish ethnic divide that also preoccupied racial scientists in this period. Whiteness had other connotations, too, in the Irish context: at least some viewers may have seen the plays *The White Boys: A Tale of the Irish Rebellion* of 1798 (Surrey Theatre, January 1862) and *The White Boys; or, Ireland in 1798* (Victoria, 30 January 1862), both of which dealt with the anti-landlord secret societies of the 1790s in Ireland (cf. Whistler's friendship with O'Leary and other Fenians in Paris in the 1850s).[31] But these are resonances that I will return to in Chapter 4.

Whistler's modernism met with considerable resistance. Until the 1880s and 1890s, when major international collectors began to buy up his paintings, it was a difficult business turning women into arrangements and symphonies, and those into money and prestige.[32] Until then his work retained the shock value of violence. The war between his vision and that of the art establishment would reach its climax some fifteen years after the first impact of *The White Girl*, when John Ruskin brought the pugnacious artist fresh notoriety in the July 1878 issue of *Fors Clavigera* by accusing him of 'ask[ing] 200 guineas for flinging a pot of paint in the public's face' with *Nocturne in Black and Gold: The Falling Rocket* (1875). Whistler took an action for libel against the great sage, but learned to his cost that juries, and even the educated public, were still closer in their views to Ruskin's moral aesthetics than to his own. One casualty of the jury's hostility to Whistler's aesthetic programme would be another symphony in white, the White House, his eye-catching new house on Tite Street in Chelsea. Sold at auction after Whistler's bankruptcy, it was bought by Harry Quilter, the *Times* art critic, who had appeared as a witness for Ruskin in the trial (we met him in Chapter 1 as an appreciative critic of Wilkie Collins).

If Whistler continued to fetishize white, by then he had long broken with his fair-skinned model: Hiffernan seems to have largely dropped out of his life in 1866–7, after his return to London from a mysterious trip to Valparaiso, Chile. Stanley Weintraub speculates that Whistler's break with Hiffernan resulted from her visit to Paris in his absence, where she posed for the explicitly lesbian work, *Le Sommeil*. We will return to Hiffernan's work with Courbet; for now let us follow the white girl's migration to another medium, a novel by Whistler's quondam room mate, George Du Maurier, and one of the first modern best-sellers, *Trilby*.

TRILBY O'FERRALL

In December of 1861, while Whistler was painting *The White Girl* in Paris, George Du Maurier had plans of his own to captivate the public, not with a painting, but with an illustrated story of left-bank life. While Whistler's progress seemed unstoppable, the sudden loss of vision in one eye had forced Du Maurier to rethink his future in fine art. Since a career as a painter seemed out of the question, like the fictional Walter Hartright he began to work as an illustrator for various London journals, eventually securing a position on the staff of *Punch*. His letters of the 1860s trace his rivalry with and admiration for Whistler, but also trace Du Maurier's progressive alienation from Whistler's Bohemian world, and attraction to the bourgeois domesticity of the Wightwicks, the family of his fiancée and later wife, Emma. At first, though, he very much lived in Whistler's shadow. In 1860, he was not only subletting Whistler's studio at 70 Newman Street, but was also making use of the dress coat and waistcoat that the latter had left behind. He describes 'Jimmy' as 'the grandest genius I ever met, a giant' (*L*, to his mother, June 1860, pp. 8–12, p. 11), though he also speaks of his 'cutting out' Jimmy at a social gathering (p. 9). In October he boasts that though Jimmy is the greater social lion of the two of them, there is no rivalry between them – and in any case he is more liked than Jimmy is, particularly because of his singing voice, his 'Horgin', as he puts it (*L*, to his mother, 3 October 1860, pp. 14–17). (His musical prowess meant a great deal to Du Maurier, and he speculated that he could make a living from his singing if his eyesight failed completely.) By September 1861, now living at 91 Newman Street, rivalry seems to have mutated into mild hostility: 'Jimmy Whistler gone to Paris – bon débarras; j'en devenais las; nothing is more fatiguing than an egotistical wit' (*L*, to his mother, pp. 65–7, p. 66). His occasional references to Jo Hiffernan in this period seem to mingle jealousy at Whistler's sexual success and snobbery at Jo's social origins. By 1862 he writes disapprovingly that she was 'de plus en plus insupportable et grande dame' (*L*, to Thomas Armstrong, May 1862, pp. 136–40, p. 139), and an 'awful tie' for the artist (*L*, to Thomas Armstrong, February 1864, pp. 226–8, p. 227).

But if Du Maurier was increasingly less the Bohemian artist and more the domesticated, professional middle-class illustrator, in 1861 he decided that he could still put his Paris years to good use by writing a semi-autobiographical tale of left-bank life in Paris. As he wrote to Thomas Armstrong in a letter of December 1861:

I took it yesterday to the *Cornhill* – 24 pages of closely written foolscap, and yet I had eliminated lots … [Thomas] Lamont is there as the wise and facetious Jerry, you as the bullnecked and sagacious Tim; the street is our Lady of the Bohemians [*sc.* Rue Notre Dame des Champs]. I shall idealize it in the illustrations (if I get them to do), make us all bigger, and develop you into strong muscularity; having insisted on our physical prowess and muscular development – the natural antidotes to morbid Quartier-Latin Romance – I shall be much surprised if it gets into the *Cornhill*... If this does succeed, I shall write lots more on the same theme, and try and embody the rather peculiar opinions of our set on art itself, and artists; and which I feel very strongly. (*L*, p. 92)

It did not get into the *Cornhill*, and we hear no more of the untitled story for thirty years, by which time Du Maurier was a well-known *Punch* cartoonist. (While the novel does not appear until 1894, we know that he had the idea of a mesmeric villain and female victim as early as March 1889, when he suggested this scenario as an idea for a novel to his friend Henry James.[33]) When he returns to his Parisian theme, the result is not a short comic tale but a full-length novel, *Trilby* (1894), perhaps inspired by the recent success of that very different tale of studio life, *The Picture of Dorian Gray* (1891). If his earlier semi-comic tale of muscular artists – a sort of *Three Men in a Studio* – provided the germ, by 1894 the story had acquired a more sinister dimension in the form of the relationship between Trilby, the beautiful model-cum-laundress turned diva, and Svengali, the novel's Austrian-born Jewish villain. (A sinister mesmerist features in the version Du Maurier offered to Henry James, so that figure must have arisen independently of *Dorian Gray*'s Lord Henry Wotton.) Svengali, of course, entered the language as a byword for manipulation and magnetism, one of a series of such figures in the nineteenth-century anti-semitic imaginary, as Daniel Pick has shown.[34] Like Whistler, Du Maurier equates the visual and the musical: Svengali is not a painter like the other young men we meet in the novel's early chapters, but a musician and composer, who takes the tone-deaf young Trilby O'Ferrall, and turns her into a singer of consummate ability. While he conducts, she spellbinds audiences with her ability to sing simple ballads and songs without words across a huge vocal range, performing almost superhuman exercises in virtuosity. At the novel's close, though, we learn that there are 'two Trilbys', and that the singing Trilby is the creation of Svengali's hypnotic powers: far from being a great singer, she is simply an instrument for his musical genius, her master's voice. When Svengali dies, his hold over her seems to be broken, and the original Trilby is briefly restored to the novel's band of heroes. But even from the grave Svengali can manipulate her, and she dies shortly after seeing his portrait.

While the novel is now best known for this sensational mesmeric subplot, which was emphasized in subsequent stage and screen versions, in the original novel far more space is devoted to the idyllic evocation of Parisian studio life, and the male camaraderie of the three young British artists: the 'Tim' (Thomas Armstrong, later director of the Art and Science Department of the South Kensington Museum) of the 1861 story has become Taffy; 'Jerry'

(Thomas Lamont, a lifelong friend of Du Maurier's) has become The Laird; and Du Maurier himself, if he is there at all, appears to have become Little Billee (later known as William Bagot). A very English version of Bohemia, their homosocial world has more in common with Jerome K. Jerome's 1889 *Three Men in a Boat* than it has with Henri Murger's novel of 1851, *Scènes de la Vie de Bohème*. Du Maurier's narrative of their left-bank life is chatty, digressive and playful: readers expecting to be gripped by a swiftly moving sensational plot must have been baffled. In this sanitized Bohemia, sexual appetency is displaced into gourmandizing, and we are treated to lovingly detailed accounts of what the three 'chums' eat and drink, rather in the manner of a school story. This all-male Eden is doomed, though, and the first half of the novel describes the gradual break-up of the male household through Little Billee's growing attraction to the beautiful and good-hearted, but fatally déclassée heroine, Trilby.[35] Trilby works as a nude model, and we are told coyly by our narrator in Latin, 'multum amavit': she has loved a lot (p. 36). The end comes when Little Billee's strait-laced mother comes from England to persuade Trilby that she will ruin his life by marrying him. Svengali appears in this first section of the novel as a friend of the trio, one of the various satellite characters who frequent the studio. Other minor characters include Lorrimer, 'the virtuous apprentice', a thinly disguised version of Edward Poynter (by the 1890s an RA, and in 1896 President of the Royal Academy), and in the magazine version, Joe Sibley, 'the idle apprentice', clearly modelled on Whistler. Whatever his theories of the autonomy of painting, Whistler was well able to see the links between life and fiction when it suited him, and he objected to his representation as Sibley. Du Maurier was forced to make changes to the subsequent book version, substituting 'the yellow-haired Antony, a Swiss' (p. 96), a witty man who never made an enemy, for Whistler's character, and removing some of the illustrations (though Whistler, complete with monocle, is still clearly visible in some of the illustrations, such as 'All as it used to be' in Part Third).

Trilby is based on Du Maurier's memories of his Bohemian years in Paris and London, refracted through the experience of the intervening thirty years, and for much of that period Du Maurier had conducted a series of skirmishes with the aesthetic movement, parodying its affectations and excesses in his series of cartoons for *Punch* featuring such characters as Maudle, Postlethwaite and the Cimabue Browns. In *Trilby*, though, it is the artistic practice of aestheticism that he attacks rather than the pretensions of the aesthetic followers. This practice is not embodied in the relationship between the talented painter, Little Billee, and Trilby, but displaced to that between the musician, Svengali, and the model.

When the homosocial world of the studio in the Rue Notre Dame des Champs breaks up, Svengali takes up Trilby as his instrument. At the novel's end we learn from Gecko, Svengali's assistant, that the mesmerist turns her into 'a singing machine – an organ to play upon ... a flexible flageolet of flesh and blood' (p. 299), through which he is able to express his own musical genius (the phrase 'singing machine' suggests that Du Maurier may have seen Thomas Alva Edison's phonographic dolls when he visited the 1889 Paris Exposition). But the novel hints that Trilby becomes Svengali's sexual instrument as well, and the sexuality repressed in the representation of Bohemia as a chummy all-male place returns here in a Gothic register: 'with one wave of his hand over her – with one look of his eye – with a word – Svengali could turn her into the other Trilby, his Trilby – and make her do whatever he liked ... you might have run a red-hot needle into her and she would not have felt it ...' (p. 298).

The spiritual love that Little Billee has for Trilby reappears here transmogrified into the barely disguised image of her brutal penetration by the swarthy foreign villain. To say that she has been reduced to a mere mouth for Svengali to sing through, then, is not the whole story: his hypnotic powers give him ready access to her whole body. That this idea was titillating as much as daring for the readers of 1894 is clear from the novel's astonishing popularity, and the letters from readers asking for further details of the exact relationship between Svengali and his obedient 'organ'.[36]

The parallel between Svengali's artistic and sexual interests in Trilby is suggested quite early on when he waxes lyrical about her unusually large mouth: 'Himmel! The roof of your mouth is like the dome of the Panthéon; there is room in it for "toutes les glories de la France", and a little to spare! The entrance to your throat is like the middle porch of St Sulpice when the doors are open for all the faithful on All Saints' Day' (p. 50). But in this respect he is in fact only continuing a morcellization of Trilby that begins much earlier. *Trilby* is a novel of fetishization, both sexual and commodity-based – people are reduced to particular body parts; sexuality is displaced into other registers; things behave like people, and people like things. Unsurprisingly, art in the novel is also fetishistic. As Leonée Ormond pointed out some years ago, Svengali's objectification of Trilby is rather belated, since she 'has already been appropriated as an object before Svengali ever sees her' by the artists for whom she sits.[37] The first thing that Little Billee does when he meets Trilby is to draw her perfect foot on the studio wall. Much later, the trio revisit their old studio, where they find this same sketch now operating as a sort of shrine. Protected 'under a square of plate glass', it is now entitled 'Souvenir de la Grande Trilby'

(p. 200), and the Laird unsuccessfully attempts to buy this piece of wall as a memento of her.

By then the three former Bohemians each 'possessed casts of Trilby's hands and feet, and photographs of herself' (p. 202), but this sketch 'was Trilbyness itself, as the Laird thought, and should not be allowed to perish' (p. 202). Du Maurier hints broadly at the species of downward displacement involved in the fascination with Trilby's foot, in a long aside about this 'wondrous thing', too often 'hidden away in disgrace, a thing to be thrust out of sight and forgotten', though 'the sudden sight of it, uncovered, comes as a very rare and singularly pleasing surprise to the eye that has learned how to see' (p. 16). Trilby, it seems, even makes a fetish of this aspect of herself: her foot, this token of 'the lordship of woman over all', is her 'one coquetry, the only real vanity she had' (p. 16). (This emphasis on Trilby's perfect feet was carried into Paul Potter's stage adaptation of the novel, and was the subject of a good deal of comic comment in the musical-hall songs of 1895.[38]) When Trilby becomes famous, it is by an advertising photograph of her in sandals that her former friends recognize her ('Look Sandy, look – *the foot! Now* have you got any doubts?' (p. 244)). The deathly and less jocular aspect of Trilby's aestheticization becomes clearer in the second half of the novel. Without Svengali's controlling power she loses all vitality, but her fading away seems to make her 'more beautiful in their eyes, in spite of her increasing pallor and emaciation – her skin was so pure and delicate, and the bones of her face so admirable' (p. 266). She becomes, indeed, a White Girl. Svengali exerts his power over her one more time from beyond the grave when his portrait arrives in the post from 'the poisonous East' (p. 282), and Trilby dies. The lines between people and things blur further when she sings one more time on her deathbed: when she stops, the doctor who examines her reveals that 'she has been dead several minutes – perhaps a quarter of an hour' (p. 284).

In *Trilby* Du Maurier may be suggesting that all art has reifying tendencies, but there is a more specific target for his animus – his former friend Whistler, and his ambitious aesthetic programme of turning women into symphonies. Whistler's presence in the novel does not, in fact, disappear with the excision of the 'the idle apprentice'; he lingers as Svengali. Critics have tended to see Svengali as Du Maurier's nightmare double for Oscar Wilde, but the sinister Austrian mesmerist and musician more closely resembles the eccentric American with the monocle, given to the composition of Harmonies, Nocturnes and Arrangements.[39] The earlier version of the novel explicitly acknowledges the kinship between the more benign Whistler character, Sibley, and his demonic

6. One of Du Maurier's illustrations for *Trilby* (1894). The old friends
contemplate Little Billee's drawing of Trilby's foot.

other: Sibley is 'always in debt, like Svengali; like Svengali, vain, witty,
and a most exquisite and original artist ... [but] The moment his friendship left off his enmity began at once. Sometimes his enmity would take
the simple and straightforward form of trying to punch his ex-friend's
head.'⁴⁰ Whistler's choice of the butterfly as his artistic signature (con-
noting transformation, beauty, artistic flight, and so on) returns in Du
Maurier's depiction of Svengali as a spider, a creature which captures its
prey in its web and then feeds on it.

7. Another of Du Maurier's illustrations for *Trilby*. Svengali as a spider.

Du Maurier even seems to have based Svengali's vampiric aspect on Whistler: for some of his sitters, such as the French dandy Count Robert de Montesquiou, whom he painted in 1892, the intensity of Whistler's gaze did indeed seem to drain them of their vitality. As he told Edmond de Goncourt, he felt that 'Whistler with his fixed attention was emptying him for life, was "pumping away" something of his individuality' (*WB*, p. 355).[41]

But if the demonic Svengali preys on Trilby O'Ferrall and lives vampiri-cally on her, who was the object of Whistler's sexual-aesthetic exploitation? Felix Moscheles, another of Du Maurier's friends from his studio days, identifies 'Carry', a Belgian girl they had befriended in Malines, as the model for Trilby, but Joanna Hiffernan is a far more plausible original.[42]

8. The cover of the 1895 Harper edition of *Trilby*, showing a
winged heart caught in a spider's web.

There are a number of indications that Du Maurier was overlaying his
memories of Paris in the 1850s with London in the 1860s. Some are links
so tenuous that they almost seem beneath notice, such as the fact that in
his letters he habitually refers to Jo Hiffernan as 'Joe', the name he later
gives to Sibley in the novel; or the fact that Trilby is a 'blanchisseuse de
fin' as well as a model. But there are stronger clues. Like Hiffernan, Trilby
is the daughter of a lapsed Irish gentleman: in Trilby's case this is the

hard-drinking 'Patrick Michael O'Ferrall, Fellow of Trinity, Cambridge', son of a Dublin physician, a classical tutor who marries a barmaid and is lost to the world of respectability (pp. 18, 37); in Hiffernan's, it is Patrick Hiffernan, 'an impulsive and passionate Irishman'. According to Du Maurier's letters, the latter gave writing lessons – the Pennells describe him as 'a sort of Captain Costigan [*sc.* an Irish character in Thackeray's *History of Pendennis*]', 'a teacher of polite chiromancy'.[43] Whistler felt that he might 'do something to disgrace Joe's sisters' after their mother's death (*L*, to Thomas Armstrong, March 1862, pp. 117–21). Trilby possesses Hiffernan's Irish complexion, 'a mass of freckles', which contrast with the 'delicate, privet-like whiteness' of her neck (p. 13). Her accent is described as 'half-Scotch', but her first question to the three artists, 'Ye're all English, now, aren't ye?' (p. 13), is more stage Irish, as apparently is her gift for compliments ('That's Irish, I suppose' (p. 91)). (In the stage version written by Paul Potter she is Irished up a bit further: her greeting is 'The top o' the morning to you, boys', and her father is described as a graduate of Trinity College, Dublin rather than Trinity College, Cambridge.[44]) Later, when rumours spread of the humble origins of the great Madame Svengali, it is said that 'she had run away from the primeval forests and lonely marshes of le Dublin, to lead a free-and-easy life among the artists of the Quartier Latin', and that she was 'blanche comme neige' (p. 238). Like Hiffernan, Trilby puts her good looks to account by modelling for young artists; and like Hiffernan, Trilby is not married to the man (in Trilby's case men) she sleeps with. Even the novel's most far-fetched feature, Svengali's occult use of Trilby, recalls Hiffernan's relationship with Whistler, since Hiffernan had acted as a medium at seances at the house of Whistler's more famous Chelsea neighbours, the Rossettis, and according to the Pennells, Whistler and Jo had tried something similar at home, with some success. Whistler later claimed that 'a cousin from the South talked to me, and told me the most wonderful things'.[45]

What, then, is Du Maurier suggesting finally about the relationships among aesthetic artist, model, canvas and viewer by transforming them into the relationships among Svengali, Trilby and their audience? What is involved in shifting the artistic modality of the novel from painting, where it begins, to mesmerism and music? At some level this may be simply a gibe at the musical metaphors beloved of Whistler and his followers; the Symphonies, Arrangements and Nocturnes. But the mesmerism suggests something else: if Whistler was wary of critics who sought to turn paintings into novels, Du Maurier gives him grounds for such wariness by turning his artistic theories and practice into the stuff of Gothic. As

Grossman, Pick and Thurschwell have argued, Svengali's mesmeric powers figure anxieties regarding questions of influence, charisma and the nature of the self. Svengali/Whistler's influence on his audience/viewers is represented as pernicious. Like Trilby, the audience is hypnotized by Svengali and Trilby in concert ('And here Little Billee begins to weep again, and so does everybody else' (p. 216)), and spellbound by Trilby's 'celestial form and face' (p. 220). No less than the popular mass culture to which it seemed to be opposed, aestheticism was about retraining consumers, but here that retraining appears as a species of black magic that can raise whole crowds to the pitch of hysteria and infatuation. The audience are not the only victims: Little Billee and the other artists may fetishize Trilby just as much as Svengali does, reducing her to a foot, or a face, but Svengali goes further by actually stealing her identity completely, or more accurately by replacing the living Trilby with a puppet, a conduit for his own personality. The instrumentalization of Trilby appears to be Du Maurier's narrative theory of what Whistler was doing in such paintings as *The White Girl*: the historical Jo Hiffernan is effaced, to be replaced by Whistler's formal arrangement; she is abstracted out of existence, turned into a sensational visual effect.[46] What Whistler presents as a pure exercise in form is for Du Maurier, then, an exploitation of model and audience alike, and one that subjugates the ontology of the represented, in this case Hiffernan, to the egotistical vision of the artist.

The Origin

And yet, there is a curious disconnect between the emplotted critique of aestheticism and the sexual menace of the relationship between Svengali and Trilby. Whistler's powerful personality may be the basis for Svengali's mesmeric powers, and the way in which everyone gets their bit of Trilby may figure the abstracting processes of Whistler's aestheticism, but there appears to be a certain narrative excess in the way in which Trilby's mouth and feet are fetishized, and in the (related) way in which we are encouraged to think of Trilby's rape over a period of years by Svengali (though Du Maurier denied that anything of the sort was intended). I think that the source material for this dimension of the novel also derives from the 1860s, but it is not the relationship between Hiffernan and Whistler that is evoked, but rather her relationship with a very different artist, Gustave Courbet, and her role not in the creation of one of the threshold works of aestheticism, *The White Girl*, but one of the most infamous works in the history of realism, *L'Origine du monde*.

In 1866 Whistler rather mysteriously embarked for Valparaiso in Chile (then engaged in a war with Spain), having told many of his friends that he was in fact going to California. Biographers have speculated that the trip was motivated by his sense of having missed his chance for heroism in the American Civil War, though he may also have been avoiding police attention in the wake of his friend John O'Leary's arrest for treason. Jo seems to have done her best to manage his affairs in his absence, selling his work when she could, but eventually she resumed her former career as a professional model. She left London for Paris, where she sat for Gustave Courbet, whom she had met in the summer of 1865 in Trouville with Whistler (and probably earlier in Paris when *The White Girl* was being painted in 1861/2). At Trouville, Courbet had produced a study of her, *Portrait de Jo* (1865), and in 1865–6 four versions of a full portrait, the three that Robert Fernier describes in his Catalogue Raisonné as: *Jo, Femme D'Irlande*, or *La Belle Irlandaise* (Stockholm, probably the original), *Jo, Femme D'Irlande*, or *La Belle Irlandaise* (Metropolitan Museum of Art) and *Jo, Femme D'Irlande* (Kansas City), and *Portrait of Jo, or The Beautiful Irishwoman* (Collection Rolf and Margit Weinberg, Zurich).[47] Art historians have speculated that she and Courbet had an affair in these months. Whether they did or not, what Jean-Jacques Fernier describes as 'un déferlement d'érotisme' swept over Courbet's studio, and he produced some of his most sensual paintings during Jo's Paris stay.[48] The Ottoman diplomat Khalil Bey, who admired Courbet's erotic *Vénus et Psyche* (1864), had asked him to produce another version of it for him to add to his already impressive collection of French art. The result was the explicit eroticism, possibly inspired by contemporary pornographic photographs, of *Paresse et Luxure*, better known as *Le Sommeil* (1866), in which one of the models is Jo (Robert Fernier identifies her as the blonde, James Rubin as the red-head).[49] As with *La Belle Irlandaise*, the Hiffernan we see here is not the ethereal beauty of *The White Girl*, a willowy figure who seems to play second fiddle to fabric, but a mature woman of flesh and blood. As with his other nudes Courbet ignores the idealizing conventions of academic painting to achieve effects of startling immediacy and physical presence.

But in 1866 Courbet also painted another work for Khalil Bey that has come to be, arguably, the most notorious painting of the nineteenth century: the unsigned *L'Origine du monde*, which shows the torso of a woman reclining with her legs apart; the edge of a sheet covers one breast, and partly covers the other, but the viewer's gaze is drawn to her exposed genitals, shown in close-up, as it were, at the centre of the composition.

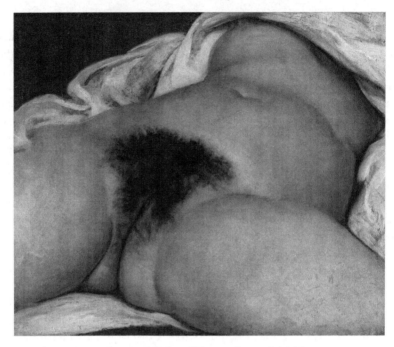

9. Gustave Courbet, *L'Origine du monde* (1866).

This was not a painting for the Salon: Khalil Bey kept it in his bathroom, behind a green curtain. Male guests were invited to view it from time to time (Maxime Du Camp and Léon Gambetta recorded seeing it in the 1860s). *L'Origine* might be considered a brilliant deconstruction of the fetishistic aspect of art, or an egregious example of it. Certainly, it makes the connection between fine art and the skin trade abundantly clear, too clear for it to work as drawing-room erotica. Contemporary opinion evinced hostility to the painting and its foreign patron. Charles Beauquier, writing in the *Revue littéraire de la Franche-Comté* in August 1866, wrote: 'The famous picture of Two Naked Women [*sc. Le Sommeil*] has been sold by M. Courbet to a Turkish diplomat. Our painter is making at the moment a pendant to this picture. I don't need to tell you that it is as indecent as the first. Dame! For a Turk!'[30]

L'Origine seems to have been a rather open secret. In June 1867 a satirical magazine, *Le Hanneton*, featured a caricature of Courbet by Léonce Petit in which the artist appears surrounded by some of his pictures; one of them is a white canvas with a solitary fig leaf in the middle. The painting disappeared after the sale of the bankrupt Khalil Bey's collection in 1867, to reappear in 1889 in the gallery of Antoine de la Narde, an art dealer. Edmond de Goncourt describes seeing it there concealed in a locked cabinet, the exterior of which showed a landscape featuring a snow-bound chateau (possibly *Le Chateau de Blonay*, according to Robert Fernier). Bought by a Hungarian sugar magnate, the Baron François de Hatvany, in 1913, it went to Budapest and dropped out of sight. Jacques Lacan and Sylvia Bataille appear to have purchased it in 1957, and they also kept it hidden behind another painting, this time a nude by Lacan's brother-in-law, André Masson. As late as 1987 Linda Nochlin, the eminent art historian, could find no trace of the painting, but in June 1995 the painting was presented to the Musée d'Orsay, where it was at first exhibited behind a glass screen.[51]

In the catalogue to the *Courbet L'Amour* exhibition held at the Courbet Museum at Ornans in 1996, a number of critics – Jean-Jacques Fernier, Michèle Haddad and Chantal Humbert – suggest that the model for this extraordinary painting is Joanna Hiffernan (an idea mooted at least as early as 1978 by Sophie Monneret), though Humbert suggests that Courbet's 'realism' is a more complex affair, and that *L'Origine* may indeed be a composite of Hiffernan and a contemporary 'star' of pornographic photography, Augustine Legaton: 'pour répondre à la commande de Khalil Bey, le peintre aurait demandé de poser á la maitresse de Whistler, Johanna Heffernan [*sic*]. Courbet aurait ensuite "peaufiné" la representation en se servant d'une épreuve semblable de nu [to meet Khalil Bey's order, the painter might have asked Johanna Heffernan, Whistler's mistress, to pose. Courbet might then have 'buffed up' the representation with a similar nude photograph].[32]

Did Du Maurier know of this picture and Hiffernan's role in its creation? Raised in Paris and himself a French-trained artist turned professional comic illustrator, it is quite possible that he would have seen or heard about the cartoon in *Le Hanneton*. By the 1890s he may have come across the rumours about the painting's existence, and he would almost certainly have heard of Hiffernan's other work for Courbet. Such knowledge of *L'Origine* would certainly illuminate the sexualized 'morcellization' of Trilby in his novel, her alternating presentation as a foot or a cavernous mouth, and indeed the suggestion of her becoming the abused private possession of a lecherous foreigner. (Trilby's description as 'blanche comme neige, avec un volcan dans le coeur' (p. 238) perhaps even suggests that he had heard of the snowy landscape cover-painting that Edmond de Goncourt describes.) In this light Svengali, then, may not be so much the Gothic version of Whistler, but Du Maurier's condensation of Whistler,

Courbet and Khalil Bey (not so much an Oriental Jew like Svengali as an Oriental Muslim).

But besides this *roman-à-clef* dimension, the novel appears to be making a serious argument about the nature of art. By conflating Whistler's publicly exhibited white symphony with Courbet's piece of private bathroom erotica, Du Maurier casts into doubt the good faith of the former. In December 1861 Du Maurier writes to Thomas Armstrong: 'I really believe that *mere female beauty* would actually make a well painted picture go down the swinish public throat, in spite of its artistic merit; indeed [John Everett] Millais is a very good instance' (*L*, pp. 92–4, p. 94). By the 1890s he has swung round to thinking that sexual interest could be used to less improving ends. Just as Svengali's musical genius parasitically depends on its living organ – Trilby's beauty, Trilby's cavernous mouth, her fascinating foot – the impact of *The Symphony in White* depends on a representation of a beautiful young woman. In both cases, sex is used to engineer attention, and to sell the grander aesthetic programme. Trilby is both the haunting young woman of *Symphony in White* and the fragmented flesh of *L'Origine*, a crotch-shot. Ultimately, Du Maurier may have thought that Whistler's work, like pornography, created a sensation only by pushing some very basic buttons for its audience, preaching not so much to the nerves as to the libido.

L'Origine resides still at the Musée D'Orsay, though no longer behind glass, and like the glass-covered drawing of Trilby's foot on the studio wall in the Rue Notre Dame des Champs, it has become a veritable shrine for art pilgrims. In this respect, Du Maurier's novel seems to demonstrate a strange prescience about the fate of Hiffernan's fragmented image. And the White Girl herself? Translated into a series of phantom doubles – first a white symphony, then an anatomical close-up, concealed beneath a snowy landscape, and then at once a singing machine and a glazed drawing of a foot – what became of the actual Joanna Hiffernan? De Montfort quotes a letter from Whistler of May 1880 to his son, Charles Hanson, in which he sends his regards to 'Auntie Jo', and Alan Cole remembered visiting her with Whistler in the 1880s.[53] According to the Pennells she was seen at Whistler's funeral in 1903, and Stanley Weintraub rather sceptically recounts Charles Freer's claim that Hiffernan came to Cheyne Walk after Whistler's death, to see him one last time, her striking hair now turning grey. As Weintraub points out, the scene is far too reminiscent of the Victorian narrative paintings that Whistler hated to be entirely plausible (pp. 463–4). It is more likely that, having lent her image to some of the key works of modern painting, she simply disappeared into the crowd.

CHAPTER 4

Black and white in the 1860s

When I say wight I mean black.
Dundreary, in *Our American Cousin*, III.

As we saw in Chapter 2, *Punch* took its usual satirical view of the arrival of sensation, identifying it as a way of advertising, or 'puffing', one or other new cultural commodity. Drama with a strong situation, or 'sensation scene', was one such product in the market for entertainment; the 'flying trapeze' artist Jules Léotard was another. The third dubious novelty mentioned in the poem under the umbrella of 'sensation' was the 'nigger minstrel [who] would deck / His wool-wig with extra green bays'.[1] The reference to 'extra green bays' remains obscure, but 'nigger minstrels' were, of course, the blackface (but not usually black) performers who became popular in the US in the 1830s, and whose popularity spread to Britain soon afterwards. By the 1860s they were a staple of Victorian entertainment, attracting a cross-class audience, appearing as music-hall acts, but also providing full variety-style shows, with their own particular conventions, characters and themes, at such venues as St James's Hall in Piccadilly and the Berners Hall (adjoining the Agricultural Hall) in Islington.

Blackface minstrelsy in the United States has been the object of a considerable degree of historical scrutiny, and has variously been seen, inter alia, as the first truly American popular form; as an unstable form that could show the fragility of race as a concept; as an oppositional discourse that questioned the boundaries of race, class and gender; as a phenomenon complexly related to the desire of such low-status immigrants as Irish Catholics to be assimilated into 'white' America; and as some combination of the above.[2] Apart from the pioneering work of J. S. Bratton and Michael Pickering, much less has been written about blackface minstrelsy in Victorian Britain, despite its enormous popularity and the longevity of its appeal.[3] While some black American performers enjoyed considerable popularity in Britain in the 1860s (e.g. the Bohee brothers), their success was greatly outweighed by that of British (or sometimes Euro-American) men pretending to be African American performers.

Why did large numbers of British people want to see other British people pretend to be black slaves, or ex-slaves, who sang, danced, played a variety of instruments and told jokes? Why did so many people purchase the sheet music to minstrel songs, and sing them at home as well as in amateur public performances, with or without blackface? At an abstract level we might speculate that there is a species of cross-ethnic identification going on here, at the same time that the audience is defining itself in opposition to the simulacrum of black identity being conjured up on stage. But we cannot simply extrapolate the findings of scholars regarding the appeal of the US phenomenon of minstrelsy – even were there any uncontroversial findings – since race and ethnicity functioned very differently in Britain, a country where in the 1860s, despite its vast empire, there was a relatively small population of colour outside of the port towns and cities. Moreover, while Britain had been deeply involved in the slave trade, slave ownership had never entered into the warp and weft of society in quite the same way as in the United States; slavery in England had ended with the Mansfield judgement of 1772, and in Britain's overseas territories had officially ended with the Slavery Abolition Act of 1833. The ethnic minority that attracted the most attention in Britain were, in fact, the Irish, more particularly the Catholic Irish, who were sometimes considered to be a race apart, and attitudes to whom became increasingly hostile during the Fenian activities of the 1860s.[4] The Murphy riots of 1867–9 further focused invidious attention on the large Catholic working-class population of the industrial towns. Active hostility was one end of the continuum of which condescension was the other: in the theatres, less benign versions of Myles-na-Coppaleen proliferated, hard-drinking and aimlessly violent, and in minstrel shows some performers moved seamlessly from plantation songs to such comic Irish numbers as 'The Ranting, Roaring Irishman' (1863) and 'Finnigans Wake' (187?). Such factors might serve to remind us that the appeal of blackface minstrelsy cannot be analysed without some sense of the more general field of British self-definition in these years.

What consequences does this racial imaginary have for the interpretation of women in white and white girls? In this chapter I want to consider a series of questions that I have largely repressed up to now: what whiteness means in terms of definitions of the national body; and how sensation and fantasies about the crowd relate to ideas of ethnicity. On one plane, the vulnerable, ethereal and even ghostly female figures of the Woman in White, the Colleen Bawn and the White Girl resemble secularized versions of the

Lourdes apparition, but their whiteness also has ethnic connotations, and they are implicitly defined against other figures: darker figures, figures defined by their corporeality rather than their purity or ethereality. While the women in white suggested that the distracted attention of the crowd could be focused through spectacle and sensation, they circulate along-side images of blackness that embody a more fearful imaginary. Whistler's *White Girl*, for example, suggests not just the logical formal corollary of a *Symphony in Black*, of a black girl in a black dress against a black back-ground, but historically evokes the black slaves who picked the cotton that went into that white muslin dress.[5] Painted during the American Civil War, when plantation slavery, and the possibility of a slave rebellion, were widely discussed in Britain as well as the United States, *The White Girl* was the work of an artist with Southern sympathies (Whistler's brother was a Confederate officer): in this context the whiteness of the White Girl takes on other resonances, as does her apparently unmotivated vulnerability. Moreover, the fact that the model for the painting, Joanna Hiffernan, was Irish, opens the painting to a broader consideration of the production of whiteness as a racial category, at a time when the racial nature of the Irish, or more accurately the peasant or working-class Catholic Irish, was being debated.[6]

But we might also consider the bodies upon whom sensation novels, plays and paintings were meant to work: if the culture of sensation was underwrit-ten by an embodied or somatic aesthetics, what sort of body was at issue? The characters in sensation novels are subject to frequent changes of colour, an index of the emotional upheavals of the characters and readers alike, but these colour shifts are generally underwritten by an assumed underlying stability: that these are white, European bodies. The biological logic that characterizes the late nineteenth century, with its vocabulary of degener-ation and decadence, its naturalist narratives and its organicist art-nouveau iconography, was still in its infancy, as it were, in the 1860s; but race was nonetheless coming to assume a new importance as a way of understanding human behaviour, national differences and dispositions, and even the pat-terns of history itself. As Catherine Hall has shown, the 1867 Reform Act was not just about class relations 'at home': the assumptions about British identity that were crystallized in the Act must be understood in relation to other contexts too.[7] The work on race of figures as diverse as Ernest Renan, the Comte de Gobineau, and Robert Knox was finding an audience, and in complex relation to this discursive turn, the events of the Indian Mutiny of 1857, the American Civil War of 1861–5 and the Morant Bay Rebellion of 1865 changed the way in which British identity came to be understood.

While the imperial contexts of Jamaica and India and the circum-Atlantic context of the American Civil War were the most obvious ones in which white Englishness was reimagined in these years, the 'internal other' of Ireland was also important. Nor were these the only factors: the 'discovery' of the gorilla in the 1860s seems to have acted as an impetus for new thinking about the place of the white European in the grand scheme of things. In short, it is not necessary to characterize the 1860s as an 'age of anxiety' to see that for a variety of reasons whiteness came into clearer focus as a category for self-definition. A number of cultural artefacts will allow us to consider the negotiation of whiteness in these years: blackface minstrelsy is one, but we will also consider the fortunes of Boucicault's racial melodrama *The Octoroon* (1859), and the craze of the gorilla in the wake of Paul Du Chaillu's reported discoveries.

* * *

In blackface minstrelsy racial difference was given its own theatrical mode, one that from its arrival in the 1830s would have major effects on the American and circum-Atlantic culture industry for at least 120 years, and whose traces linger still. (Its substantial, as opposed to vestigial, presence on this side of the Atlantic is not historically remote: in Britain, a blackface revival, the *Black and White Minstrel Show*, was last broadcast by the BBC in 1978; the stage show derived from it continued to tour until 1987.[8]) White men rubbed their faces with burnt cork or greasepaint, dressed as ragged but happy plantation hands or as over-dressed black northern dandies, adopted putatively black accents, facial expressions and speech-patterns, and told jokes, sang songs and danced on stage: veering between comedy and sentiment, this was the minstrel show, arguably the first uniquely American popular cultural form. Curiously enough, the new form did not evolve in the Southern slave-owning states of the US, but in the north. Thomas Dartmouth Rice, a New York-born apprentice woodworker turned entertainer, is generally seen as the first major blackface star in the US, and New York long remained a centre of minstrel innovation. Rice brought blackface to Britain in 1836, when he appeared at the Surrey and Adelphi theatres. His legendary 'Jim Crow' routine, in which he adopted the character of a scarecrow-like black plantation worker, was supposedly copied from a black stableman, whom he saw singing and performing a distinctive shuffle in the early 1830s:

> Wheel about and turn about, an' do jis so,
> An' eb'ry time I wheel about, I jump Jim Crow.[9]

The legend describes how Rice turns this accidental meeting into a proper stage act – in some versions he is even good enough to pay the stable-hand for his contribution, presumably to assuage any doubts we might have about the ethics of cultural appropriation.[10] Recent scholarship, however, argues for a more complex process of cultural transmission. W. T. Lhamon, for example, argues that Rice carefully built up his comic Jim Crow character over a number of years from various sources, rather than simply copying a randomly glimpsed dance. Moreover, if Rice imitated black performers – such figures as the New Orleans street-singer Pickiune Butler – some black performers probably copied him. Minstrelsy was not, that is, a distortion of some pure 'folk' material, but culturally syncretic, though it was a form of syncretism that would enormously benefit white performers rather than black ones.[11] Rice was not the first practitioner of this combination of simultaneous admiration for and exploitation of blackness and black culture, which Eric Lott calls 'love and theft': the English comedian and actor Charles Mathews, for example, performed a number of blackface comic roles that he in part derived from his visits to the African Grove Theatre in New York. But while other performers also played Jim Crow in the 1830s, the figure became synonymous with Rice.

Rice's dancing scarecrow soon crossed the Atlantic, and his first performance was at the Surrey Theatre on 9 June 1836, where he appeared in a piece of his own composition, *Bone Squash Diabolo*.[12] He appeared at the Adelphi Theatre on 7 November 1836, when he appeared in William Leman Rede's *A Flight to America*, which featured a scene that celebrated Emancipation (J. S. Bratton suggests that, curiously, some of the early enthusiasm for blackface in Britain was related to the widespread support for Abolition). He stayed for twenty-one weeks, the management devising a number of other vehicles for Rice's singing and dancing black character: a burletta, *The Peacock and the Crow*, and a farce, *The Virginian Mummy*.[13] Rede somehow found a part for him even in his unauthorized adaptation of *The Pickwick Papers*, *The Peregrinations of Pickwick*. According to Alicia Kae Koger's summary of the 1836–7 season at the Adelphi, a Jim Crow craze 'swept through London', spread by concerts, but also by street singers and barrel organists.[14] Bratton notes that the visiting star married the daughter of one of the theatre's proprietors, Thomas Gladstane (p. 134). Rice returned to the London theatre in December of 1838 and was again a tremendous draw, appearing in *A Flight to America, Jim Crow in his New Place*, by Thomas P. Taylor, and the anonymous *A Foreign Prince*. His last London appearances were in 1842–3, when he played in a number of comic pieces at the Adelphi, including *Yankee Notes for English Circulation*, in which he played the part of Julius Caesar Washington Hickory Dick, 'a nigger help'.[15] As Michael Pickering notes, Rice/Jim Crow captured the public imagination to such an extent that he created a market for spin-offs, from Jim Crow hats to cigars, but he also 'inaugurated a whole new and long-durable form of entertainment' in a show based on the figure of the blackface minstrel.[16] The Jim Crow song was the first of many black-face songs in England that lent itself easily to what one might term locali-zation: topical verses were soon added to the original (Bratton, pp. 134–5). Rice would have many imitators, including the English performers John Dunn and J. A. Cave, and the Americans Ned Harper and Joe Sweeney.

The next significant innovation in blackface entertainment in Britain was the arrival in 1843 of the Irish-American performer Dan Emmett and his Virginia Minstrels, who were already hugely popular in the US.[17] Emmett, a former printer's apprentice, was later associated with some of the best-known of the minstrel songs, such as 'Old Dan Tucker' and 'I Wish I Was in Dixie's Land' (1859), with its famous evocation of the South as a pastoral heterotopia.[18] With the Virginia Minstrels the minstrel show assumed the general form it was to keep for the rest of the century, if not longer. Four or five minstrels formed a line or semicircle facing the audi-ence, with a tambourine-player ('Tambo') at one end, and a bones-player ('Bones') at the other.

These were the comic 'end men' or 'corner men' (the British usage) who, together with the central master of ceremonies ('Mr Interlocutor'), entertained the audience with jokes, puns and banter, the Interlocutor generally playing the straight man to the end men. (Other instruments usually included the banjo and the fiddle.) The show usually comprised three or four segments: an introductory piece, or 'overture', incorporating repartee, music, and often a selection of plantation songs; a central 'olio', which often incorporated a comic – and often satirical – 'stump speech', but could also contain other variety material; and a final farce; there was sometimes an afterpiece consisting of a group musical number, often with a 'walkaround' to showcase individual players.[19] Within this basic frame-work considerable variation was possible, and the music, songs and dances were drawn from disparate sources: clog dances, Irish jigs and light opera might all feature as well as, more predictably, the sentimental plantation songs of Stephen Foster and others (Toll suggests that much of the min-strel music was itself of European origin).

Over time, as with music hall, the form became closer to the modern 'variety' show, with big production numbers and elaborate costumes. Solo artists, following in the tradition created by Rice, could be incorporated

10. Illustrated cover for 'Lucy Neal', performed at the St. James's
Theatre by the Ethiopian Serenaders (*c.* 1846).

into other entertainment forms, such as theatre and music hall, but the minstrel groups often created stand-alone shows, and sometimes had long residencies at particular theatres.[20] E. P. Christy's minstrel show ran for many years at the Mechanics' Hall, New York, and the Mohawk Minstrels and the Christy Minstrels (later the Moore and Burgess Minstrels) had long-running shows in London – the former at the Agricultural Hall in Islington, the latter at Saint James's Hall in Piccadilly.[21] There were also far less prestigious versions of blackface performance, including street acts, and performers at festivals, fairs and (as time went by) the seaside, as well as amateur performers at various local events. As early as 1847, as Michael Pickering records, a song called 'Niggermania' lamented the 'glut' of blackface acts.[22]

It might be useful at this point to look at some actual blackface material from the period, while bearing in mind that with the minstrel show – even more than with the theatre – we are faced with the problem of trying to recover and understand the dynamics of live performance through look-ing at printed artefacts. But even from the texts, one general feature stands out at once when we consider the plantation songs in the context of British reception: these songs invite their British audience to be nostalgic for a world that they could hardly have known themselves; while this must have been true of many US audiences too, of course, it is particularly obvious in the transatlantic context. That world, the minstrel South, is a very curi-ous form of pre-industrial pastoral Eden: it is a place where people have been turned into commodities, but paradoxically also a place where the bonds of human affection, and simple human pleasures, are paramount. Old times there are not forgotten: loyal slaves love their masters and mis-tresses more than their own freedom; and there is a pleasure in the life of the body, in spontaneous singing and dancing, as well as in sexuality. But these are hardly songs of undiluted happiness: emotional crises caused by separation (often as a consequence of slavery) and death are common. Stephen Foster's 'Angelina Baker' (1850) is a good example of the more pathetic type of song:

> Way down on de old plantation
> Dah's where I was born
> I used to beat the whole creation
> Hoein' in the corn
> Oh den I work and den I sing
> So happy all de day
> Till Angelina Baker came
> And stole my heart away.

Angelina steals his heart, only to disappear one day: she has presumably been sold to another plantation, perhaps because of her dangerous habit of asking 'Massa' to free his slaves. The singer is left to weep and 'beat on the old jaw-bone', a rather tragi-comic figure; any emotional investment we might make is rendered difficult because of his comic traits.

In other songs nostalgia rather than pathos is the dominant effect strived for, as with 'I Wish I Was In Dixie's Land', often called simply 'Dixie'. When performed in 1859 by Bryant's Minstrels at the Mechanics' Hall on Broadway in New York, it became one of the best-known minstrel songs of the 1860s. The Bryants were led by the O'Neill brothers, who were, like Dan Emmett, of Irish immigrant stock, which might seem to support David Roediger's theory that blackface provided a way for immigrant populations to become white Americans; Dan Bryant, though, was also willing to play up his Irishness, and he starred as Myles-na-Coppaleen in a New York production of *The Colleen Bawn*.[23] At any rate, Dixie became the most famous evocation of the South as a realm outside of industrial modernity: 'Old times dar am not forgotten'.[24] The song crossed to Britain in the early 1860s, possibly brought there by the Buckleys (English emigrants turned American minstrels) when they visited in 1860. As with other songs of this type, it is tempting to speculate that its form of pastoral was attractive in Britain to working-class urban audiences who were often themselves only a generation away from rural life, and who might have felt some ambivalence about the benefits of an industrial, urban existence. If there is a clear utopianism to such nostalgia, it should also be borne in mind that part of the appeal for a middle-class audience might have been not so much the representation of a carefree life of the body as the image of a society free from class conflict, one where the franchise was the undisputed possession of the masters rather than the hands. One of the things apparently not forgotten in the minstrel South is a form of quasi-feudal loyalty, and the original lyrics celebrate the faithfulness of Southern slaves as much as the joyful and sensually promising life of Dixie itself: 'Now here's a health to the next old Missus / An all de gals dat want to kiss us'. (It is curious, of course, that the singer does not appear to have actually *left* the plantation life for which he already seems nostalgic.) In this light, blackface minstrelsy might be seen to carry different and even contradictory utopian impulses to the various sections of its audience, those who could at least in part recognize their own subalternity in the lot of the slaves, translating race into class, and those who could more easily fantasize about their place at the top of an organic social order.

During the Civil War, nostalgic minstrelsy shades into largely pro-South propaganda. 'Dixie' naturally became associated with the Confederate side, though counter-versions, such as Frances J. Crosby's 'Dixie for the Union' (1861) and A. W. Muzzy's 'Dixie Union-Ized' ('Oh, I'm glad I live in a land of freedom / Where we have no slaves nor do we need them'), appropriated the melody for the Union side. The songs of the Confederate states, sometimes in the pastoral plantation vein, sometimes more strident patriotic hymns, enjoyed a considerable vogue in Britain during the war years, as we see from such publications as Hopwood and Crew's *Celebrated Songs of the Confederate States of America, Dedicated to the Confederate Exiles in Europe* (c. 1865).[25] This included stirring martial songs – 'My Maryland', 'Bonnie Blue Flag', 'God Save the South' and 'It is My Country's Call' – as well as lighter minstrel fare: 'Down Among the Cotton' and, of course, 'Dixie'.[26] 'Maryland, My Maryland' (sung to the tune of 'O Tannenbaum') was, like 'Dixie', a song that existed in pro- and anti-union versions, but the version printed by Hopwood and Crew makes it quite clear which side it is on: 'Huzza, she [*sc.* Maryland] spurns the Northern scum / She breathes, she burns – she'll come, she'll come.' Such songs, besides providing material for minstrel shows, must have also provided the staples of shows like that of the American singer Henri Drayton, who is described by the *Times* round-up of London Easter amusements for 1863 as continuing to 'sing and tell stories in the Confederate interest at the Polygraphic [*sc.* Hall]', Charing Cross.[27] Drayton and his wife were also among the performers at the charity Confederate Bazaar held at St George's Hall in Liverpool in October 1864 in aid of the Southern Prisoners' Relief Fund, where again 'Dixie' and 'Maryland, My Maryland' were on the programme.

The popularity of minstrel songs during the war years might suggest a degree of displaced nostalgia for a pre-industrial Britain, but it evidently also indicates a level of British sympathy for the underdog South (it is usually assumed that in the early years there was considerable support for the South among Britain's educated classes, as well as its newspapers, but that such support diminished as the war continued). However, English artists also directly transformed American material to their own ends, as we see in Frank Hall's 1861 rewriting of 'Dixie' as 'In the Strand, or, I Wish I Was With Nancy', popularized by the blackface performer E. W. Mackney, a former supper-room performer who had been promoted by Charles Morton, the music-hall impresario. Far from being a celebration of the pastoral, 'In the Strand' is a paean to the romantic pleasures of the modern city:

For the last three weeks I've been a dodging
A girl I know who has a lodging
In the Strand, In the Strand, In the Strand, In the Strand

The first thing that put my heart in a flutter
Was a Balmoral Boot as she cross'd the gutter, etc.

I wish I was with Nancy, Oh! Hi! Hi! Oh!
In a second floor forever more
To live and die with Nancy.[28]

Subsequent verses continue to dwell on Nancy's sartorial charms, with more than a hint of sexual interest that may have been further developed in performance:

A porkpie hat with a little feather
And new knickerbockers for the dirty weather, etc.
Some pretty petticoats too she's got 'em
Trimm'd with embroidery round the bottom, etc.

Another edition of this song, describing itself as the '100th edition', appears in the British Library Catalogue with an accession date of 1863, which suggests that Mackney's version enjoyed something of the same vogue as the original.

Mackney also sang Hall's 'Oxford Street', which, like 'In the Strand', and indeed many of the original plantation melodies, does not appear to have been sung in mock-plantation dialect. It is one of the many comic songs of the 1860s that deal with romantic street encounters that somehow go awry (see Chapter 5): in this case the protagonist falls for one Nelly Brew in Oxford Street, and courts her assiduously, only for her to subsequently run off with a swell. But what is most striking about 'Oxford Street' is its illustrated cover, which shows the encounter between Nelly and Mackney on Oxford Street; he is in blackface, dressed rather as a swell himself, or like Zip Coon, the dandy blackface character. Here we seem to be very far away indeed from the land of cotton. Indeed, it is difficult to imagine this cover being allowed to circulate anywhere in the United States in this period.

Clearly, then, if blackface negro minstrelsy in Britain sometimes summoned up for audiences its putative Southern origins, it could also float relatively free of them, as J. S. Bratton has argued, citing Mackney's work as a case in point.[29] To this extent is can be very difficult to interpret the theatre of race that is on show: Mackney's urban blackface scarcely evokes the pastoral South, but the song does not reference the character of Zip Coon either. The music cover, which shows a 'black' man accosting a white woman

11. Illustrated cover for E. W. Mackney, 'Oxford Street' (1862).
Chromolithograph by R. J. Hamerton.

in the street, is clearly meant to be comic, but we might have expected it to be rather edgy material for a reading public that was also being entertained in the early 1860s with speculation about the potential threat to American womanhood in the event of a 'servile insurrection' in the course of the Civil War. That such a cover was produced at all suggests, perhaps, that in British blackface the racial imaginary was very complex, or very deeply submerged.

This 'localization' of minstrel material also characterizes another comic song of the 1860s, 'Am I Right, Or Any Other Man', a song 'sung with unbounded applause' by W. West (1817–76) 'of the Harmoneons, "Farrenberg and West"'. What makes this piece interesting is that besides the music it features 'West's Celebrated Stump Speech'. The sung part commences:

> Now Free Enlightened White Folks, Wise foolish short and tall
> I've come here to indress you on what concerns you all
> Some talk of this, some talk of that in State of Blusteration
> Then list to me and then you'll see my nigger stump oration
> I'm a Slick and Learned nigger, tho I cut a funny figger
> Deny what I says no one can – Am I right, 'Or any other man'.[30]

The speech itself is a rambling, mock political oration, full of seemingly random topical references that, together with the malapropisms and the repetition of the catchphrase 'or any other man', were meant to get the laughs:

'White Folks' – 'Feller Citizens' – 'Brudders' and Englishmen, unacustom'd as I am to Public Speaking – I stand afore you as a Misrepresentative of the Houses of Parliament – or any sort of Houses – that is to say, that when a man gets up to say something – he says so – at the same time by saying what he says – and having said so, whey then it's said and there's an end to it – but if he means to say some-think and don't say so, that at once proves beyond doubt – that he's said nothing at all – eh – Am I right – 'Or any other man'.

Return to subject – As I before observed, when a man gets up to indress you on his Political Pinions, and says so, and understands what he's talking about, he's a Man – Am I right – 'Or any other man'.

Return to subject ...

The politics of the day, and the debates over Reform, come in for mention: 'What did Lord Pummistone say the other day – eh – didn't he say that if things remained in the state they was – there's be no alteration whatsom-dever – and wasn't he right ...' Whether the turning of Lord Palmerston into an abrasive pumice stone here is meant to be satirical, or merely an amusing homonymic effect, is difficult to establish, but the general defla-tion of political rhetoric is clear enough.

Most of the topical references are to the other forms of entertainment competing for the interest of the Londoner:

What did 'Henry the Eighth' say to 'Julius Caesar' when he saw the 'O' Donoghue' – eh – and what did the 'Colleen Bawn' say to 'Alexander the Great' when he led the 'Sardines' across Blackfriars Bridge to 'Seeblastapool' – eh – and wasn't she right when she said so – 'Or any other man'.

12. Illustrated cover for W. West, 'Am I Right, Or Any Other Man'.
Chromolithograph by R. J. Hamerton.

Shakespeare and sensation plays, Royal Academy pictures and the newspaper reports of the war in Italy are all jumbled together here. But plays
and pictures are not the only form of entertainment singled out for mention. The Stump Speech is being presented as a comic variation on the
lecture form, and West throws in a rather acerbic reference to the surfeit of
such improving entertainment on offer:

Dere am Lectures on 'Gorillas'
As well as Shakespeares play
And Lectures too on 'Counterfeits'
Which seems in 'Spurgeons' way [*sc.* C. H. Spurgeon, the popular preacher][31]
And then dere's Temperance Lectures
That comes from Mister Gough [*sc.* John Gough, temperance lecturer]
So one way and de oder
We get Lectured well enough.

The 'lecture' ends with another sung verse that seems to underline that this particular lecturer is a wise fool:

My Lecture now am over
So I'll amputate [*sc.* absquatulate?] away
And hopes you is enlightened
By what Ise had to say
I gives you useless knowledge
Free – gratis – not for pelf
If you understand what I has said
I really don't myself
But I'm a slick and Learned Nigger
Although I cuts a funny figger
Deny what I've said no one can
Am I right 'Or any other man'.

The audience, of course, cannot deny what he has said, insofar as with a certain sort of political rhetoric, it is hard to extract any positive state-ments out of it. We are meant to laugh at the character's garbled account of London life, and the tortuous malapropisms that suggest he has no real understanding of what he is saying. But at the same time, we are invited to see past the blackface character to the entertainer behind, and his know-ing listing of the competing novelties of London as if to say, 'Yes, I know that you have been to too many plays, seen too many new pictures and been lectured to in too many halls, until you have had enough entertain-ment, and especially enough improvement.' The performance acknow-ledges itself as part of this flood of commodified entertainment while also winking at the audience to sign that it doesn't take itself very seriously. The use of blackface contributes to the overall effect by saving West from directly taking up the position of a superior insider who can see past the cant of the times, a position that might make some of the audience think he is rather too full of himself. By adopting his limited stage persona this superiority is not actually removed, since the more thoughtful sections of the audience are invited to see him pulling the strings, as it were, but that is not what they have to engage with directly.

In one of the few discussions of the tremendous popularity of blackface minstrelsy in Britain, Michael Pickering suggests a number of possible ways in which we might interpret its evident appeal. In the case of stump speeches he suggests that their comic success is based on the 'incongruity of blackface entertainment' (p. 79). The same incongruity, he argues, is evident in blackface love songs, 'which in varying degrees comically subverted the tone and content of the Victorian parlour ballad, not only by treating the theme of romance with a flippant lightheartedness, but also by using the coon buffoon caricature to ironically send up a mawkish sentimentalism' (p. 79). Pickering is writing here of later blackface material, but his interpretation is persuasive for the material of the 1860s too, which mines existing modes and themes for their comic potential. To this extent, he argues, there is a continuity between negro minstrelsy and various earlier popular practices – for example, mumming and other forms of seasonal vernacular drama – that involve burnt-cork make-up, cross-dressing and analogous inversions of the norm. This suggests one reason why performances such as Mackney's, which often strayed far from plantation themes, could be easily assimilated. What this entailed for the understanding of race and ethnicity among audiences is harder to establish. If minstrelsy provided a theatre of race in the United States, in which (particularly Northern) ambivalence around race could be expressed and managed, or alternatively, acted as a rebellious form that imagined cross-ethnic solidarities, what did it mean in a Britain that, as both Bratton and Pickering point out, had a very small black population? Bratton argues that blackface comes to be a relatively autonomous entity in Britain, with little if any actual reference to actual people of colour, though it did occasionally reference Britain's eighteenth-century slave-owning past, as in the vogue for court-dress minstrel groups (p. 139). Pickering argues that it is the nature of Victorian Britain rather than that of the plantation South that is being staged, in however oblique a form, in the minstrel show: 'What was being symbolically worked out in minstrelsy, at a metalevel of commentary, were questions about the status of white Victorian society in the whole human social and biological order' (p. 85). The minstrel acts popularized certain images of black America, images that would linger, and would have real consequences for the ways in which blacks were perceived in Britain subsequently, but it is far more of a theatre of whiteness than a theatre of blackness. To an extent this is also true of the American stage, of course, but there the racial stakes were high from the start, and the impact of theatrical representations on the lived reality of black Americans considerably more direct, not to say more brutal.

As with the enormous body of Orientalist writing and representation, then, British blackface acts might in general terms be best read as a species of projection of more local fears, anxieties and longings, as much or more than any real encounter with alterity. What this may have meant in practice for audiences must have depended on the composition of those audiences (which spanned the social range from the East End to Windsor). In the figure of the happy-to-lucky but intellectually limited plantation slave, working-class audiences may have been provided with a parodic form of humanity to which they might feel superior, reassuring them that even their lowly place in the order of things put them immeasurably above others. But working-class audiences may also, of course, have felt some sense of solidarity with such comedy figures, as we have seen. The representation of a lowly form of otherness, of a form of abjection, was counterbalanced by the more utopian aspect of minstrelsy, evinced not only through its evocation of a world of strong affective bonds, but in the sheer delight in the physical world, and in aesthetic expression (song, dance) in the face of adversity. For other audiences, especially for the 'respectable' middle-class audience, as Bratton has speculated, the cultivation of a sense of natural superiority may have been accompanied by a form of physical release and spontaneity unavailable to them through other forms of entertainment, since blackface enjoyed a species of respectability that made it available and 'safe' fare for middle-class women, as well as for the most strait-laced of non-conformists. That such a release could be effected by the contemplation of white men pretending to be happy black slaves is only one of the many curious ironies created by blackface. Nor, as I noted above, should we discount the extent to which the plantation provided a comforting image of an organic society to middle-class and aristocratic audiences who were concerned that their own 'hands' were likely to get more power than was good for them through the 'leap in the dark' of Reform. Black slaves and British labourers were frequently compared in contemporary debates, and US Emancipation and the British Reform Act were collated by middle-class commentators.[32] (To enfranchise, of course, means to free a slave as well as to endow with a vote.) The minstrel world of comical but loyal field hands and kind and gentlemanly owners must have seemed quite appealing to some. The political threat represented by the working class could be defused, rendered the stuff of breakdowns and comic Jim Crow gaits: in the minstrel show, calls for enfranchisement are rare.

Nonetheless, if blackface had more to do with the lives of its immediate audience than those it purported to represent, we should not altogether discount the real effects on black subjects outside of this rather self-referential theatre of colour. As Pickering observes in a more recent article, 'John Bull in Blackface', if Britain did not have a substantial black population, it had a very substantial empire. Seeing a happy subject population on stage, even through the self-revealing theatricality of the minstrel show, may not only have offered British audiences a reassuring glimpse of those less fortunate than themselves, or held out a model of a more solidary form of subjection than their own; it may also have helped to assure them that their own subject peoples, those in far-off colonies, were in the main happy in their primitive way.

Pickering is no doubt correct, but we do not have to go quite so far to find another 'race' who might have been more directly affected by the minstrel show: that comic blackface material sometimes shaded into comic Irish material suggests that one local population directly affected by such performances were the working-class, Catholic Irish. In this respect, high and low culture were not so very far apart. At a time when Darwin's ideas on evolution were being twisted into Eurocentric ideologies of manifest racial destiny, the representation of other, less industrialized, and more 'superstitious', populations as backward and childlike was gaining the force of scientific fact as well as the support of 'common knowledge'. Even those who did not always directly link physical characteristics and intellectual and moral development took part in a more general project of isolating the racial types of Great Britain and Ireland: among these was John Beddoe, President of the Anthropological Society, who toured Ireland to see how the Irish related ethnographically to 'other so-called Kelts, and to our own English nation', studying skulls and categorizing subjects according to his 'index of nigrescence', a measure of the darkness of hair and eyes rather than skin.[33] Others in the Society felt readier to move on to the moral qualities of the 'Celtic Race', such as Henry Hudson who suggested that the government should pay attention to racial characteristics when dealing with the 'Celtic Race' of Ireland. Because of a nature that combines, inter alia, courage, rashness, generosity, but also dreaminess, superstition, a propensity for squalour, and a strong sense of injustice, 'they require a paternal government, with a strong and firm hand to put down the slightest disobedience or resistance to the laws of the land'.[34] Popular entertainment produced a similar division of Anglo-Saxon Englishness and a darkened Irishness. If, in the United States, Irish-American blackface provided a way for Irish immigrants to 'whiten' themselves, as David Roediger has argued, in Britain they may have found themselves identified with plantation blacks in ways that militated against any such assimilation. The 'backward' Irish peasant or labourer thus could provide a missing link, or an imaginary cordon sanitaire, not between the gorilla and the black slave, as *Punch* joked in 1862, but between black slave and working-class Englishman.[35]

THE OCTOROON

The performance of blackness, and the evocation of Southern plantation life, were not confined to minstrel shows, of course. After the unprecedented success of *The Colleen Bawn*, Boucicault's next major London production was *The Octoroon; or, Life in Louisiana* (Adelphi, 18 November 1861), a play that, like the Colleen, he had already staged in New York (Winter Garden, 6 December 1859). Boucicault took the part of Salem Scudder, a Yankee overseer; his wife, Agnes Robertson, who had most recently played an Irish peasant, now took on a rather baroque blackface part, appearing as Zoe, a young black woman who looks white. While Zoe appears white, she invites her lover to note the 'bluish tinge' of her nails and of the sclera, or white, of her eyes, and 'the same dark, fatal mark' in the roots of her hair – presumably details left to the audience's imagination rather than made visible on stage.[36] The London public was given some notice of the arrival of the new mortgage melodrama, and even an explanation of its title and origins, in the theatre ads of *The Times*:

Theatre Royal, New Adelphi.
Next Monday, November 18, the new play, in five acts, by the author of *The Colleen Bawn*, entitled *The Octoroon; or, Life in Louisiana*, will be produced; in which Mr Dion Boucicault will appear as Salem Scudder, the Yankee Overseer, and Mrs Dion Boucicault as Zoe, the Octoroon. The word Octoroon signifies 'eighth blood', or the child of a quadroon by a white. The Octoroons have no apparent trace of the negro in their appearance, but still are subject to the legal disabilities which attach them to the condition of the blacks.

Boucicault probably borrowed his plot for the play from Mayne Reid's novel of 1856, *The Quadroon*, but this ad goes on to offer quite a different source of inspiration:[37]

The plot of this drama was suggested to the author by the following incident, which occurred in Louisiana, and came under his notice during his residence in that State. The laws of Louisiana forbid the marriage of a white man with any woman having the smallest trace of black blood in her veins. The Quadroon and Octoroon girls, proud of their white blood, revolt from union with the black, and are unable to form marriages with the white. They are thus driven into an equivocal position, and form a section of New Orleans society resembling the demi-monde of Paris. A young and wealthy planter of Louisiana fell deeply and sincerely in love with a Quadroon girl of great beauty and purity. The lovers found their union opposed by the law; but love knows no obstacles. The young man, in the presence of two friends, who acted as witnesses, opened a vein in his arm, and introduced into it a few drops of his mistress's blood; thus he was able to make oath that he had black blood in his veins, and being attested, the marriage was performed. The great interest now so broadly felt in American affairs induces the author to present *The Octoroon* as the only American drama which has hitherto attempted to portray American homes, American scenery, characters, and manners, without either exaggeration or prejudice ... New scenery faithfully delineating the plantation life, will be presented.[38]

There is much that could be commented on here, but taken simply as an account of Boucicault's inspiration, the episode described does not prepare us for the plot of *The Octoroon*, which ends with a tragic death rather than the cleverly managed marriage of comedy. Zoe, the Octoroon, is the illegitimate daughter of the deceased Judge Peyton, a plantation owner, who has left his embarrassed estate to his nephew, George Peyton, and when George arrives in Louisiana from Paris, he promptly falls in love with her. M'Closky is the estate's wicked Yankee overseer, foil to Salem Scudder, the good-hearted Yankee overseer. He has already contrived to obtain half of the plantation, but he also covets Zoe, and discovers that she has not been properly emancipated by the Judge; she is thus effectively part of the estate, and will be sold off if the estate's debts are not paid. The overseer makes sure that this happens by stealing money destined for George Peyton, in the process killing Paul, a young black slave, and throwing suspicion for the murder on Paul's native American friend, Wahnotee. In the slave auction that follows, the play's most famous sensation scene, M'Closky buys Zoe. But his murder of Paul is revealed by a dagurreotype taken at the scene (Salem Scudder, conveniently, is an amateur daguerreotypist), and he is imprisoned aboard a paddle steamer. He escapes by starting a fire on the boat (the play's other great sensation scene), but is pursued by Wahnotee. Ignorant of these events, Zoe takes poison, and dies in George's arms. The curtain descends on Wahnotee, standing over the dead M'Closkey at Paul's grave.

Joseph Roach has written brilliantly about the way in which *The Octoroon* dramatizes race in America, and re-enacts the historical reduction in Louisiana of the recognition of ethnic diversity to the absolute binary logic of black/white. Roach demonstrates that part of the play's power derives from its theatrical reinvention of a form of actual, non-theatrical spectacle. 'Fancy-girl' auctions, sales of quadroon or octoroon girls and women, were 'an exceptionally popular' New Orleans 'specialty', as well as the subject of a good deal of prurient interest elsewhere; Boucicault's slave auction draws on these 'violent, triangular conjunctions of money, property, and flesh', working to titillate as much as to horrify its audience at what happens when people become property.[39] At the centre of the play as well as of the auction is the figure of the beautiful but doomed female of mixed race, Boucicault's drama resonating with many other cultural narratives in which this figure 'condenses hatred and desire in the same imaginary liquid – mixed blood'.[40] Racial difference is thus reimagined as sexual difference in a way that allows desire for otherness to be staged – some amalgam of George's romantic love and M'Closky's rape fantasy – but ultimately kills off that desired other.

But does this reading hold true for the play's London production? As is well known to theatre historians, Boucicault rewrote the play in London after it had run to a mixed reception for a few weeks.[41] This reception was in marked contrast to its success at the Winter Garden in New York, where the *New York Times* had dubbed it 'the great dramatic "sensation" of the season ... Everybody talks about the *Octoroon*, wonders about the *Octoroon*, goes to see the *Octoroon*, and the *Octoroon* thus becomes ... the work of the public mind.'[42] Interest in the play was, of course, due in no small part to the questions it raised about slavery, at a time when the gap between North and South was widening, but it was also kept alive by the 'Octoroon War', the dispute between the Boucicaults and the management of the Winter Garden, which ended up in the US Circuit Court.[43] (By the time the *New York Times* was dubbing the play the sensation of the season, the Boucicault's had been refused entry to the Winter Garden, and were suing their former business partners for breach of copyright.) A centrepiece of the trial was a letter in which Agnes Robertson withdrew her services, claiming that she was in fear for the safety of herself and her husband because of the violent reaction to the play in some quarters, and that she had received written threats.[44] It seems more likely, though, that differences over money dictated her withdrawal.

In London there was neither an imminent Civil War nor a legal war, and *The Octoroon*'s handling of race did not initially excite anything like the same levels of interest. In the end Boucicault felt he had to take action. On 12 December, *The Times* announced that 'The Octoroon dies no more!'[45] Such a course had been determined by the audience's hostility to Zoe's demise in the last act, in contrast to their enthusiasm for what went before, as is clear from the *Times*'s review of opening night:

Mrs Boucicault, as Zoe, has occasion for far more intense pathos than in the *Colleen Bawn*, and last night surprised the public by the force of her delineation.

Indeed, such a popular person was the Octoroon in her hands that several of the audience were dissatisfied with her unfortunate end, and refused to understand why George could not marry his devoted 'Yellow Girl' in one of the many states where Louisiana law does not prevail ... To this feeling alone can we ascribe the few sounds of disapprobation which followed the descent of the curtain last night, and contrasted so strangely with the enthusiastic applause that had accompanied the first four acts.[46]

Though often thought of as a dramatist who was rather too eager to please the public, Boucicault held out for some weeks, writing a letter to *The Times* to defend his ending. He criticizes the audience for its inconsistency: where in the 1850s the death of Uncle Tom in the Adelphi production of Harriet Beecher Stowe's novel provoked only sympathy, now the suicide of Zoe to avoid rape provokes none:

Since the Uncle Tom mania, the sentiments of the English public on the subject of slavery have seemed to be undergoing a great change; but I confess that I was not prepared to find that change so radical as it appeared to be when the experiment was tried upon the feelings of a miscellaneous audience ... The audience hailed with every mark of enthusiasm the sunny views of negro life; they were pleased with the happy relations existing between the slaves and the family of which they were the dependents; they enjoyed the heartiness with which the slaves were sold, and cheered the planters who bought them. But when the Octoroon girl was purchased by the ruffianly overseer to become his paramour, her suicide to preserve her purity provoked no sympathy whatever. Yet, a few years ago, the same public, in the same theatre, witnessed with deep emotion the death of Uncle Tom under the lash ... In the death of the Octoroon lies the moral teaching of the whole work. Had this girl been saved, and the drama brought to a happy end, the horrors of her position, irremediable from the very nature of the institution of slavery, would subside into the condition of a temporary annoyance. While I admit most fully the truth of your statement that the public was disappointed with the termination of the play, and would have been pleased with a happier issue, I feel strangely bewildered by such a change of feeling. Has public sentiment veered so diametrically on this subject?[47]

Rather than assume that his audience simply wants a happy ending, Boucicault interprets such a wish not in generic terms but as a moral failing, a symptom of a change in 'the sentiments of the English public on the subject of slavery'. Of course, we cannot take Boucicault's complaints entirely at face value. As John A. Degen notes, when the play had been performed in New York, mindful of his audience, the playwright had gone out of his way to state that the Octoroon was not an abolitionist drama. The ads in the *New York Times* had announced the impartiality of the production with quotes from Shakespeare and Virgil: 'Nothing extenuate, nor aught set down in malice' and 'Tros Tyriusque mihi nullo discrimine agetur' [as Degen translates, 'Both Trojan and Tyrian I shall treat with no partiality'].[48] In a letter to the *New York Herald* he had averred that slavery was included as part of the fabric of Southern society, not for any propaganda purposes: 'I felt capable of writing a work upon society in America. I have laid the scene in the South, and, as slavery is an essential element of society there, insomuch I have been obliged to admit it into my scheme'.[49] (The court case reveals that his agreement with the proprietors of the Winter Garden was for a 'Mississippi piece', presumably meaning a local-colour drama.)

In America, then, Boucicault represents himself as a social chronicler who does not take sides; in London he declares himself a moral commentator, whose audience has failed him by not grasping the 'moral teaching' of his abolitionist drama engagée. And yet, Boucicault's letter should not be lightly dismissed. He remarks that although during his stay in Louisiana he saw no ill-treatment of slaves, this is not the point:

A visitor to Louisiana, who might expect to find his vulgar sympathies aroused by the exhibition of corporal punishment and physical torture, would be much disappointed ... But, behind all this, there are features in slavery far more objectionable than any of those hitherto held up to human execration, by the side of which physical suffering appears as a vulgar detail.[50]

It is not that physical suffering is unimportant, but that to focus only on the treatment of slaves may be to miss the real horror of slavery, the transformation of a person into property, into a thing. There is an implicit criticism here of the shock tactics of plays like *Uncle Tom's Cabin,* which, Boucicault seems to suggest, appealed to rather dubious 'vulgar sympathies' by making a spectacle of torture rather than of the institution of slavery as a whole. That Boucicault himself expects to get to the existential horrors of slavery by encouraging us to imagine the almost-white Zoe stripped at auction, and to picture her as M'Closky's sexual plaything, suggests that he has not escaped the appeal of sensation: *The Octoroon* makes no less an appeal to sadomasochism than did the Adelphi production of *Uncle Tom's Cabin.* In the end, Boucicault's alterations were not enough to make the play a real success, and for much of its run it played alongside *The Colleen Bawn,* which meant that Agnes Roberston played colleen and octoroon, lily-white Irish girl, and not-quite-white American girl, in the one evening, as Boucicault played both wily Irish trickster and Yankee overseer.[51] While I argued in Chapter 2 that whiteness in the Irish play is overdetermined by the secular performance of religious spectacle, we should not ignore its ethnic resonances. It is difficult to imagine that audiences did not view Robertson's performances stereoscopically, as it were, seeing Irish colleen and American octoroon as two versions of non-British identity that yet seemed curiously close to home. In its London version, the ending of *The Octoroon* converges with that of *The Colleen Bawn*. The happy ending allowed the almost-white Zoe suggests, perhaps, that desire of the other produced less psychic strain for British audiences because Agnes Robertson's slave girl seemed just a costume-change away from being Irish.

Changing views

Whatever the contradictions of his vision of life in Louisiana, the point Boucicault makes in the letter is still irrefutable: that even an ostensibly benign slavery is still slavery. Nor can we dismiss his claim that audiences had changed since the 1850s in their attitudes to slavery, or more accurately, towards slaves and towards race, though it is more probable that such attitudes were already changing even at the moment that *Uncle Tom's Cabin* was packing them in. As Christine Bolt, Douglas Lorimer and Nancy Stepan have all argued, there appears to be a shift in thinking about race between the early and mid-nineteenth century.[52] To put it crudely, there is more scientific support for the idea that there are separate and distinct races of people in 1850 than there was in 1800, and although the circulation of Darwin's ideas after 1859 complicates this picture, it does not fundamentally alter it. The development of a 'science' of race was underpinned by the more general rise to prestige of the biological and human sciences – the term 'biology' itself was not used until 1802, and comparative anatomy, physiology and histology were all new sciences (Stepan, p. 5). But although scientific discourses operate according to their own rules and protocols, they do not enjoy complete autonomy, and scientific attitudes to race in this period cannot be divorced from, for example, the existence of the modern slave trade (distinct from earlier forms of slavery insofar as it was based on perceived race, as opposed to the fortunes of war), and indeed opposition to it; or from the industrial revolution that accentuated the differences between the European and American powers and the rest of the world. In general terms, nature was given precedence over culture in the explanation of human behaviour. In Nancy Stepan's words, 'The scientists' deepest commitment seems to have been to the notion that the social and cultural differences observed between peoples should be understood as realities of nature' (p. xx).

One symptom of this shift was the appearance in London in 1863 of the Anthropological Society, under the presidency of Dr James Hunt, a firm believer not only in a hierarchy of peoples, but in the idea that the Negro and the European were distinct races. (There had been an Ethnological Society since 1843, but its numbers had declined by the 1860s, seemingly as the humanitarian interest in other peoples that had accompanied the successes of the Abolition movement began to fade; Hunt and others felt that the new Anthropological Society would be free to discuss certain topics because of its exclusion of women and split from the Ethological Society.) Hunt was a disciple of Robert Knox, a Scottish doctor whose career had been derailed by his involvement in the Burke and Hare grave-robbing scandal, and who had turned to essay-writing. In 1850 Knox published *The Races of Men: A Fragment*, in which he argued that the fates of the various races as he presents them – Saxon, Celts, Jews, Gypsies, as well as Negroes – were determined by their innate character. (His work anticipates such continental works as De Gobineau's *The Inequality of Races* (1852–3), and had more currency in the English-speaking world.) He also prophesied that there would be a race-war, again driven by biological rather than cultural factors (an idea that was seen by some to be borne out by the Indian Mutiny of 1857). Indeed cultural factors, including nationality, counted for much less than racial nature in Knox's vision of things. The mixing of peoples through intermarriage was removed as a factor: like some other theorists of race such as the Frenchman Paul de Broca, and in the face of all evidence to the contrary, he believed that such 'crosses' tended towards sterility (Lorimer, pp. 139–40). Knox, Hunt and others, including the celebrated Victorian traveller Richard Burton, were in fact reviving the polygenetic account of human diversity that had enjoyed some popularity in the eighteenth century, but had largely been displaced by monogenetic accounts. Monogenesis thrived in the abolitionist era, when the natural brotherhood of humankind was stressed as a fundamental reason why slavery was an abomination. The proponents of polygenesis believed in no such basic unity: there existed distinct races that had developed separately in their various parts of the world. Between 1863 and 1866 Hunt, for example, argued that Negroes were a separate species, that they were intellectually inferior to Europeans, and that they could best be humanized and civilized by Europeans, though they were in fact closer to the ape than the European (Lorimer, pp. 138–9; Bolt, p. 18). On 17 November 1863, Hunt argued before a largely appreciative audience of members of the Anthropological Society that 'there is as good reason for classifying the Negro as a distinct species from the European as there is for making the ass a distinct species from the zebra'.[53] Under Hunt's leadership, the Society became a bully pulpit for polygenetic theory and scientific racism;

although its proponents remained a minority voice within the British scientific community, they were far from being an insignificant one. Even those scientists, like Thomas Huxley, who pointed out the pseudo-scientific nature of Hunt's arguments, and who supported emancipation during the American Civil War, did not entirely disagree with him on the comparative abilities of white and black peoples. During the Governor Eyre controversy of 1866–9, unsurprisingly, the Anthropological Society was staunchly pro-Eyre (Stepan, p. 45).

The reception of Darwin's work illuminates the way in which racial science operated according to a logic that depended on an a priori assumption of racial hierarchy. Where Darwin's *Origin of Species* actually outflanks the monogenetic/polygenetic debate (species are mutable over a long historical timespan, and interrelated, and not formed for all time in one place, or in many places), it was initially seen to offer support to the polygenetic camp (Bolt, p. 11). Even when it was realized that the thrust of Darwin's theories was against such a hypothesis, those who were convinced of the innate superiority of the European found other ways of harnessing them to fit their own opinions. Paleontology had already given a new currency to the older idea of a 'chain of being' that united Europeans (on the top) and Africans (on the bottom); now it could be polished up and given a more scientific lustre through ideas of natural selection and the struggle for survival (Stepan, pp. 6, 55). If humans and animals were part of a continuum, the link was readily identified, even by Darwin himself, in savage human societies. From this it appeared to be only a short step for others to assume that black Africans, or black Americans, might also represent a link between the drawing room and the jungle. As Douglas A. Lorimer concludes about the porosity of scientific discourse in this period, 'it would appear that science followed rather than led opinion on the racial question' (p. 149). Of course such debates also provided a shadowy double to the controversies surrounding the Reform Act, and there were many who believed that there were domestic populations, as well as international ones, that needed to be guided and firmly ruled by their innate superiors.

British responses to the American Civil War show a fascination with race, and also indicate the extent to which an older Abolitionist humanitarianism had been eroded. In 1852 *Uncle Tom's Cabin*, as Boucicault pointed out in his letter to *The Times*, had been an enormous success in Britain, both as a novel and in various dramatic versions, and much of this success can be attributed to its effective marshalling of sympathy at the plight of the slaves. Such sympathy, of course, may have been a complex matter. Bolt suggests that at least some of the attacks on American

slavery were 'animated by a general hostility towards American institutions masquerading as a respectable concern for the American Negro'
(p. 31), though it cannot be doubted that there was genuine antipathy
towards slavery, and a pride in Britain as a 'free' land. And yet during
the Civil War, there was considerable support in Britain for the South.
According to Christine Bolt, 'British newspapers friendly to the Union
remained in a minority throughout the war; Lincoln's administration was
ridiculed until his death; while Southern Independence societies flourished – with at least eighteen in Lancashire alone' (p. 33). The war, like the
issue of Reform in Britain, had been long brewing. It had finally erupted
after a long period of dispute between the slave-owning states of the South
who wished the new Western states to also be slave-owning, and those in
the North who argued that slavery should stay within its existing state
confines. (The emancipation of existing slaves was not one of the original
war aims of the Union, but it became one after Lincoln's Proclamation of
September 1861.) It is sometimes argued that North and South were chiasmatically linked between the two countries, with the North of England
being strongly pro-South. The North of England was certainly heavily
dependent on the cotton-producing slave states for its factories (according to *The Times* in 1861, one fifth of the population of England depended
directly or indirectly on the cotton industry, and most of this cotton came
from the US (Bolt, p. 51)); in the southern counties this was not a factor,
though support for the Southern planters was still quite widespread in the
war's early years. Some of the support the South attracted reflected the general distrust of the good faith of the Union (Lorimer, pp. 163–4, 167). The
New York Draft Riots of July 1863 added to the perception of Northern
hypocrisy regarding slavery: angry at what they saw as the empowerment
of blacks at their own expense in Lincoln's Emancipation Proclamation,
and fearing displacement in the labour market by freed black slaves, white
workers, many of them Irish immigrants, went on a bloody rampage. In
five days mobs lynched eleven black men and seriously assaulted countless
more, terrorized 'mixed' married couples, burnt black homes and businesses, and drove black men out of mixed workplaces, such as the dockyards.[54] Such events did little to convince the British press that the North
was on a crusade to help the oppressed. But the South also benefited from
its perception as a place where the good times are not forgotten, a pastoral space where chivalric values survived, though it is difficult to see how
this pastoral/chivalric image squared with the knowledge that the South
was closely tied to the cotton industry of the North of England. In economic terms there was concern in the industrial North that emancipation

would see black field hands withdraw from cotton production (an anxiety presumably based on what had happened in the West Indies, when freed slaves took to subsistence farming rather than exploitative work on the sugar plantations). If the caricature of the plantation slaves depicted in minstrel shows suggested that they were essentially happy with their lot, it also suggested that they were innately lazy, and this image of the idle and sensual plantation worker was widespread in the 1860s press (Bolt, pp. 41, 58). Even the relatively liberal *Spectator*, which supported emancipation as well as the black franchise, followed this line to some extent: 'like all the dark races except the Chinese, like the nations of India, and the Italian peasantry [African Americans] are extremely industrious when they work for themselves, and grossly negligent when working for hire' (Bolt, p. 60).

However, we cannot take the newspapers as an unproblematic guide to popular opinion in this period. Particularly towards the end of the war it is possible to trace a deep divide between the reaction of the press (and Britain's upper- and middle-class educated public) to the war and the high levels of support for the North, and for abolition, that are registered in popular meetings, and in the reception accorded to pro-Northern (and pro-Reform) speakers like John Bright.[55] Nor is the history of the press coverage of the war by any means straightforward. The opening of the rift between the Union and the Confederate states in fact sees considerable press sympathy for the North, but when Lincoln made it clear in his inaugural address that his administration did not intend to interfere with existing slave-holding states, some of that sympathy evaporated, and there arose distrust in the good faith of the North. When it became clear that there was going to be an actual war (generally considered to be a war that the North could not win), there was a further ebbing of support for the Union, a change that may have been exacerbated by the perceived economic threat to Britain's manufacturing interests. *The Times* led the way in the swing towards the South, a position that it maintained until the end of the war. John Bright's paper, the *Morning Star*, and the *Daily News*, were the only daily papers that consistently supported the North between 1861 and 1865. But among the disenfranchised workers of Britain there was widespread and genuine support for the North. Certainly, there were Southern Clubs in Manchester and some of the other northern towns, and a Southern Independence Association was formed as a London equivalent. But these do not seem to have commanded the same intensity of working-class commitment as the abolitionist/pro-Northern side. (The Southern Independence Association in particular seems to have been a rather late effort on the part of pro-Southern sympathizers to harness the support of the disenfranchised, having long concentrated on winning over those with official influence.) An abolitionist mass meeting in Exeter Hall on 29 January 1863 blocked the traffic in the Strand; in 1863 as a whole there were no fewer than eighty-two pro-Northern meetings, twenty-six of them religious/abolitionist in character, fifty-six of them held by working-class supporters of the North (Adams, pp. 111, 123). In fact the affiliation of the industrial North of England to the cotton-producing South does not seem to have been as powerful a factor as one might expect, with working-class support for the North and for abolition being far more prevalent. Indeed the Southern Clubs of the North were organized by James Spence (and funded by the blockade-running firms) in 1863 to offset the effects of Bright in the manufacturing towns. The economics of Confederate sympathy in the manufacturing districts also needs careful scrutiny: the extent to which the 'Cotton Famine' of 1861–2 was caused by the Civil War is open to question; as Douglass Adams points out, there were other factors, including over-production after the bumper crop of 1860, and fluctuating foreign demand (Adams, pp. 6–13).[56] In the parliamentary debates of July 1862 on the possibility of British intervention in the war, none of the Northern representatives spoke in favour of such a move; the workers, of course, had little voice in such debates (Adams, pp. 20–1).

But the most telling reasons for working-class support for the North, and press partisanship for the South, have to do with the political landscape at home. The broad support of the disenfranchised for the North was an explicit endorsement of Northern democracy, and an implicit endorsement of democracy per se; just as the press's hostility to the North, and to Lincoln himself, was an often undisguised reflection of attitudes to Reform at home. One contemporary commentator, an American living in London, noted that the venom of *The Times* was an index of 'their hatred, not to America, so much as to democracy in England' (cited Adams, pp. 280–1). Among the more conservative periodicals, the war was held up as an example of the bitter fruit of giving the working classes the vote, with *Blackwood's* pointing to the fall of the Union as the inevitable end of that 'spoiled child, Democracy' (Adams, p. 281). The most weighty of the conservative journals, the *Quarterly Review*, ponderously opined that 'political equality is not merely a folly, it is a chimera' (Adams, p. 286). Lincoln's relatively humble origins were seen to offer further proof that the ending of traditional hierarchies would issue in chaos; internecine warfare was what happened when you elected a rural attorney as effective sovereign. The London-based Confederate propaganda paper, *The Index*, stoked such feelings by playing up the gentlemanly nature of Southern society

(Adams, p. 287), with Jefferson Davis as the cultured foil to Lincoln's bumptiousness.[57] The equation of the South with gentlemanliness, and with pastoral/chivalric ideals, chimed of course with the version of plantation life celebrated in minstrel shows, and indeed in such productions as *The Octoroon*.

A more coded, and more hysterical, fear of democracy reveals itself in the initial reaction to Lincoln's Proclamation of 22 September 1862, which promised freedom to the slaves of those states in rebellion against the Union (not, it might be noted, the slaves of the loyal border states). From the beginning there sounded occasional doom-laden warnings of a 'negro Garibaldi calling his country-men to arms' (Adams, p. 80, citing the *Saturday Review* of 17 November 1860). But the Proclamation gave these relatively insubstantial fears a startling reality, and the phrase 'servile insurrection' gained a wide currency. (Such fears were voiced in the US too, of course.) The press was not convinced that the Proclamation amounted to final proof that the North was on a genuine moral crusade against slavery. On the contrary, as Adams states, 'the London newspaper press was very nearly a unit in treating the proclamation with derision and contempt, and no other one situation in the Civil War came in for such vigorous denunciation' (p. 102). In general, one disenfranchised landless group without much formal education acted as a stalking horse for another. *The Index* played on British perceptions of the sensual negro, suggesting the possible consequences for the planters when 'a race naturally licentious, of weak intellect, and strong animal impulses' was unleashed (Lorimer, p. 165). The more sensationalist end of the press coverage, perhaps influenced by Knox, and by the still vivid memories of the Indian Mutiny, saw Lincoln's Emancipation Proclamation as presaging a race war, in which the 'passions' of the Negro would be roused (though events in New York seemed to suggest that blacks were the ones most at risk of racial violence). The *Daily Telegraph* saw the Proclamation as an 'illegal incitement to servile war' (Lorimer, p. 165). For *The Times* of 21 October 1862, Lincoln's action was the desperate last card of a thwarted presidency, and it envisaged nothing less than a bloodthirsty slave rebellion succeeded by a retributive genocide: 'horrible massacres of white women and children ... followed by the extermination of the black race of the South' (Adams, pp. 102–3). For other commentators it was either a 'brutum fulmen', or empty threat, or a 'cry of despair'; *Blackwood's* presented it as 'monstrous, reckless, devilish' (Adams, p. 103).

Some of this hysterical rhetoric may have been driven by more local fears of the enfranchisement of the British working class, but not all of it.

The minstrel show had not entirely convinced the public of the harmless and happy-go-lucky qualities of the plantation slaves. But as time went by, and no servile insurrection followed, the supporters of abolition and of the North, including John Bright, grew more confident. Bright openly criticized the hostility of the ruling classes to the Union as the corollary of their antipathy to democracy at home. By early 1863 there had been a groundswell of support for the North, and a revival of abolitionist feeling, with old hands like George Thompson and Harriet Beecher Stowe attracting large and enthusiastic crowds.

On the whole, then, Boucicault was correct in 1861 to assume that there had been a sea change in British opinion, though it had come about over a longer period than he allowed. While the views of Hunt and Knox remained those of a minority, they were not so far outside the fold as they might once have been. Yet the appearance of many Freedmen's Aid Societies in England suggested that part of the population still thought of African Americans as their brothers, and kept up the earlier ideals of the Abolition movement. Nor is there any straightforward relationship between the emergent science of race and the burgeoning entertainment industry. Audiences at the Adelphi *wanted* to see the Octoroon united with George Peyton, not, like their American counterparts, to briefly imagine this possibility before seeing Zoe conveniently killed off. Even blackface minstrel acts, which could hardly be seen to produce progressive images of ethnicity, sometimes performed in the abolitionist cause.

The debates about race that were brought into everyday discourse by the American Civil War, and which were put to work by Boucicault for his own dramatic purposes, were given fresh impetus by the events of October 1865 in Jamaica. When black Jamaicans protested in Morant Bay at the heavy sentences handed down to 'squatters' on uncultivated land, part of the ongoing war of position between the planters and the freed black population, the Riot Act was read, and shooting broke out. Soon there was a real riot, in which the Chief Magistrate, or Custos, was killed, along with fifteen others. In subsequent raids on estates, two overseers were killed. But the martial law that followed, under the orders of Governor Edward Eyre, exacted a terrible and disproportionate retribution: 439 black West Indians were killed; 600 savagely flogged; and many homes were razed. George William Gordon, a politician of mixed ethnicity who had fallen foul of Eyre, was transported from Kingston, which was not under martial law, to Morant Bay, which was, and executed there after a 'trial'.[58] The immediate reaction in Britain was that strong measures were called for: again, memories of the 1857 Mutiny were still fresh, and were revived further by press coverage; others saw parallels with Fenian activities closer to home (Lorimer. p. 184). In the aftermath, unsurprisingly, there was a feeling that Eyre might have over-reacted. In particular his treatment of Gordon attracted condemnation: Gordon was a gentleman; his father was Scottish, and he had been educated in Scotland. Eyre was recalled, and a Royal Commission appointed to investigate his handling of the situation. The Commission's report, issued in 1866, criticized Eyre, but no further measures were taken, which led John Stuart Mill and the Jamaica Committee to proceed with a private action against him.

As with the American Civil War, attitudes to Morant Bay were heavily overdetermined by the emotions raised by Reform. On the radical side, Eyre was burnt in effigy at the Reform demonstration at Clerkenwell in September 1866; on the conservative side there were many who saw links between unruly black bodies overseas and unruly working-class bodies at home. As Catherine Hall phrases it: 'The potential anarchy at home suffused the conservative discourses on the heroic Eyre who had saved the beleaguered white people.'[59] Those who came to the defence of Eyre included the Earl of Shrewsbury, Thomas Carlyle, John Ruskin, Charles Dickens and Alfred Lord Tennyson. As Hall also makes clear, though, anti-Reform feeling was not the only factor, and an earlier hardening of racial attitudes made it easier to support brutal colonial action: 'The assumption that black men and women were part of the same universal family as white people, an assumption that many did not share but few would openly debate in the high moment of abolitionism, no longer held a position of hegemonic power.'[60] The Eyre controversy was to last for the rest of the decade, and indeed for a long time after that.

GORILLAS IN OUR MIDST

The ongoing need to define the exact place of the white Briton in the order of things also underlies one of the other great debates of the 1860s, albeit one with more inherent comedy than those over the Civil War, or the Eyre affair. This was the flurry of excitement and subsequent controversy created by the arrival from Africa in 1861 of the self-styled explorer and naturalist Paul Du Chaillu, who soon became the talk of the town with his accounts of the gorilla, a then relatively unknown creature. It was relatively unknown, insofar as many major museums had stuffed gorillas, the skins of which had been showing up in Europe for at least fifteen years; but Du Chaillu seems to have created the impression that he was bringing something radically new to his public, whom he captivated with lectures at the Royal Institution and elsewhere. The Royal Geographical Society was impressed enough to offer him rooms in which to display his collection of stuffed gorillas. Du Chaillu's narrative account of his explorations in the remote forests of Gaboon (now Gabon), his encounters with cannibal peoples, and his descriptions of the fierce gorillas and hundreds of other species he had shot, appeared in April 1861 as *Exploration and Adventure in Equatorial Africa (1856–9); with Accounts of the Manners and Customs of the People and the Chase of the Gorilla, Leopard, Hippopotamus, Chimpanzee, and Other Animals*, and became a great success. But as Joel Mandelstam describes, the book's initial success received a considerable fillip from the controversy in which Du Chaillu became embroiled.[61] In part this was to do with the highly charged field into which he entered, since in these post-Darwinian years the gorilla was pointed to by some (notably T. H. Huxley) as one of humankind's nearest kin in the animal kingdom, and seen by others (notably Sir Richard Owen, Superintendent of Natural History at the British Museum) to be a distinct and separate species. Upon his arrival in London, Du Chaillu had been befriended by Owen, and also patronized by another powerful advocate, Sir Roderick Murchison, President of the Royal Geographical Society, who nominated him for Fellowship of the Society. In Owen's Royal Institution lecture of March 1861 on 'The Negro and the Gorilla' (which also appeared in *The Athenaeum*), generous reference was made to Du Chaillu's work; and he was similarly cited in Huxley's response to Owen. But then, Mandelstam relates, Du Chaillu's star began to wane: a rivulet of minor critiques of the details of his book developed into a torrent, and those critiques based on close reading of the book's claims were soon supported by letters from Gaboon from those who knew its author that completely discredited his accounts of himself as an explorer, linguist, and hunter of and expert on gorillas. (Du Chaillu's account of the ferocity of young gorillas was undermined by a letter from R. B. Walker, a friend of his, who noted that Du Chaillu had visited him on several occasions and seen the perfectly tame young gorilla he kept as a pet.) One of the gorilla hunter's greatest adversaries in this period was in fact one of Sir Richard Owen's colleagues at the Museum, Dr John Edward Gray, Keeper of the Zoological Collection. Gray noted the inconsistencies in Du Chaillu's travelogue, but he also poured cold water on the explorer's claims to have brought back the preserved remains of unknown species, arguing that there was not a single species in his collection that was not already known to science. In particular he suggested that some of the book's drawings had been plagiarized from another book, and that a drawing of a gorilla skeleton was clearly based on an image, readily purchasable in the British Museum, of one of its own exhibits. Owen rushed to Du Chaillu's defence, but realized his rashness when *The Athenaeum* began to publish the letters from Gaboon that discredited many of the explorer's claims. Curiously, this controversy did very little harm to Du Chaillu: he returned to Africa, where he undertook further explorations with the blessings of the Royal Geographical Society, and wrote a series of other successful books, though ones that depended more on their histories of adventure than their natural history.

Much of the Du Chaillu story unfolds in the pages of *The Athenaeum*, but as a 'sensation' the gorilla overran the banks of gentlemanly scientific discussion, and began to turn up in a variety of other cultural media. We have already seen that *Punch* made fun of Du Chaillu's 'Gorilla Book' as one of the major sensational draws of 1861 in the dialogue of the 'Mild Youth' and the 'Horrid Girl'; and that Du Chaillu's gorilla lectures appear in the Stump Speech quoted above. The gorilla also found its way into the popular music of the 1860s, such as C. H. R. Marriott's 'Gorilla Quadrille' (*c*.1862), with an illustrated cover by Concanen and Lee.

Other gorilla-themed dance tunes included Wellington Guernsey's 'Gorilla Galop' (1861), and H. J. Byron and Frank Musgrave's 'Mr. Gorilla: The Lion of the Season' (Hopwood and Crew (*c*.1870)), with a chromolithographic cover by Concanen and Lee. Pantomimes and burlesques, always reliable for topical references, also put the supposedly savage beast to work, and throwaway gorilla references find their way into a number of the burlesques of the 1860s, including Henry R. Addison's 'Mr Gorilla' (1862) and Henry J. Byron's 'Esmeralda; or, The "Sensation" Goat' (1861).[62]

Why was the gorilla such a sensation? Du Chaillu arrived at a time when there was a ready-made audience for material that would contribute to Darwinian controversy; but since, as Gray pointed out, major museums already possessed stuffed gorillas, and had done so for some fifteen years, we do have to wonder why the self-promoting explorer was given such a warm welcome. We might assume that the public was in need of a savage gorilla, and that they were enchanted by Du Chaillu's tales of a ferocious misanthropic beast in way that they had not been by the stuffed skins and articulated skeletons otherwise available. In light of the way in which Huxley and others were prepared to speculate about the possible links between black Africans and the gorilla, it is tempting to suggest that this fantasy of a ferocious quasi-human beast who dwelled in the forest came from the same fevered imagination that produced apocalyptic visions of servile insurrection abroad, and proletarian revolt at home.

The gorilla could also be used to connect up the putative savagery of Africa, the degradation of the American slave, and Britain's largest ethnic

13. Illustrated cover for Marriott, 'The Gorilla Quadrille' (186?).
Chromolithograph by Concanen.

minority, the Irish.[63] This connection could take playful forms, as in H. J. Byron's parodic version of *The Colleen Bawn*, *Miss Eily O' Connor* (1861), where Danny Mann assures Mrs Cregan that he will be 'remorseless as the gorilla' in carrying out his mission. She replies:

> Gorilla! Good! The simile's refined,
> And that the water's not too shallow [*sc.* Du Chaillu], mind.

But the gorilla could also be used to, quite literally, put the Irish in their place in the order of things. The Hyde Park riots (including the 'Hyde

Park Aspromonte') of September 1862 saw a series of clashes between tens of thousands of supporters of Garibaldi and Irish Catholics anxious to defend the Papacy.[64] (The riots of 1862 should not be confused with the Reform-driven demonstrations of 1866, which inspired Matthew Arnold's *Culture and Anarchy*). Garibaldi's efforts to unite Italy were opposed by Pope Pius IX, who called on Catholics everywhere to come to the defence of the Church. The Irish were among the keenest, and a Papal Irish Brigade, the 'Papal Battalion of Saint Patrick', was formed in 1860 (Catholic volunteers also came from other countries, including Canada). Events in Italy gave fresh impetus to 'No Popery' lecturers in Britain and Ireland, and there were a number of relatively minor disturbances in Bradford, Leeds, Belfast, Tralee and elsewhere.

There had already been a resurgence of anti-Catholic feeling in 1850 following the restoration of the Catholic hierarchy in Britain, and a series of firebrand lecturers stirred up resentment throughout the 1860s: Alessandro Gavazzi, the Baron de Caumin and, infamously, shoe salesman turned demagogue William Murphy (Gilley, p. 700). The Hyde Park riots of 1862, though, were not caused by the more familiar religious factions of Orange and Green, but by a clash between working-class Secularist supporters of Garibaldi (whose march on Rome suffered a setback when he was imprisoned after a clash with government troops at Aspromonte in Calabria) and London's working-class Irish Catholics. On Sunday, 28 September, the Secularists, who were more inclined to denounce the supporter of the Papal States, Napoleon III, rather than the Pope, were charged by angry crowds of Irishmen and women defending 'God and Rome', some of them wielding clubs and throwing stones. Among those on the mound, or 'Redan', as it came to be called, was the radical activist and editor of the *National Reformer*, Charles Bradlaugh. Sporadic violence continued throughout the afternoon, with off-duty guardsmen weighing in on the Garibaldi side. After the first clash, Sir Richard Mayne, the Police Commissioner, sought to keep any conflagration within the park's boundaries on the following Sunday by stationing large numbers of police around the park, while leaving the park itself relatively lightly policed. This time the pro-Garibaldi working men lay low, and the fighting that ensued was between the Irish and the off-duty soldiers, though some pro-Garibaldi Italians also took part. Although *The Times* described it as a 'battle' (cited in Gilley, p. 710), there were only seventeen arrests: two Italians, four English and thirteen Irish 'White Jackets', so styled for their white labourers' smocks (Gilley, p. 711). Sporadic fighting continued for weeks afterwards in the Irish districts of London. While not all of this was linked to the Hyde Park events – some of it was internecine faction fighting – the English press saw a pattern of violence. It was in this context that *Punch* of 4 October 1862 compared the Irish of the London rookeries to 'savages', and that of 18 October described the 'Irish Yahoo' as the 'missing link' between the negro and the gorilla (cited in Gilley, pp. 713–14). As Gilley points out, though, the English poor of the rookeries, the source of the garroting scare of the same year, were also criticized in the press, as were the soldiers who ran amok.

There was more serious fighting in Birkenhead on 7 October, this time stirred up by an Irish Protestant clergyman, the Reverend Joseph Baylee. The press were again inclined to perceive an orchestrated campaign of Catholic violence where there was almost certainly no such pattern. The Catholic Church, it was felt, must be responsible for manipulating its people, since they were on their own incapable of such organized action. It was *The Times* on this occasion who put the gorilla metaphor to use:

Surprise could scarcely have been greater if gorillas had issued from the arches of the Adelphi to revenge ... the open exhibition of the skins of murdered gorillas ... the poor, savage, Irish drudges ... so ignorant, so quarrelsome ... and so utterly untaught in morals or religion. (cited in Gilley, p. 722).

The representation of the poor Catholic Irish as a subhuman population continued for the rest of the decade.

At the same time, the Hyde Park events gave the Irish in Britain and elsewhere a sense of their own power, as well as renewing their sense of grievance. Some of this new energy fed into Fenianism. Fenian activities in England, Ireland and Canada served to further crystallize hostility to the Catholic Irish – ironic in light of the Catholic Church's own hostility to the Fenians. There was a disastrous rising in Ireland in March 1867, and in the same year an attempt to raid Chester Castle for arms and an abortive 'invasion' of Canada. Two sensational rescue attempts excited enormous interest: one in Manchester, in September, in which a guard was killed, and one on Clerkenwell prison in London in December, in which a number of local people were killed or injured. (When Fenian activities had died down in the 1870s, Boucicault included a Fenian prison escape in *The Shaughraun* (1874), and used the play's success to lobby for the release of Fenian prisoners.[65]) As Catherine Hall points out, it is against the background of this Fenian surge that the Murphy riots took place, culminating in the events of June 1867 in Birmingham, when an angry mob destroyed the largely Catholic Park Street, and attacked a Catholic chapel, singing *John Brown's Body* (Hall, pp. 218–19).

In the 1860s, an aggressive working-class Protestantism was given a fresh lease of life, and directed at the enemy within: Irish Catholics. Violence was clearly used on all sides, though the press reportage usually assumed that it was the Irish who were innately violent. As Hall puts it, 'In the imagined nation as it was reconstituted in 1867, "Paddy", the racialized Irishman, stood as a potent "other" to the respectable Englishman' (p. 220). One of the things that was frightening about this simianized Paddy, this white gorilla who was also kin to the black American slave, was that his attention could not be held, or it could only be held by foreign agents, priests with the authority of Rome.

Structuralism has taught us that language can be understood as a system of differences, and the same is true of colours, which as they exist in historical context have cultural qualities as well as physical ones. In the 1860s whiteness can only be understood in just such a relational, and indeed oppositional, way. We can trace the prehistory of such figures as the Woman in White, the Colleen Bawn and the White Girl to the grotto of Massabielle, to that scenario in which a crowd was held spellbound by a young woman's vision of the Virgin. But we need to consider that the sensation culture of the 1860s also depended on the imagination of other crowds and other bodies: pastoral images of a carefree, more sensuous plantation world, which was also reassuringly hierarchical; and more troubling images of dangerous and libidinous black masses, which doubled the threatening crowds closer to home, the violent and superstitious Irish as well as the franchise-hungry natives. The savage gorilla appears at just this moment as a condensation of the fears and longings of a society on the threshold of a limited democracy, the foil of the singing, dancing – and always smiling – plantation black of the minstrel show.

We might note in closing that such a dangerous beast appears again in 1933, when the monstrous Kong figures forth the anger and frustration of the Depression-era crowd. This is not a pure coincidence: *King Kong's* co-director, Merian C. Cooper, had been given a copy of Du Chaillu's 1861 *Exploration and Adventures in Equatorial Africa* as a boy, and its fantastical representation of the predatory gorilla had stayed with him.[66] But by then the power of Ann Darrow's (Fay Wray) blonde beauty to kill the beast is more assured, for which we might read the confidence of the entertainment industry in its own power to hold the restless crowd in thrall.[67]

CHAPTER 5

The chromolithographers of modern life

And when life's prospects may at times appear dreary to ye,
Remember Alois Senefelder, the discoverer of Lithography.
William McGonagall, 'The Sprig of Moss'

According to Maurice Willson Disher there was a lot of singing in the London of the 1940s: not only was there a more general resurgence of morale-boosting, professional variety entertainment during the war years, but amateur singing offered a way of passing the time in the darkness of an underground shelter, while bombs and rockets fell from the skies.[1] They sang the popular songs of the moment, but also those of the Edwardian and Victorian years: just as collapsing buildings must have occasionally revealed the underlying fabric of an older city, people sometimes found themselves remembering fragments of lyrics and snatches of melody that floated up out of the past, *disjecta membra* of the comic music-hall songs and drawing-room ballads of an earlier London. This welling-up of memory was not, of course, confined to music. In a number of her short stories from these years, Elizabeth Bowen dramatizes the way in which the war, for all the importunacy it gave to the present, set the past free in the imagination. Thus the central character in 'The Demon Lover' visits her eerily empty, bomb-damaged London house, only to find herself pursued there by a ghost from her youth, a soldier to whom she had once been engaged, before his death in the First World War.[2] In 'The Happy Autumn Fields' a woman in war-time London finds herself projected back into a nineteenth-century rural landscape by a set of family letters that she finds in her bomb-shaken house, though in this case the story suggests that it is she who haunts the people of the past. In both stories the cracks in the physical fabric of the city seem to stand for rifts in the fabric of time: in one story the war evokes the previous war, the one that was supposed to end wars; in the other, it is a version of Victorian pastoral that is evoked, though the violence of the present seems to cast its shadow over it.

147

This folding back on itself of linear history may suggest one reason why in August 1944 Sacheverell Sitwell took up his pen to take an imaginary walk through London by taking a tour through the music of another age. The result, *Morning, Noon and Night in London*, is something of a curiosity, a slim book that sets out to capture the 'genius loci' of London, by looking not at the present, or even the proximate past, but at the London of the 1860s, and it aims to do so not through the high culture of the period, or even its middle-brow novels or drawing-room ballads, but through its popular, illustrated sheet music, which brought the comic songs of the music hall, and the quadrilles, polkas and waltzes of the fashionable resorts, into the Victorian home.³ The chromolithographic illustrations provide Sitwell's focus rather than the songs and melodies themselves, and the book provides colour reproductions of a number of eye-catching covers: 'The Bond Street Beau', 'Kleptomania', 'The Dark Girl Dress'd in Blue' and 'The Age of Paper', among others. Sitwell uses the characters portrayed on these covers to take us on a guided tour through the air-raid-free, cobbled streets, and to bring the 1860s vividly to life, while in the present 'the streets of London are in daily and nightly peril from the flying bombs' (p. 1). We are some way along in this idiosyncratic narrative before Sitwell reveals to us the name of the man whose work these covers are, his painter of mid-Victorian life, the artist and lithographer, Alfred Concanen (1835–86), often paired with John Brandard as the most gifted of the nineteenth-century music-cover illustrators.

Concanen, Brandard and their peers are by no means alien figures to the literary and theatrical worlds of 'sensation' that we surveyed in earlier chapters. In the 1870s, Concanen, for example, illustrated a number of the Chatto and Windus editions of Wilkie Collins's works, including *Antonina*, *The Law and the Lady* and *My Miscellanies*. But more importantly, illustrated sheet music reflects almost all other aspects of Victorian culture, including many theatrical and literary sensations of the 1860s. Concanen produced covers for popular music derived from Dion Boucicault's plays of the 1860s, such as William Forde's 'Colleen Bawn Quadrille' (1861), George Richardson's 'Flying Scud Quadrilles' (1867?) and Charles Coote's 'After Dark Galop' (1869); Brandard illustrated C. H. R. Marriott's 'Colleen Bawn Waltz' (*c*.1861) and the same composer's 'Woman in White Waltz' (1860); R. J. Hamerton illustrated a comic song, 'The Woman in White' (dedicated to Collins, but independent of the novel); and Thomas Packer illustrated Thomas Browne's 'The Colleen Bawn Galop'.⁴ Blackface minstrelsy features in many illustrated covers, including pieces sung by the Moore and Burgess Minstrels ('Please Give

Me a Penny Sir' (*c.*1870)), illustrated by Concanen, and E. W. Mackney ('In the Strand' (1861)), illustrated by Hamerton. Even the Gorilla craze found its musical expression, in Marriott's 'Gorilla Quadrille' (1864), vividly illustrated by Concanen. Fine art featured less often in such covers, though by the 1880s the aestheticism popularized by Whistler and others had become widespread enough to feature in a number of comic songs illustrated by Concanen, including T. S. Lonsdale's 'My Aesthetic Love' (1881), Harry Adams's 'Flippity Flop Young Man' (*c.*1882) and Robert Coote's 'Quite Too Utterly Utter' (1882), the cover of which features an aesthetic type who looks decidedly like Whistler.

For Sitwell, Concanen's pictures are in a class of their own in terms of their artistic achievement. He treats them as self-contained cultural artefacts, while also stressing the importance of their connection to popular music. In fact, he argues, it is their relationship to the popular music of the time that allows these illustrations to capture the city's inhabitants and their way of being in the city – quite literally the street life of the 1860s. In the case of our first 'guide' through these streets, the man-about-town caricatured in the song 'The Bond Street Beau', the lithograph, even though based on a caricature, provides access to aspects of the history of everyday life otherwise lost:[5]

The Bond Street Beau['s] walk and attitude are not to be found in the pages of any novelist or historian. His are the characteristics that they do not set out to capture, or that escape them. No full-length biography could tell us as much as this meeting with him upon the pavement. It is because he is living and moving, which never happens, or is only hinted at, in fiction. Music is the secret. It is music to which he walks and moves, and which explains and makes probable his attitude. (p. 12)

It is these muted echoes of the secret harmonies of the past, of the forgotten rhythms, gestures and attitudes of everyday life, that give these chromolithographic covers their evocative power.

If Sitwell's is not a fully developed theory of mediation, an account of a lost 'structure of feeling' that might be recovered in fossil form, or a material unconscious to be brought back to consciousness, neither is it a view of how cultural forms capture history that we should lightly dismiss. In this chapter I want to follow in Sitwell's footsteps, as it were, and to consider how the work of Concanen and his collaborators and peers might complicate the version of the 1860s that I have presented in previous chapters. Here we leave the sensational world of secularized apparitions, of women in white, White Girls and Colleen Bawns, and their dark others, for a world of colour, the bright colours of 1860s chromolithography: the

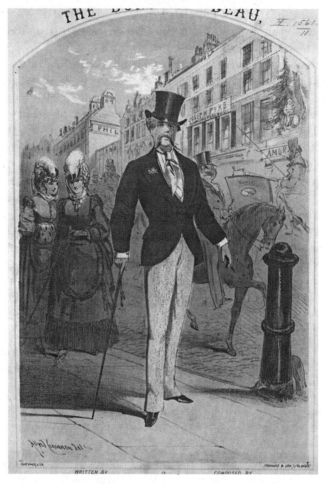

14. Illustrated cover for Alfred Lee's 'The Bond St. Beau' [1873?].
Chromolithograph by Concanen and Lee.

mustard yellows, indigo blues, dazzling checks, and the newly popular
aniline-based mauves and magentas that almost literally seize the viewers attention. In earlier chapters I have discussed the ways in which the
writers and artists in the years of Reform meditated upon the crowd as
a category made visible by both social and political modernization, and
evaluated their own ambivalent position relative to this new potential
audience, sometimes trying to capture its attention, sometimes trying
to evade it. The recurrence of the term 'sensation' in the 1860s provided

a convenient way of tracing shifts in the market for cultural goods, and its relationship to transformations in the world of formal politics. In this chapter we will be examining a cultural form aimed at the crowd, and in which the crowd, as the condition for modern urban experience, is regularly evoked. But here we step outside of the problematic of 'sensation', for in the work of Concanen and his peers the crowd, and issues of social and political modernity, do not primarily appear as problems. The key to this difference is the form of entertainment that did most to sustain the work of Concanen and company: the music hall, the major source of popular songs and popular dance tunes in the 1860s. Although anchored in the experience of the urban working class, the music halls were part of a nascent culture industry as much as an expression of popular feeling, and we should avoid romanticizing them. Nonetheless, as we shall see, they are the centres from which emanate a set of images, narratives, tastes and dispositions different from the ones we have hitherto encountered. For the core audience of the halls, Reform represented an opportunity more than a threat, and the crowd a form of solidarity more than an engulfing mass.

In the 1940s Sitwell wished to recover Concanen as a lost auteur working in an ephemeral mode. But Concanen was not a solitary auteur working in a popular form: he collaborated with other artists (notably T. W. Lee), as well as with lithographers like the Hanharts, and even though his best work is remarkable, he was not the only chromolithographic artist who produced interesting work in this period – we shall also see examples of the work of Hamerton, Packer and Siebe. The interesting thing about these artists is not that they transcended their materials and circumstances; the latter are perhaps the key to the interest of their work. They produced non-auratic 'mass' art out of the new technique of chromolithography, and created a popular form for an industrial age that was at once up-to-the-minute, accessible and visually sophisticated. But Sitwell is right to stress the musical factor: through their ties to the music hall, these artists provide access to a counter-vision of the 1860s.

LITHOGRAPHY AND CHROMOLITHOGRAPHY

Since illustrated sheet music is a relatively understudied cultural form, it may be as well here to consider its visual and musical nature, and its probable conditions of reception, before moving on to look at the covers themselves. That illustrated music covers were produced using lithography and later chromolithography gave them a particular place in the hierarchy of nineteenth-century visual culture, and indeed has to some extent determined their comparative neglect in the present. Lithography is a late arrival as a means of mechanical reproduction, not appearing until the end of the eighteenth century, when Aloys (sometimes Alois) Senefelder, working in Germany, developed a technique for printing from stone plates. Lithographs are produced by a planographic method, that is to say one that does not depend on intaglio (as with engravings, including mezzotint, aquatint and drypoint) or relief (as with woodcuts and wood engraving), and the image to be reproduced can be drawn directly onto the stone plate, rather than carved or etched, as in woodcuts or steel engraving. The basis of lithography is the tendency for water and grease to repel each other. First the image to be reproduced is drawn on a stone surface with a crayon (also called lithographic chalk) or greasy ink – Martin Hardie describes a mixture of 'tallow, wax, soap, shellac, and Paris black'.[6] The stone is then washed in a weak acid, a solution of gum arabic is applied to it, and it is moistened with water. When the stone is then inked with a roller the ink is taken up only by the greasy part of the surface (i.e. the drawing). In colour lithography, or chromolithography, there is only one colour per stone, and a coloured print is built up from successive applications of different stones, or colours are built up from individual tones, again using successive applications of stones (the most suitable form of stone for the purpose proved to be the compact Solenhofen limestone that Senefelder found in the quarries of Bavaria). Lithography is obviously not a simple method of reproduction, and it required commercial printers to have tons of stone in stock, but it was more economical than existing methods because of the possibility of direct drawing, and the greater numbers of good-quality imprints that could be produced from a plate. Senefelder himself visited England to establish a patent, and the first lithographic (or 'polyautographic') book, *Specimens of Polyautography*, was published in London in 1803 by his associate, Philipp André. Rudolph Ackermann and Charles Hullmandel are generally associated with the use of the new technique in the 1820s. The former translated into English Senefelder's *Complete Course of Lithography*, and published lithographs. Hullmandel set up a printing shop, and published the *Art of Drawing on Stone* (1824); he is also credited with the invention in 1840 of the lithotint, a technique for imitating the washes of watercolour by painting diluted ink directly onto the block.[7]

The new technique was by no means an immediate success. Ackermann returned to the use of aquatint and engraving for his illustrated publications (e.g. the *Repository of Arts, Literature, Fashions, &c.*); Hullmandel persisted, but complained that lithography was 'despised and abused by artists of talent'.[8] For the next few decades lithography was used primarily for gift books, and for illustrated travel books. Hullmandel's invention of the lithotint resulted in a wave of topographical books illustrated by such artists as J. D. Harding, Thomas Shotter Boys, John Nash and Louis Haghe. Some of the landmark publications of these years are Samuel Prout's Facsimiles of *Sketches Made in Flanders and Germany* (1833) and David Roberts's extraordinary *The Holy Land, Syria, Idumea, Arabia, Egypt and Nubia* (1842–9) and *Egypt and Nubia* (1846–9), both lithographed by Louis Haghe; the tinted lithographs of the latter two publications, in particular, showed the sophisticated effects that could be achieved in the new medium (fully coloured images from Roberts's work are often to be seen, but these are hand-coloured rather than chromolithographed). Although some limited use was made of it for printing playing cards (by the firm of De la Rue), chromolithography proper does not really make much of an impact until the 1840s, when Owen Jones uses it in his illustrated account of the Alhambra (1842–5), as well as in John Gibson Lockhart's *Ancient Spanish Ballads* (1841), William Sleeman's *Rambles and Recollections of an Indian Official* (1844) and *The Song of Songs* (1849). (Even in this period colour printing was more associated with George Baxter's patented colour printing process, which combined chromo-xylography – woodblock colour printing – and steel engraving.)[9]

Godefroy Engelmann had patented a chromolithographic process in France in 1836, but this had no legal purchase in England (he had established a business in England, but this closed in 1830), which allowed the technique to be widely copied. One of Engelmann's former managers, Michael Hanhart, set up his own printing business in London, and the Hanhart name is to be found more than any other on the chromolithographs of the 1850s and 1860s, including much of the sheet music.[10] Yet, the status of the new art remained uncertain: that two of the best-known chromolithographed books of the 1850s are Owen Jones's *The Grammar of Ornament* (1856) and Matthew Digby Wyatt's sumptuous record of the 1851 Exhibition, *The Industrial Arts of the Nineteenth Century* (1851–3), suggests the extent to which the new technique was something associated with design rather than fine art. Its use for illustrated sheet music may have helped to popularize it, but it did little to add to its prestige. The use of lithography in nineteenth-century France by such figures as Odilon Redon, Henri Fantin-Latour and Edgar Degas has no real equivalent in England, with the possible exception of Whistler, who produced a small number of lithographs in the 1870s and 1880s.[11]

Why was lithography pigeon-holed in this way? While it did not always produce the subtle effects of aquatints or mezzotints, it could produce fine work, and was economical. The Pennells insist that 'snobbishness was the obstacle to the success of [*sc.* fine art] lithography' (though they themselves were not free from such condescension), and their argument is supported by the comments of the *Quarterly Review* regarding the 'greasy daubs of lithography' used as book illustrations.[12] The use of lithography to make affordable, if not always ideal, reproductions of the fine art of the past presumably lies behind John Ruskin's urgent 1857 warning to would-be artists that they should 'let no lithographic work come into the house if you can help it, nor even look at any', which seems in keeping with his dim moral view of industrial reproduction in general.[13] Yet Ruskin's attitude was more complex: it should be noted that just before this passage from his *Elements of Drawing* he praises the lithographic work of Samuel Prout and John Lewis, and he also employed Samuel Rosenthal to make lithographs of his drawings for *The Stones of Venice* (1851–3). Through the Arundel Society he became involved in the publication of limited-edition, high-quality chromolithographs of Renaissance art. But it is his distrust of lithographic reproduction, shorn of its complexity, that finds many echoes. Fifty years later a similar distrust of industrial methods and of popular taste seem to underlie the views of Martin Hardie (subsequently Keeper of the Departments of Painting, Engraving, Illustration, and Design at the Victoria and Albert Museum), writing in 1906, who considered that lithography had declined in the later decades of the nineteenth century because 'easiness of imitation led the mechanical and commercial lithographer to the cheap and vulgar reproduction of the worst types of popular pictures'.[14] Where other more labour-intensive methods of mechanical reproduction were somehow assumed to allow a vestige of artistic aura to remain, this was not the case with lithography. It is tempting to speculate that printing from stone was considered too easy, too cheap, too industrial and altogether too democratic a visual form, and that the greasiness of the technique was equated with the putative greasiness of the populace.[15]

Some of the assumptions underlying this hierarchy of the arts were made more explicit in the United States, as Peter C. Marzio has chronicled in his study of American chromolithography, *The Democratic Art*. Marzio traces the way in which, from the 1860s onwards, chromolithography became widespread as a means of image reproduction: in trade cards, advertisements and music covers, as colour magazine supplements and in the varnished reproductions of high art generally known as oleographs in Europe. The working and lower middle classes could thus afford to have pictures in their houses, and companies such as Currier and Ives thrived. But as chromolithography spread, cultural commentators increasingly linked it to what they saw as the degraded tendencies of modernity, or what the New York-based *Nation* called a 'chromo-civilization'. For Edwin L. Godkin, *The Nation*'s Irish-born editor, chromolithography was one of a number of pernicious media that 'diffused through the community a kind of smattering of all sorts of knowledge, a taste for "art" – that is a desire to see and own pictures – which taken together pass with a large number of slenderly equipped persons as culture, and give them an unprecedented self-confidence'.[16] The democratization of the visual, and of culture more generally, for some at least, meant a dilution. Such attitudes can easily be interpreted in light of Pierre Bourdieu's *Distinction*, but Marzio makes clear the more general historical context of such attitudes: chromolithography comes to act as shorthand for a seismic social shift, as a small, hierarchized America was replaced by a giant, urban and relatively democratic nation. Over time the popularity of chromolithographs was succeeded by their devaluation even among those who had once eagerly purchased them. By the 1890s, as Marzio records, 'chromo' becomes American slang for 'a person or object that is ugly or offensive'.[17]

Marzio's work cannot simply be extrapolated to the British case: chromolithography never reached the same degree of saturation in Britain; and it never attracted quite the same level of high-cultural hostility, or created the same eventual popular distaste. Yet the battles over popular taste that we have traced around the term 'sensation' had their equivalent in attitudes to the mechanical reproduction of the image. The place of chromolithography in the hierarchy of the arts remained a lowly one in the nineteenth century, and this has had consequences for the way in which it has been studied. Even today an informed British commentator can write that 'it is clearly out of the question to describe a colour lithograph by Picasso as a chromolithograph'.[18] Specialist collectors and music historians have considered illustrated covers (e.g. Ronald Pearsall, and the Spellmans), but such figures as Concanen rarely appear in general accounts of the Victorian visual arts, such as the Pennells' *Lithography and Lithographers* (1915); or of book and magazine illustration, such as Forrest Reid's *Illustrators of the Sixties* (1928) or Gordon N. Ray's *The Illustrator and the Book in England from 1790 to 1914* (1976); though a more recent study, Simon Houfe's *Dictionary of Nineteenth-Century British Book Illustrators and Caricaturists* (1996), does contain brief entries on Concanen, R. J. Hamerton, and others.[19] Cultural history has not done so much better: one of the best cultural histories of the visual field in the nineteenth century to appear in recent years, Kate Flint's *The Victorians and the Visual Imagination* (2000), does not consider the impact of chromolithography.

The most detailed recent account of urban experience and the visual arts in 1860s London, Lynda Nead's *Victorian Babylon: People, Streets, and Images in Nineteenth-Century London* (2000), does feature a number of chromo-lithographs, and contains a discussion of a particular Concanen cover in the context of Cremorne Gardens, but there is a good deal more to be said about chromolithographs as part of the 'frenzy of the visible' of the nineteenth century.[20] With the exception of an essay on music-hall comic songs by Jane Traies that appeared in 1986, Victorian studies has effect-ively ignored Concanen and his peers: Sitwell's 1944 attempt to show the significance of Concanen as an interpreter of modern urban experience, as a chromolithographer of modern life, was exceptional, and contemporary cultural studies has done little to build on it.

FROM JULLIEN TO THE LION COMIQUE

It is pointless to consider the illustrated popular music of the 1860s with-out some understanding of its musical origins. There are at least four over-lapping factors that lead to the efflorescence of the chromolithographic cover: to the three major factors listed by Ronald Pearsall – the popular-ity of the 1840s composer and conductor, Jullien; the affordability of the piano; and the rise of the music hall – we might add a fourth, the rise of the drawing-room ballad.

Let us take the last factor first, since according to Derek B. Scott, the drawing-room ballad was 'the stimulus behind the first flowering of the commercial popular music industry in Britain and North America'.[21] (The profitable marketing of sheet music was underwritten not just by improvements in mechanical reproduction, but by the 1842 Copyright Act, which allowed an author to sell the performing rights and reproduc-tion rights separately.) Such ballads, often dealing with patriotic themes as well as with thwarted love, maintained their place in the middle-class home throughout the nineteenth-century, and sometimes featured litho-graphic and chromolithographic covers. Although they are somewhat out-side the scope of this chapter, their co-existence with the more strident tones of music hall should not be forgotten.

That there was also an increasing appetite for instrumental music in the home was in part thanks to the efforts of Louis Antoine Jullien. Jullien was a French composer and conductor who had left Paris in 1838 for London, where he brought his verve and showmanship to promenade concerts held at the Surrey Zoological Gardens and at Drury Lane, among other London venues. These large-scale entertainments featured his arrangements of the great classical and Romantic composers in the same programmes with more popular fare: polkas, waltzes and quadrilles composed and arranged by himself. Promenade concerts, with their relatively low ticket prices, targeted a wider audience than existing orchestral concerts; they came into their own in the summer, when the aristocracy left London.[22] As *The Musical World* put it, 'Jullien broke down the barriers and let in the crowd.'[23] He was also a great showman, who conducted Beethoven with a special, jewel-encrusted baton, and who would grab an instrument and join in at climactic moments. From 1844 he began to widen his appeal by publishing the sheet music to his popular quadrilles and other pieces with illustrated covers, and selling these from his music shop in Maddox Street. Some of these covers were chromolithographs or, more often, hand-tinted lithographs, many of them drawn by John Brandard. Jullien's were by no means the first musical illustrations, of course: woodcut illustrations appeared on printed song sheets from the fifteenth century, and engraved illustrated covers appear at least as early as the seventeenth century.[24] They were not even the first lithographed covers, as these begin to appear with some frequency from the 1820s. Brandard produced covers from the mid-1830s, some of them closer to the comic spirit of Concanen than the more dignified work he created for Jullien, and he produced chromolithographed covers for Nelson and Jeffrey's musical annual, *The Queen's Boudoir*, from 1841. (Brandard himself was influenced by the earlier work of such figures as Maxim Gauci and H. C. Maguire.) But Jullien's cross-class appeal helped to make the lithographic music cover a significant component of Victorian life from the 1840s onwards, part of that intensification of visual culture that came to characterize nineteenth-century urban experience more generally. Nor was his influence confined to England, as by 1844 he had agencies in New York, Leipzig, Madrid, St Petersburg, Vienna, Bonn and Milan.[25] Jullien had a stand at the 1851 Great Exhibition to display his illustrated musical covers, as did rival music publishers, Chappell.[26]

One reason for Jullien's success, Ronald Pearsall suggests, was the popularity of carpet dancing, or ballroom dancing – these were the years of polkamania. But another significant factor he notes is pianomania: not just the widespread popularity of piano music, but the relative affordability from about 1840 of the overstrung piano, which fitted into even modest houses as the grand piano could not.[27] Jullien's music thus became reproducible – to some extent at least – in the middle-class home. The piano also facilitated the popularity of salon singing: many of the early illustrated covers are not for dance music, but for genteel drawing-room ballads, different in appearance and content from the broadside ballads that were sold in the streets by popular ballad singers, and which were already going into a decline by the 1850s.[28]

If the piano underpinned the musical evening in, a new form of musical night out was offered by the appearance of the music hall, a mode of entertainment that came from working-class culture, not that of the middle classes. The halls were preceded by a variety of other sorts of musical venues: London had singing saloons and saloon theatres, like the Royal Brittania in Hoxton, the Union Saloon in Shoreditch, or the Grecian, attached to the Eagle Tavern, City Road; and somewhat more upmarket West End singing rooms such as Rhodes's, or the Cyder Cellars, in Maiden Lane at the back of the Adelphi Theatre, or the Coal Hole in the Strand; or supper rooms like Evans's in Covent Garden. The last four catered to a relatively well-to-do and often Bohemian crowd, but many ordinary pubs had occasional 'harmonic meetings', or sing-songs – as they occasionally still do in some places – and a number of these featured turns by professional singers. Over time the surging urban population made the music business seem lucrative enough for some enterprising types to build substantial separate premises that charged entrance fees, usually adjoining or replacing public houses, and still selling alcoholic drinks for a major part of their revenues.

In the more industrial towns and cities music hall takes off early. Dagmar Kift has shown that establishments like the Star in Bolton (opened in 1832) possessed all the characteristics, being large, commercial, professional and permanent entertainment centres, though they did not style themselves as music halls.[29] The regional halls have a somewhat different history from the metropolitan ones, in part owing to the fact that they faced less competition from the minor theatres.

In London, the Surrey Music Hall opens in 1848, but the first major London instance is usually seen to be Charles Morton's 700-seat Canterbury Hall on the Westminster Bridge Road in Lambeth, built in 1852 next to the Canterbury Tavern. The first West-End music hall, the Weston, appeared in 1857 in Holborn on the site of the Seven Tankards and Punch Bowl Tavern.[30] In London the halls really only come into their own in the late 1850s and 1860s. John Wilton founded Wilton's Music Hall in the East End in 1850, but it reopened after a £20,000 renovation in 1859 with a capacity of 1,500. Morton's second venue, the famous Oxford Music Hall, opened in 1861 on the corner of Oxford Street and the Tottenham Court Road on the site of an old coaching inn, the Boar and Castle, and the London Pavilion appeared that same year, on the site of the Black Horse Inn in Tichbourne Street (later Great Windmill Street). The year

1860 sees the founding of the London Music-Hall Association to defend the interests of the music halls, which were under constant attack by the theatres as well as by the temperance movement. While the rapid spread of the halls was by no means confined to London, the capital saw a particularly dramatic increase in their numbers, with some forty new halls appearing in the 1860s, most of these thriving concerns that weathered the economic depression that began in the early 1870s, though a number succumbed to 1878 legislation that introduced expensive changes to the lay-out of the halls. The part played by alcohol in the halls gradually diminished, and by the end of the nineteenth century they had to a considerable extent been gentrified: by then they were closer to the less class-specific ethos of 'variety'.

In the early 1860s the music halls were still a comparative novelty in London, and considered to be largely a working-class or Bohemian preserve, so much so that in an article in *All the Year Round* from 1861, Dickens felt the need to explain to his readers what exactly the music halls were:

A large proportion of our readers may be probably in need of some preliminary explanation on the subject of music halls, and of the quality of the performances which are exhibited in them. These places of entertainment may be roughly described as the growth of the last 10 years, both in London and in the large towns throughout England. They are, for the most part, spacious rooms, attached to large public-houses, but having special entrance-passages of their own. The prices of admission are generally sixpence for one kind of place, and a shilling for another. Both sexes (except, we believe, at Evans's supper-room in Covent-garden, where men only are admitted) are allowed the right of entry – there are female, as well as male performers at the entertainments – and the audience have the privilege of ordering what they please to eat or drink, and of smoking as well, at any period of the evening's amusements, from their beginning about seven o'clock to their end a little before twelve.[31]

The writer proceeds to give a description of a typical evening's entertainment at Weston's Music Hall in Holborn, where some 1,500 people gathered to enjoy 'a clever nigger vocalist with a blackened face, and nimble feet at a jig', instrumental music 'played by a full band of wind instruments', 'a young lady who sang "serio-comic" songs', 'ladies and gentlemen who sang sentimental songs', 'a real Chinaman' who juggled knives and an excerpt from Donizetti's opera *Lucia di Lammermoor*. In addition to these there was 'another comic singer, preserving his natural complexion [*sc.* unlike the "nigger vocalist"] – a slim inexhaustible man, who accompanied himself (if the expression may be allowed) by a St. Vitus's Dance of incessant jumping, continued throughout his song, until the jumps were counted by the thousand' (p. 559). This latter unnamed figure was in fact James Stead, and his bizarre jumping routine, performed in his trademark costume, accompanied his best-known comic song, 'The Perfect Cure', which describes the misadventures of a young man in love. Maurice Willson Disher quotes some of the lyrics, by F. C. Perry:

> I wasted on her lots of cash
> In hopes her love to share,
> I with her used to cut a dash,
> And all things went on the square
> Until I caught another chap
> Who on his knees did woo her;
> She cried as she my face did slap,
> You're a perfect cure, a cure, a cure, a cure, a cure,
> Now isn't I a cure,
> For here I go,
> My high gee wo,
> For I'm a perfect cure.
>
> ...
>
> I was laid up for sev'n long months,
> Indeed I'm not romancing,
> Which brought me on Mr Antinny's dance,
> That's why I keep on dancing.

At which point, as Disher describes, 'in fool's cap and a red-and-white suit, like pyjamas, Stead kept bobbing up and down, feet together, arms to sides, before a delighted audience'.[32]

Who comprised the audiences that flocked to see Stead's comic turn? Were the halls the exclusive haunt of the urban working class? One view of music-hall demographics can be deduced from Dickens's article, which was inspired by the attempt by the managers of the theatres to legally challenge the right of the music halls to stage performances that were, they considered, the province of the theatres. Specifically, Benjamin Webster of the Adelphi (whom we met in Chapter 2) took Morton to court for contravening the Theatre Act by staging a 'pantomimic dialogue named *The Enchanted Hash*'.[33] As Dickens sees it, this was simply an attempt by the established theatres to curb competition, an unnecessary effort not only because the theatres were enjoying good business, but because they were courting a different public, and employing more sophisticated material and greater resources. Some of the theatres had themselves only been properly able to stage legitimate drama since the 1843 Theatre Act, for which Dickens, among other writers, had campaigned. Thus he regards it as ironic that Webster was the named plaintiff for the theatres, when 'his

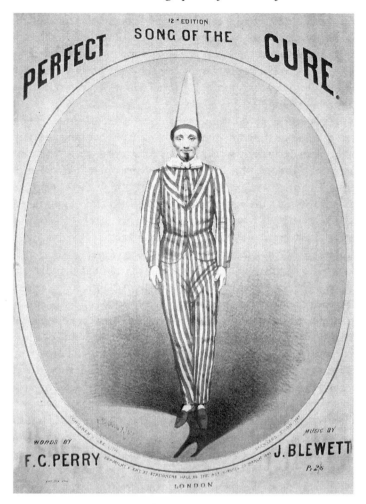

15. Illustrated cover for J. H. Stead's 'The Perfect Cure'.

theatre has been literally besieged by the public for the last hundred and fifty nights, and is likely to be besieged in the future for a hundred and fifty more' (p. 561), thanks to the success of *The Colleen Bawn*. Besides which, the theatres 'have a refined, intelligent, and wealthy public to appeal to, from which the music halls are separated by the great social gulf which we all know there is no crossing' (p. 561). Despite this gulf, he suggests that the music halls will ultimately send some of their audience to the theatres, an audience that they have in effect created, just as the cheap newspapers and penny-a-week novels have created new audiences: 'the music-halls have unquestionably raised up *their* new public; and in doing so will indirectly help to improve the prospects of the theatres, by increasing the number of people who look to public amusements as the occupation of their evening'; a small but significant proportion of these will 'drift into theatres from a natural love of change' (p. 561).

It is an interesting account, but not one to take entirely at face value: it has been quite some time since cultural historians have believed music hall to have been an exclusively working-class or working-class/petit-bourgeois phenomenon.[34] Indeed, the archival evidence suggests that what the article terms 'the great social gulf which we all know there is no crossing' between the music halls and a more 'refined' audience could be and was crossed: the music halls were not attended by the working class and petit bourgeois alone (even the attendance of the article's writer suggests as much), though they were its principal audience; and as the article contradicts itself by admitting, at least some of that principal audience might attend the 'legitimate' theatre too. Dagmar Kift claims that the West End halls 'had always attracted an audience of aristocrats and students', a view that is supported by memoirs of the 1860s.[35] Writing in February of 1863, the barrister and diarist Sir William Hardman (later editor of the conservative *Morning Post*) opines that 'the Music Halls are the one great incubus that sits on the souls of the young and old England; they give the cue to the Extravaganzas, they furnish the tunes for our barrel organs': even given Hardman's general cultural pessimism, this suggests that the reach of the Halls extended beyond the working and lower middle classes.[36]

If we consider the action by the theatre owners that inspired Dickens's article, we have further cause to question his assumptions: if there was no significant overlap between the audience of the theatre and that of the music hall, why were Webster and the other theatre managers at all concerned? Did they simply not know their own business? Dickens, the man who did most to vastly expand the ordinary readership of the Victorian novel, and who had with *Household Words* and *All the Year Round* clearly eschewed the more exclusive (or expensive) magazine formats for a tuppenny weekly magazine, must have known better than most that class and taste were neither as stratified nor as fixed as his article suggests. As with 'sensation' culture, the reaction to the halls suggests anxieties about cultural dilution, and the blurring of class boundaries: the halls were a threat to middle-class distinction. By the end of the 1860s the war between the 'legitimate' theatres and the music halls should have been over, since a Select Committee of the House of Committee had investigated the latter, and concluded that, following the example of the French music halls, they should be allowed to offer most kinds of 'light' entertainment, such as operetta, ballet and pantomime, and not just acrobatic acts and singing. But no legislative changes followed, and cultural turf wars between the minor theatres and the halls continued for several more decades.

The lions comiques and their female equivalents (lionesses comiques?) were the main draw for the halls, and the principal targets for the cultural jeremiads directed against them. The first generation were such figures as Arthur Lloyd, Harry Clifton, Alfred 'The Great' Vance, George Leybourne and G. H. MacDermott, and their female counterparts: Kate Harley and Fanny Edwards, among others. One middle-class commentator, writing in the satirical magazine *The Tomahawk*, saw these lions as diminishing the earlier promise of the halls, which he sees as having provided working-class audiences with a knowledge, however bastardized, of 'good' music:

Operatic selections, it is true, are still to be heard, but they are, as a rule, so badly sung and vulgarly accompanied, that it were better for the cause of art that they should be omitted ... Nothing is listened to now-a-days but the so-called 'comic songs', and, in sober earnestness, we must express our astonishment that human beings, endowed with the ordinary gift of reason, should be found to go night after night in order to witness such humiliating exhibitions ... A man appears on the platform, dressed in outlandish clothes, and ornamented with whiskers of ferocious length and hideous hue, and proceeds to sing, verse after verse, of pointless twaddle, interspersed with a blatant 'chorus', in which the audience is requested to join.[37]

But even worse, he believes, is the 'serio-comic' female singer:

Her very title is assuredly a misnomer, for there is nought of seriousness in her performance, whilst as for comedy – Heaven save the mark! – she knows not the meaning of the word! She appears on the platform and, with saucy bearing and shrill voice, howls forth some ditty about 'cards in the Guards', or some 'swell in Pall Mall', or, perhaps, she will tell you a domestic romance in which omnibus conductors, or policemen, or costermongers, form the important features. Wanting, alike, in point, grace, or humour, these songs can have no purpose save to indulge the degraded taste of the majority of those who nightly fill the Music Halls; amongst such of the audience as have been attracted in the idea that they would hear a rational performance, there can be but one feeling – pity.[38]

These comic and serio-comic singers were the successors to the singers of the song-and-supper rooms and singing taverns, but they also owed more than a little to the popular entertainment of the street. As Peter Bailey notes, they may have derived at least part of their performance technique from the physical style of the street singers, though in their repertoire the ballad was often replaced by more episodic or situational forms.[39] Attention-grabbing volume and physicality, and vivid dress were some of the techniques that were employed to hold a lively, smoking, drinking audience at least partially spellbound, when they were not being encouraged to join in. A certain physical jerkiness was used to give emphasis to particular lines (a street-singing technique deployed to memorable effect by Captain Cuttle in *Dombey and Son*), and the song lyrics were usually glossed with improvised patter, almost all of which is now lost to us, though the acts of such later performers as Marie Lloyd and Vesta Tilley would suggest that this was sometimes sexually suggestive. Bailey has given us the most persuasive account of the male comic singers of this period – and indeed of music-hall culture in general – in his article on the 'swell song', the best-known of which, perhaps, is Leybourne's hit of 1866, 'Champagne Charlie', an extraordinary hymn to the life of the man-about-town, that links extravagant and even heroic consumption with explosive sexual potency ('Good for any game at night, my boys / Who'll come and join me in a spree'). Bailey suggests that we can only understand the success of the song in the light of various contexts: Leybourne's performance, with its knowing appropriation of the signs of aristocratic display; the class tensions within the halls themselves, with their mixed audiences of would-be 'gents' and artisans as well as Bohemians; and a negotiation between a traditional utopianism and the prosperity and political power tantalizingly held out by liberalism in the 1860s (Bailey points out that these were years of comparatively high wages as well as the extension of the franchise).[40]

Clearly, then, while the colourful illustrated covers helped to sell sheet music, we also have to understand them as part of the advertising that built up the star personas of such figures as Leybourne and his rival, Alfred Vance ('The Great Vance'), whose 'Clicquot' was a riposte to 'Champagne Charlie'. To this extent the illustrations belong with the posters, press notices, signed cartes de visites, and larger-than-life lifestyles that were increasingly necessary to keep one's place in a crowded and competitive entertainment industry.[41] It is a particular version of the larger than life, though, one in which the trappings of the landed classes are appropriated, and given a new set of meanings: they become emblems of 'bling' rather than the markers of blood. Not only did Leybourne sing of the swell life, for example, but he was also, according to his 1868 contract with the Hall owner Billy Holland, to 'appear in a carriage, drawn by four horses, driven by two postilions, and attended by his grooms'.[42] Leybourne's life/performance literalizes the term 'labour aristocracy'. In their songs as well as in their star personas, the lions and serio-comic female vocalists offered the working and lower-middle classes lessons in how to take part in consumer society, how to be streetwise, and how to be a modern man or woman of the world. Small wonder that to conservative commentators the halls were an 'incubus'; from Hardman's standpoint the self-promoting music-hall swell that featured on so many sheet-music covers looked more like a dangerous counter-jumper.

FROM THE HALLS TO THE COVERS

But there were other kinds of songs too, as the *Tomahawk* columnist notes, songs that were not always quite so coterminous with the singer's stage persona – songs about street encounters, railway encounters, and the perils and pleasures of domesticity, to say nothing of such topical songs as 'Banting' (1870; *sc.* dieting), 'Kleptomania' (1863) and 'Have you Seen the Ghost?' ([1870] *sc.* Pepper's Ghost).[43] Nor were all of the most elaborate illustrated covers for comic songs: if the Spellman Collection at Reading University is representative, there are as many or more lithographed covers for instrumental music, specifically dances – galops, quadrilles, schottisches, polkas, waltzes, lancers and the occasional varsoviana. To this extent we cannot always rely on lyrics to frame how we might 'read' the images. Even where we have lyrics, as with the comic songs, the images do not always simply correspond to them. In Martin Meisel's terms, we are dealing with illustrations that interpret, expand and sometimes change the meanings of the songs rather than straightforward realizations of the lyricists' intentions (or those of the performers).[44]

There is a further problem in viewing the illustrated covers as exclusively tied to the halls themselves and to the lions comiques. Admission to the Canterbury in the 1860s was from six pence to a shilling, and Wilton's charged four pence to eight pence, with boxes available for a shilling. But illustrated sheet music in the 1860s might cost between two shillings and four shillings per piece, at a time when a London labourer might make twenty shillings a week, and a male mill worker thirty-two, with women's wages ranging from ten to twenty shillings.[45] Pearsall notes that it was the practice of the music sellers to sell the sheets at half price shortly after publication, but this would still mean that a four-shilling colour piece would cost two shillings, or one tenth of the weekly wage of a London labourer. And this is to pass lightly over the cost of buying a piano, in an age when the ten-guinea piano was generally thought to be the bottom of the market. We cannot deduce from these factors, of course, that the working

class were not buying sheet music, but such constraints do strongly suggest that they could only do so by making a considerable financial investment. It seems more than likely that of the majority audience of the halls
in the 1860s it was only the very well paid artisans and the lower middle
class who could regularly buy such music, though we might assume that
the Bohemians, students and young bloods who also patronized the halls
could have been buying it too. Where working-class consumers were buying music it was probably, as Jacky Bratton suggests, in the form of popular compendia or 'songsters' rather than illustrated sheets.[46] This is not, of
course, to say that they rarely or never saw such music, since the illustrated
sheets filled the windows of London's many music shops and thus became
part of the lived environment; we might also guess that pubs bought sheet
music for sing-alongs.

Other evidence supports the assumption that illustrated sheet music
bridges the world of the halls and the middle-class home: much of the
music that survives from the 1860s comes from privately bound volumes,
which suggests the post-purchase practices of a relatively affluent consumer group.[47] Ronald Pearsall's advice from the early 1970s on where to
find Victorian illustrated covers in London stresses that some of the best
hunting grounds are the suburbs, since 'East Enders frequented the music
halls but they did not buy the music; the middle-classes in the fashionable
suburbs of Balham, Hornsey, or Sydenham did.'[48] In this light it is worth
noting that the domestic scenes in which Concanen and his collaborators
show the greatest virtuosity are scenes of middle and lower-middle class
life, and as Jane Traies has shown, there is a significant number of comic
songs that deal with such themes.[49] The domestic interiors in particular
summon up the detail of lower-middle class life with extraordinary detail,
for example in such covers as 'Oh Lor, Oh Lor! Oh Dear, Oh Dear!', 'I'm
a Happy Little Wife and I Don't Care' and 'Mrs Watkin's Evening Party'
(the street scenes, by contrast, appear to be more varied in character, and
cover the social gamut from mouse-catchers to Burlington Arcade toffs).
We cannot, of course, assume that purchasers of sheet music were drawn
exclusively to comic representations of the domestic life of their own
class, any more than we can assume that the original readers of *Diary of A
Nobody* were themselves all Pooters; but I think Traies is correct in arguing that some of the comic details of these interiors depend upon a degree
of recognition – that this is the comedy of the familiar.

The covers, then, can be considered as a popular visual form, with many
illustrated songs achieving sales of over 10,000 copies, but popular here
cannot be taken to be synonymous with 'working-class', and we must

assume that the majority of the buyers of sheet music were likely to be the lower middle class of clerks and small shopkeepers, or Bohemians, as well as the middle and upper tiers of the middle class.[50] This is of crucial importance insofar as it suggests that the counter-vision of the 1860s that we can extrapolate from illustrated music is not an exclusively working-class phenomenon. Rather, it is something that develops in the shifting cultural terrain where the mixed-class world of the halls, mediated by professional illustrators, shades into the world of the middle-class home.

But what of the covers themselves? We might first consider those covers that were more directly linked to the music halls, before examining the illustrated dance music. There are various subdivisions of such illustrated music. The categories employed by one of the most prolific publishers, Hopwood and Crew, in an advertisement of 1860 are 'Comic, Motto, and Topical Songs'.[51] The motto songs, where illustrated at all, are often simply illustrated by portraits of the performers (there are many Harry Clifton covers of this sort, for such nautically inspired sermons as 'Wait for the Turn of the Tide' (1866) and 'Paddle Your Own Canoe' (1866)).[52] The popular comic songs and the topical tend to converge, since many of the comic songs deal with modern, urban life, including fads and current events. I will return to these below. The other comic songs, which I will deal with first, are, broadly speaking, about love and marriage: some are vignettes of the ups and downs of domesticity (Watkin Williams's 'I'm a Happy Little Wife and I Don't Care' (1863); W. H. Witt's 'The Parlour Blind' (1865)); John W. Roe's 'Mrs Watkin's Evening Party' (1871); and such later songs as Harry Hunter's 'Money Matters' (1883?)), but the most common type deal with romantic or erotic encounters, usually in urban settings. This category includes some of the best-known covers of the period: e.g., 'The Dark Girl Dress'd in Blue' (1862) and various responses to it such as 'I am the Dark Girl Dress'd in Blue' (1863), 'The Dark Man Dress'd in Blue' and 'The Young Chap Dress'd in Blue'; 'Down in Piccadilly' (1863); 'The Sewing Machine'; 'Jemima Brown, or, The Queen of a Sewing Machine'; 'The Properest Thing to Do' (1863); 'Oxford Street' (1863); 'The Charming Young Widow I Met in the Train' (1863) and its close imitation, 'She'd a Black and Rolling Eye'; 'I Really Couldn't Help It' (1863); 'It's a Way the Girl's Have Got'; and 'Up to the Knocker'.

What most of these songs have in common is that they make of the street (or the railway carriage, or the omnibus) a realm full of erotic possibilities, even if many of them turn on the (comically) adverse consequence of such possibilities. They are, in fact, recognizably descended from the 'as I roved out' type of folk ballad, often presumed to be a descendant of the medieval pastourelle form, though in these city versions roving tends to end in comic reverses rather than successful wooing.[53] Here the city provides the landscape, and the pretty maids of the folk ballad have been transformed into worldly-wise city girls, just as the young men who go roving out are often married, and on a 'spree'.[54] In 'The Properest Thing to Do', for example, the protagonist leaves his wife and family to go out on the town. Temptation is not long in coming:

> I jumped into an omnibus
> That soon came passing by
> And sat opposite to a pretty girl
> Who giggled at me so sly
> I caught a glimpse of her dear little foot
> And somehow I hardly know
> But I found that I was actually
> Treading upon her toe.[55]

He quickly establishes that she, like himself, is ready for some erotically-tinged fun: 'That she was game for a bit of a spree / I saw at half a glimpse', and they head off to Rosherville (a pleasure garden at Gravesend), and go dancing. As Jacky Bratton notes, the way in which the women in these songs are as eager for such encounters links them to the folk ballad tradition, and also marks them off from the conventions of middle-class culture.[56] In this case it is the young woman who suggests to our protagonist, the delightfully named 'Mr Fitzplantagenet' ('that's my name when I'm out'), that they go for 'a lark in the maze'. But then, he tells us, she faints, and just as he is cutting her stays (presumably we are not meant to take this at face value, but as a way of suggesting sexual activity) the reality principle intervenes, in the form of his mother-in-law, wife and child. The fight that ensues is the subject of the comic lithograph by Hamerton, which neatly encapsulates the change in our hero's fortunes.

Our frisky hero has now been apprehended by his wife, ably assisted by his umbrella-wielding and hatchet-faced mother-in-law. More or less brought to his knees, the once bold man-about-town now holds in his hand his slightly crushed hat, symbol of the deflation of his sexual ambitions. The policeman in the background, by contrast, not only wears a rather phallic hat, but also holds his truncheon in an upright position: he is now the man in charge here, though even he is dwarfed by the wife, who, clad in a capacious crinoline, dominates the composition as well as her cowed husband. The latter's striped trousers suggest the costume worn by Victorian convicts rather than vivid self-display.

16. Illustrated cover for Frank Hall's 'The Properest Thing to Do' (1863).
Chromolithograph by R. J. Hamerton.

Frank Hall seems to have made something of a specialty of such cautionary tales of urban encounters. His 'I Really Couldn't Help It' follows a similar narrative pattern. This time our urban lover is on foot when he comes to an understanding with a young woman:

> I met a girl the other night
> As I was for a walk
> She winked at me, I winked at her
> We then began to talk.[57]

He buys her drinks: he can't help it 'as she was such a scrumptious girl'. She gets drunk and rolls in the gutter, and makes a spectacle of herself: 'And her crinoline stuck round about / 'Twas such a dreadful sight', whereupon his wife appears and again a fight ensues. The song ends with a warning about the dangers of flirting on the streets:

> Now married men attend to me
> Just mind when you go out
> Don't wink as pretty girls pass by
> Take care what you're about.

This time, though, the illustrators (Concanen and Lee) have ignored the narrative elements and confined themselves to the production of a portrait of Hall himself as fashionable gentleman, or possibly a 'gent' who dresses the part of a man of leisure, more in keeping with the collapse of singer and swell persona described by Peter Bailey. The same illustrators gave themselves more scope with Hall's 'Down in Piccadilly', another tale of erotic urban adventure, but one with a happier ending. Again, our hero is the susceptible type, with little of the cool distance of the flaneur:

> I'm fond of pretty girls whose lovely glances Burke us [*sc.* kill us][58]
> Sweetest I e'er did meet was down by Regent Circus [*sc.* Oxford Circus]
> Eyes as black as sloes
> They almost knocked me silly
> As I met her round the corner
> Down in Piccadilly.[59]

This time we learn a useful bit of 'chaff' for picking up strangers:

> I scarce knew what to do I felt in such a tremor
> So I rais'd my hat and said
> How do you do Miss Emma
> Says she there's some mistake
> I happen to be Milly
> Said I never mind your name
> Let's walk down Piccadilly.

He takes his chance, and throws his arms around her, but at that very moment her father appears and throws him in the gutter, where he is jeered by the crowd that gathers. The police arrive and he is bound to the peace in court, but he is also bound to the 'piece', when he proposes to and is accepted by Milly. The streets of London are quite literally brought into the family when their first son is named Piccadilly to 'celebrate the happy day'. As with the previous two songs, the conflict appears to be between the realm of erotic pleasure and the world of the family and duty.

17. Illustrated cover for Frank Hall's 'Down in Piccadilly' (1863).
Chromolithograph by Concanen and Lee.

In this case, the lyrics tell us that the couple's illicit desire will be channelled into proper courses, and the young swell will become a protective father himself.

Concanen and Lee's detailed lithograph illustrates the moment when the irate father appears, and shows him with umbrella raised to bring down a blow on the head (or at least hat) of the fashionably clad young man. The latter is clearly in a different walk of life from the protagonist of 'The Properest Thing to Do': he looks in fact more of a real swell than the 'gent' that the song suggests, which supports Jane Traies's contention that the illustrated covers sometimes alter the class of the characters represented in the songs, in line with the likely sympathies of the more affluent group who were buying sheet music.[60] Piccadilly itself is evoked in some detail, with the corner of Clarges Street shown in the background, and a group of cab drivers clustered in the background, on the edge of Green Park. As with many such lithographs, a great deal of care is taken with the clothes: the young woman wears a ribboned bonnet, crinoline and elaborate shawl; our hero wears a morning coat, cravat and chalk-stripe trousers. The attractive young couple in fact seem to belong to a different visual register from the father, who is a rotund and red-faced cartoon type, complete with umbrella-as-axe, ready for slapstick violence. Concanen and Lee have pursued an effect of dramatic irony: the couple enjoy a flirtatious moment, oblivious to the figure of authority that looms behind them.

In a subgroup of these songs the young woman turns out to be other than she seems; and the protagonists are often innocents up from the country rather than young men about town, or married men looking for some fun on the side. 'The Dark Girl Dress'd in Blue', one of the covers discussed by Sitwell, belongs to this type, as does 'The Charming Young Widow I Met in the Train'. The former begins:

> From a village away in Leicestershire
> To London here I came
> To see the Exhibition and
> All places of great fame.[61]

This time our man loses his heart (and his head) because of the romantic potential of public transport:[62]

> I went in a six-penny omnibus
> To the Exhibition of 'sixty-two
> On a seat by the right hand side of the door
> Sat a dark girl dress'd in blue.

When they get as far as the Brompton Road, the dark girl has no change for the conductor, so our protagonist pays her fare. They fall into conversation, and she describes herself as the 'chief engineer in a milliner's shop'.[63] They walk about the Exhibition for a couple of hours, but things go badly wrong when she gets him to change a five-pound note at the refreshment room. She slips away, but another figure dressed in blue, a policeman from 'X-division' appears, and reveals the note to have been a forgery. The countryman's story is believed, but he has to pay up anyway, and the song finishes with a warning to all young men who encounter 'Ladies strange'.

If the model for the previous type of song is the comic folk treatment of the pastourelle, here we are closer to the tales of urban deceit that go back at least as far as Robert Greene's sixteenth-century *The Art of Coney Catching*.[64] We might also think of them as comic treatments of the alone-in-the-city narratives that are such a prominent part of popular melo-drama, and which broadly speaking map the more general shift from a rural to an urban society. In these comic inversions it is the lad up from the country rather than the young female who finds himself quite literally seduced – or had – by the city. For the audience, whether in the music hall or at home at the piano, such rural innocence is presumably offered as a comic foil to their own worldliness and common sense. The 'Dark Girl' was evidently a successful song, since it spawned at least two serio-comic sequels written for female vocalists by Watkin Williams, 'I'm the Dark Girl Dress'd in Blue', sung by Kate Harley, and 'The Dark Man Dress'd in Blue'; and a parody written by Charles Sloman, 'The Young Chap Dress'd In Blue'.[65] In the first the girl explains that it has all been a misunderstanding; in the second, city guile comes to the country, and a man who claims to be a former officer tries to deceive a young countrywoman; in the last the young chap in blue is actually a policeman. (There is also an American adaptation of the original by Billy Morris, in which the young man comes from New Hampshire to see the Boston Exhibition.) Jane Traies has suggested that songs like these negotiate ambivalent responses to the independence of the 'working girl', a figure who can be related to the actual historical forces that drew working-class women into the lower reaches of the expanding middle class as shopgirls and sewing-machinists, just as it drew working-class men into positions as shop assistants and clerks.[66] As part of this negotiation, the female serio-comic response to Clifton's song, 'I'm the Dark Girl Dress'd in Blue', sung by Kate Harley, contests the assumption of the original that the girl is a criminal who uses her sexual attractiveness to bait her trap, though its portrayal of the Dark Girl's innocence also has ambiguities that might have been developed in performance.

Concanen and Lee's chromolithograph to 'The Dark Girl' takes considerable licence with the story: it appears to represent the moment when the dark girl (Kate Harley) is slipping away from our man (Harry Clifton), while the policeman – ubiquitous in these covers – advances in the background. But instead of being in the refreshment room they are on the pavement outside the Exhibition building, which is clearly shown

18. Illustrated cover for Harry Clifton's 'The Dark Girl Dress'd in Blue' (1862).
Chromolithograph by Concanen and Lee. Hamerton and for C. Sloman,
'The Young Chap Dress'd in Blue' by Concanen and Lee.

in the background, with a bustling street scene (including an Exhibition omnibus) in the middle distance. This, of course, has the benefit of great visual economy, since the setting is immediately clear, and the nature of the brief encounter of the two is telescoped neatly by showing the dark girl flitting away into the crowd. The principal effect, as in 'Down in Piccadilly', is dramatic irony, since at this point the countryman does not realise what their encounter has actually been about, and he still holds his

18. (*Cont.*)

whip in a rather dashing fashion. She looks coyly behind her, but whether this is a parting glance at him, or a precaution against the appearance of the police, is not clear. Again, clothing is elaborately detailed: he is well dressed in a black top coat, though he does not look like a West End swell, and his riding boots suggest his country origins; she is the more fashionable figure, wearing a crinoline of shimmering blue silk, a black shawl, and a blue and white bonnet, and carrying a matching parasol. We might, as Traies suggests in other cases, see the Girl's finery as evidence that the illustrators tend to move the characters of the songs up a social notch. But the visual impact of the clothes is also in keeping with the more general tendency of these covers to make the streets of London look like a visual and tactile feast, a place for sexual display, a message not entirely fitted to the moralizing endings of the songs: where the songs tell us that London is full of traps for the unwary, and that we will lose our purse, or worse, the covers seem to tell us that it is well worth the risk.

'The Charming Young Widow I Met in the Train' is a similar piece that shows the vulnerability of countrymen to the guile of pretty young women. A man from North Wales inherits some money, and buys a first-class train ticket to London. He falls into conversation with a pretty young woman with a baby, who gets him to hold the child while they are stopped at a station, as she claims to see her late husband's brother on the platform. She never returns, and he finds that his watch, purse, ticket and other valuables have disappeared. The baby turns out to be dummy, and the final verse turns to admonition:

> And I now wish to counsel young men from the country
> Lest they should get served in a similar way
> Beware of young widows you meet on the railway
> Who lean on your shoulder – whose tears fall like rain
> Look out for your pockets in case they resemble
> The charming young widow I met in the train.[67]

This song also exists in an American version, and the blackface singer Mackney sang a similar song, 'She'd a Black and a Rolling Eye', in which the hapless traveller is left holding a real baby.[68]

But countrymen were not the only gulls in these songs, as we see in Harry Clifton's 'Jemima Brown, or The Queen of a Sewing Machine'; Frank Hall's 'Oxford Street'; G. W. Hunt's 'Oh! She Had Such Taking Ways'; and 'The Sewing Machine'. 'The Sewing Machine', for example, shows that London has its perils even for young *flâneurs*. In this case the victim is smitten through glass, as the young woman that catches his eye works at a sewing machine in the window of a dress shop. This is a phenomenon of the 1860s that is explained and critiqued in an article in *Once a Week*:

It will be an advantage when the particular style of advertising common to sewing-machine warehouses can be dispensed with – the highly dressed young ladies sitting at their supposed work in elegant attitudes framed and glazed within plate-glass windows almost extending to the pavement. A crowd of male admirers, not purchasers, clusters round the charming picture of domestic virtue, and one salesman, with a higher appreciation than others of advertising effect, divided his premises on the dioecious principle. In one window were seen refined and interesting young gentlemen – in the other, ornately fascinating females. Outside the effect was truly galvanic. The public instantly arranged itself like the oxygen and hydrogen at the two poles of a battery. The former window was obscured by a compression of crinolines; the other by a queue wearing hats. There was certainly in this case no occasion for the notice seen in many shop-fronts – 'You are requested to choose from the window'.[69]

In this song this phenomenon is replicated in a simplified fashion, with just one young man replacing the street crowd:

> I saw her first on Regent Street, in such a dashing shop
> Workin' Thomas No. 2, at the window I did stop[70]
> By the signs that passed between us
> Cremorne gardens she'd not seen
> But she promised to meet if I'd stand treat
> When she'd done at the Sewing Machine.[71]

It is not quite clear how this exchange of signs works (what, one wonders, is the sign language for Cremorne Gardens?), nor is it really clear why she asks him to mind her purse when they get to Cremorne Gardens. But when he does, a cry of 'Stop, Thief' is heard, and he is apprehended. The purse turns out to have a ticket of leave in it (another topical reference), and he finds himself in Wandsworth prison, 'Where [he] learnt to tread a machine'. In the imaginary of popular song, the road from Regent-Street flirtation to imprisonment with hard labour seems very short indeed, and if there are many music-hall songs that mock at policemen (like mothers-in-law), there appear to be just as many that assume the efficiency and omnipresence of the police – and indeed mothers-in-law.

Thomas Packer's fine chromolithograph to 'The Sewing Machine' freezes the action in Regent Street. Our hero is a swell in a cutaway morning coat, fitted waistcoat, contrasting peg-top trousers and stove-pipe hat. He sports Dundreary whiskers and flourishes a cigar.[72] The young woman casts a coy sidelong glance at him from behind the large plate-glass window, in which she sits at her sewing machine, apparently working on a narrow band of cloth. While her position in the window is rationalized by her occupation (cf. Dreiser's *Sister Carrie* as well as Benjamin on the Arcades), she is clearly also being presented as merchandise; she is thus none-too-subtly being equated with other available goods, like the dress on show in another part of the window, or the sewing machine itself. And yet, she is not really available, kept out of reach by the plate-glass window,

19. Illustrated cover for Frank Hall's 'The Sewing Machine' (1864).
Chromolithograph by Thomas Packer.

and presumably carefully watched by the shop's manager. She is, in fact, an example of the deployment of the 'parasexuality' that Peter Bailey discusses in relation to the Victorian barmaid, a form of open, licensed and regulated sexual display turned to commercial ends.[73] Here the sewing-machine 'Queen' is elaborately dressed, and wearing a day dress with full crinoline and voluminous sleeves, but she wears no hat or bonnet as she would in the street, and her long, curled tresses add a further element of sexual display. He looks down at her, and points with one hand, presumably gesturing towards the idea of al fresco fun in Cremorne Gardens. Those who knew the lyrics of the song might see this as a scene charged with dramatic irony – he will be the one working a machine shortly, and in a barred cage rather than a glass one. But unlike in 'The Dark Girl Dressed in Blue' there is no policeman in the background here to throw the scene into Foucauldian relief, and the scene can be read on its own as a vignette of sex in the city, equating window-shopping with sexual *flâneur*ship; linking sexual difference to the difference between viewing subject and fetishized commodity; and blending sexual difference with class difference.

In this respect it closely resembles 'Jemima Brown, or the Queen of a Sewing Machine', which also features a young man who is tricked by a shopgirl whom he meets initially at a variety of stock locations – first at a railway station, then at a haberdasher's in the Burlington Arcade, where she looks 'the Queen of a sewing machine'. When he meets her for the last time she has used his money to buy a shop for herself and her real love ('That shop was bought and I was sold by naughty Jemima Brown'). In the Concanen, Lee and Siebe chromolithograph, we are taken inside the haberdasher's shop to see the swell leaning on the counter and eyeing up the young woman behind the counter, Jemima, like so many yards of cloth. There too the trajectory of the song shows a comic reverse to the swell's expectations, but the image contains nothing that anticipates such an end to the protagonist's assumptions about his own class-based powers, and as with the Packer image we are placed on the side of the swell, looking over the counter at the young woman, who is flanked by the other goods on display. We might see this as another example of 'parasexuality', but we are also on fairly familiar territory here in terms of the way that cultural history has interpreted the *flâneur* in gendered terms: to be male is to be empowered to look; to be female in the urban environment is to be an object of a commoditizing gaze; to be behind a counter or behind glass is to be all the more commoditized (familiar examples might include the barmaid, Suzon, in Manet's *A Bar at the Folies-Bergère*).[74]

But is this exactly what is happening here? It is possible to read the shopgirl images as simply embodying an ideology of class and gender privilege – in this case, perhaps, offering a fantasy of this perspective even to those who may not really have it. However, it is also possible to argue that the feast for the eyes on offer to the men in these images is also available to us with respect to the men, who are put on display at least as carefully as the women. In both images the point of view does not align us directly

20. Illustrated cover for Harry Clifton's 'Jemima Brown, Or the Queen of a Sewing Machine' (1865). Chromolithograph by Concanen, Lee and Siebe.

with the men; rather, it places us at an angle to them that renders them just as much on display – more so, in fact, in the 'Jemima Brown' cover – as the shopgirls. This is in keeping with the way in which the Victorian comic ballads view sexual appetite as a field of equal opportunity, and not as a male prerogative: we are a long way here from the middle-class ideologies of the 'angel in the house', or Ruskin's 'Of Queen's Gardens'; would-be male seducers encounter women who will meet them halfway, or who are rather too much for them.

Both men and women are put on display here, and both are represented as much through their clothes as through face and figure. This is consistent with the prominent part played by clothes and social display more generally in the illustrated covers, which seem to delight in the fabrics as much as the fabric of everyday life, celebrating the vanities of the Victorian street, defamiliarizing it, and offering it up as a kaleidoscopic landscape. In the illustrated covers, a world of mauve, magenta and solferino comes to life. In this respect the illustrated covers offer a valuable corrective to accounts of the Victorian period that read it as an age of mourning wear, or more accurately of men in black and women in white. John Harvey, for example, taking Dickens, Doré and Brontë as his guides, sees black as the dominant colour, or non-colour, of the Victorian years, and he sees this as in keeping with the idea of the 'great renunciation' (the term coined by J. C. Flugel) in men's dress, a rejection of colour that Harvey considers to be complexly related in this period to an austere male dandyism, professional ideologies of knowledge/power, and to Weberian capitalist asceticism, among other things.[75] But, with the exception of those that simply show male performers in evening dress, one struggles to find any images from that austere imaginary in the illustrated covers of this period. It is not that Harvey's account is simply wrong – the renunciation that he describes is certainly part of the mid-Victorian world – but it offers only a partial truth, one that fails to do justice to the counter-perspective of music hall and other popular forms. If we start with Concanen rather than Doré, we get a very different sense of the structure of feeling of Victorian life in the 1860s. Nor is this simply an issue of colour versus asceticism: the colourful street clothes of the characters we meet in these tales of the city suggest a much less fearful attitude to the street, and to the crowd, than we have encountered in previous chapters. Notwithstanding their cautionary endings and tableaux, these songs, and these covers, celebrate modern urban life.

While many of the romantic/erotic encounter songs touch on topical themes, there is also a sizeable category of purely topical numbers. One of Concanen and Lee's most dazzling chromolithographs is for Frank Hall's song, 'Kleptomania' (1863), which pokes fun at what it sees as a cover for good old-fashioned thieving:

> Of course you know the newest dodge
> If not I will explain here
> When rich people prig and steal
> They call is Kleptomania
> If you pay the income tax
> No policeman will detain you

If you nail a watch or rob a till
But say its Kleptomania
...
The complaint comes on in many ways
But it first excites alarm sir
When the symptoms show the patient has
An itching in the palm sir.[76]

Much could be said about the attitude to upper-class morality displayed here, to say nothing of the scepticism regarding the nascent science of psychology. With the benefit of historical perspective, it is, of course, a song that should remind us that city life, with its random encounters with not only attractive strangers but also alluring goods, brought with it its own psychopathology.[77] But the cover is our principal concern here. This represents a scene in Regent Street, outside Lewis and Allenby, high-class silk mercers, and shows two glamorous young women who appear to have just left the shop with their shoplifted goods (one of them is carrying a parcel half-concealed beneath her paisley shawl). In the background we see the large plate-glass windows, behind which lies an array of clothing and fabrics. A young boy – Sitwell notes that he is a crossing-sweeper – points out the two ladies to the rather stunned-looking manager and his assistants, who stand in the shop entrance. As often is the case with Concanen, there is a sort of 'sub-plot' as well, in which the young ladies are almost tripped up by a poodle, a fashionably clipped creature, who has also just stolen something (a bone? a glove?). An immaculately dressed gentleman (he wears a blue tailcoat, matching yellow waistcoat, a blue patterned necktie and grey top hat) with Dundreary whiskers seems to be intervening, but he is using a brush (presumably that of the crossing-sweeper) to stop the dog rather than the young ladies, one of whom casts a glance back at him, allowing us to see her face more clearly. The presence of a policeman in the background walking obliviously in the other direction bears out the lyrics of the song, that some forms of criminality escape the reach of the law. As Sitwell points out, the two ladies appear to be moving at some speed: one holds her crinoline up by a loop to allow her to walk more quickly, and her shawl and crinoline skirt seem to billow out behind her; the other is leaning forward, like a runner trying to cross the finishing line – or a shoplifter trying not to be recognized. But the chief impression of the cover is not of a socio-historical or moral commentary, but of a virtuoso presentation of colour and movement. It is quite literally a picture of the fugitive beauty of modernity, in that the composition is dominated by two fugitive beauties, one brunette, one blonde, and their sumptuous

21. Illustrated cover for Frank Hall's 'Kleptomania' (1863).
Chromolithograph by Concanen and Lee.

clothes. The elaborate fringed paisley shawl worn by the first young lady, together with her voluminous crinoline, makes her resemble nothing so much as a peacock (an effect heightened by her companion's hat feather).

As with the romantic/erotic covers I have discussed above, this brings the Victorian street to life in kaleidoscopic colour: it quite literally dazzles the viewer before he or she is able to make out the various narratives unfolding within the picture. Like the young ladies, or indeed like the dog, we are being tempted by the bright colours and sensuous promise of city life. It is hard to do justice to the vivid effect of this picture in words;

we do not have to agree with Sitwell's assessment ('we have, what we never get in any history or work of fiction, two living figures moving before our eyes') to recognize it as a piece that dramatizes modern life with the colour and dash of a Vincent Minelli Technicolor musical. It is as spellbinding as any woman in white, but there is no hint of the numinous here: rather than being held captive, we are invited to step into the picture, to take part in the life of the street. This piece of illustrated sheet music is a plate-glass window, advertising the delights of modernity.

PICTURES WITHOUT WORDS

With illustrated covers for popular dance music, the artist had more freedom since there were no lyrical constraints. In some cases, of course, there were narratives to be followed, as with dance music based on popular plays. Thus pieces like 'The Colleen Bawn Quadrille', the 'After Dark Galop' and the '*As You Like It* Polka' all illustrate scenes from those plays; in the case of the first two the climactic 'sensation scenes' are illustrated. Similarly, those pieces that derived from new music-hall songs, like 'The Cure Lancers', tend to picture the singer, or illustrate the original song. There were also topical items like the 'Eclipse Galop'; or the many dances inspired by the Volunteer movement; or those pieces inspired by current crazes, for example the 'Gorilla Quadrille', the 'Mormons Quadrille' and the 'Croquet Galop'. In many cases, one suspects, the topicality of the titles and illustrations may have deflected attention away from the recycling that often went on in the melodies themselves.

Concanen created covers for many dramatically inspired pieces. Adam Wright's '*As You Like It* Polka' [1865?] is one of the most detailed of these, featuring an elaborate medievalized representation of a scene from the play, with Orlando standing before the Duke and Touchstone, who are flanked by the court. For H. Bernhoff's 'Lord Dundreary's Galop' (1862), Concanen and Lee produce an image of Dundreary that is not particularly dramatic, representing him solus in a morning room, in a splendidly coloured smoking jacket.[78] Of course, this is a cover appropriate to the cultural phenomenon of Lord Dundreary, since the role of Dundreary, as interpreted by E. A. Sothern, came to overshadow the play in which it appears, Tom Taylor's *Our American Cousin*, which is largely remembered today as the play Lincoln was attending when he was assassinated.

The tendency for songs to generate instrumental spin-offs seems to have grown as the lion comique became the dominant figure of the music-hall stage. 'The Cure Lancers' (1864) derived from J. H. Stead's 'The Perfect

'Cure', is an early example from the 1860s. An advertisement for Charles Sheard's from the early 1870s offering 'Copyright Comic Songs, and Dance Music ... With handsomely coloured title pages, by Concanen and Co.', includes quite a number of such parallel pieces: Leybourne's song 'I Always was a Swell' [1870?] and the instrumental piece, 'The Swell Waltz'; The Great Vance's 'The King of Trumps' and Marriott's 'The King of Trumps Polka'; and The Jolly Nash's 'Jog Along Boys, with a Rattle and a Noise' ([*c*.1867] 'it is impossible to hear it and stand still') also exists as a polka, quadrille and galop. George Leybourne's song 'Up in a Balloon', written by the prolific G. W. Hunt, presumably inspired George Roe's 'Up in a Balloon Schottische'. The cover of the song is quite a plain portrait of Leybourne pointing upwards, but the latter is a striking picture by Packer and Griffin, which features a huge striped hot-air balloon carrying a number of passengers, who wave from the basket hanging beneath; in deference to its origins, the balloon itself carries the legend LEYBOURNE.[79]

It can be difficult to establish precedence between songs and dance instrumentals: in the case of George Leybourne's 'The Mouse-Trap Man' (1868) there also exists 'The Mouse-Trap Man Waltz' (1870), but the advertisement tells us that the latter 'is the beautiful composition from which the favourite comic song ... is taken. It is the most charming set of waltzes ever written, and creates the greatest furore, nightly, at Mr Alfred Mellon's Concerts.'[80] The publication dates are confusing here, but the waltz may have been played at concerts long before publication – nor can we assume that even the British Library has the earliest version in print.

Two of the topics that inspired a range of illustrated instrumental musical responses were the Rifle Volunteers, which drew tens of thousands of middle-class men into an amateur militia, and the Mormon community in Utah. An enfranchised working class was not the only national spectre in the 1860s, and the Rifle Volunteers Corps appeared as a civil response to perceived threats to Britain from the military power of Napoleon III (notwithstanding the military alliance between Britain and France during the Crimean War). The Corps had been mooted from the time of Louis Napoleon's *coup d'état* of 1851, and had been given fresh impetus by the Orsini assassination attempt in January 1858. In 1859 the Volunteers were finally given an official basis, and they were formed into battalions by a rather reluctant government in the early 1860s. Throughout the 1860s the amateur soldiers who were to defend the coast of England were the subject of a good deal of humorous comment, in *Punch*, and to a lesser extent in the music halls, though they also had their defenders, including the Poet Laureate.[81] Henry Walker's song, 'The Awkward Squad, or the Experience of a Volunteer Rifleman' (1865), with a cover by Thomas Packer, is an example of the popular music-hall view:

> A cry was raised for Volunteers
> To set at rest invasion fears
> For Rifle Corps we gave three cheers
> And started out recruiting;
> We muster'd strong: all sizes we
> From four feet nine, to six feet three,
> And short and crooked, slim and stout
> For hearts and homes turn'd boldly out.[82]

But there are actually greater numbers of 'serious' instrumental pieces, perhaps meant to appeal to general patriotic sentiments. Examples include R. Andrews's 'The Volunteer Rifle Corps Grand March' [186?], which has a cover by John Brandard; John Blockley's 'The Riflemen Polka' (c.1860); the 'Bristol Volunteer March' (1865); Stephen Glover's 'The Riflemen's March' (c. 1860), which has a cover by Concanen and Lee; and J. Callcott's 'The First Surrey Volunteer Rifle Quadrille' (c. 1860), also with a cover by Concanen and Lee. These Volunteer-themed covers (like the music itself) would presumably have appealed to a middle-class audience, the same group who made up the vast majority of the Rifle Corps, so it is not surprising that most of them present flattering portraits of the week-end soldiers. Indeed, the number of local variations suggests that they were targeted at the Volunteers themselves and their families. There are, though, some comic pieces that undermine the seriousness of the part-timers. One of the more curious pieces of this sort is C. C. Amos's 'The Irresistible Rifle Corps Polka' (1860), with a cover by Concanen and Lee that shows three attractive young women dressed as soldiers and carrying rifles, with Lincoln-green tunics, rather short red pantaloons and elaborate feathered hats. We can only assume that this is Concanen's visual pun on the 'irresistible' of the title, which presumably was originally meant to qualify 'polka' rather than 'rifle corps'.

Interest in the Mormons in 1866–7 seems to have been sparked by the American humorist Artemus Ward, who gave a series of illustrated comic lectures on his visit to Salt Lake City at the Egyptian Hall in Piccadilly in November 1866. Ward combined a comic deconstruction of the illustrated lecture (his illustrative panorama was deliberately awful) with a deadpan account of his experience among the polygamist community led by Brigham Young. As the *Times* review by John Oxenford noted, to most English people 'Mormonism is still a mystery', though Ward was by no means the first traveller to have brought back tales.[83] Presumably much of the appeal lay in the sexual heterotopia that Salt Lake City appeared to represent, rather than interest in the theology of the Latter Day Saints. Charles Coote cashed in on the Mormon craze with his 'Mormons Quadrille, Dedicated to Artemus Ward' (1867). (This time the comic song version comes later, in the form of George Leybourne's 'My Wife Has Join'd the Mormons' [1870?], which features such lines as, 'Oh! Brigham Young, I'd have you hung'.) Concanen produced one of his most fluidly comic covers for this piece. The main picture shows a cartoon patriarch, a heavily bearded and rather sombre Mormon, wielding an umbrella, who marches from left to right across the picture, flanked by an army of his contented-looking wives and children. In the background a self-satisfied patriarch stands, as if for inspection, with his many wives lined up with him, the bonnets of the furthest off ones disappearing into the distance. The 'Mormons' of the title divides the composition at an oblique angle, creating space for two further vignettes of Mormon life. The smaller shows a happy father playing with his numerous children, watched by a clutch of his wives; the larger presents an unhappy husband covering his ears while his wives bicker and his children howl and cry in the background.

Other dance pieces are equally attuned to the times, and recall some of the more obscure fads of the 1860s. One such is banting, a term that originated in William Banting's *Letter on Corpulence, Addressed to the Public* (1863), in which the author extols the benefits of dieting. Banting (1796/7–1878), an undertaker by trade, was a rather short man who grew increasingly obese with age, despite various exercise regimens. In his sixties he suffered hearing loss, which his doctor attributed to his being overweight. The prescription was a major change of diet, particularly the abstention from fatty and sugary foods, and their substitution with more protein (not unlike the Atkins diet of more recent years), and the resulting weight loss was dramatic enough to inspire Banting to share his diet with the public. His *Letter* became a cause célèbre in England, attracting articles in *The Times* and *Blackwood's*, and it was translated into a number of other languages. The term 'banting' or 'to bant' passed into the language, and indeed remains in use in Swedish.[84] Not everyone took the new idea seriously: as Alfred Rosling Bennett recalls, the 'comic papers and singers made themselves merry; every burlesque and pantomime scored its joke'.[85] Among the comedy spin-offs were Howard Paul's song, 'Banting' (1864), with a cover by R. J. Hamerton, and a farce by William Brough and Andrew Halliday, *Doing Banting* (1864). Concanen, Lee and Siebe produced a cover for C. H. R. Marriott's 'The Banting Quadrille' (1866).

22. Illustrated cover for Charles Coote's 'Mormons Quadrille' (1867).
Chromolithograph by Concanen.

Unusually, this quadrille has lyrics, perhaps intended to be spoken rather than sung:

> It's very well for you to stare
> At my enormous figure
> Unless I take to Banting's plan
> I surely shall get bigger

Forsaking all good things
Will cause me great dejection
I soon shall get as thin
As Pepper's Ghost [*sic*] reflection.
Now Banting's system you can see
Tried on me
Now of flesh I'm almost free
Don't you see
Should I get so fat again
It down must come by Banting's plan
'Tis the only way you see
If you wish to slender be.

The reference to Pepper's Ghost evokes a cause celèbre of the 1860s that we have already encountered, the famous plate-glass optical illusion designed by Henry Dircks, and perfected by him and John Henry Pepper. This debuted at the Royal Polytechnic in Regent Street in December 1862, and later appeared at the Adelphi in the revival of the stage version of Dickens's *Haunted Man*.[86] Concanen, Lee and Siebe's cover for 'The Banting Quadrille' shows a very fat man conducting an orchestra on stage, with an audience synecdochically evoked by their hats. In a vignette in the bottom right-hand corner, framed by the edge of the stage curtain, we see the same man after a bout of banting: he is rail-thin, and is frightened by his own shadow, which has a rather Satanic aspect. It is, in other words, an early comic version of a stock device of later advertising: the montage of before and after. This is entirely apt, insofar as the vogue of Banting is a mid-Victorian instance of that narrative of physical self-transformation on which the growth of modern consumer culture depends. It is worth noticing, though, that in this early version the enormous pre-Banting conductor, with his baton held aloft, dominates the composition, and even allowing for his greater weight, he is out of scale with the diminutive post-Banting figure. The lyrics, then, may suggest, however comically, the benefits of dieting, but the picture tells quite a different story: to lose flesh may be to lose self as well. (A similar cover by Concanen, Lee and Siebe for 'The Banting Galop' shows a portly man who in multiple images shrinks down to an exclamation mark – the author is significantly named 'A. Lessermann'.)[87]

There are covers that do not fit any of these categories, of course. Among the most striking of these is Concanen and Lee's extraordinary cover for 'The Bow Bells Polka' (1862), which appears to be purely a work of the artists' imagination (it pre-dates H. J. Byron's comic play, *Bow Bells* (1880)).[88] The cover presents a sumptuously detailed medieval street with Bow church in the background, a military procession advancing through

23. Illustrated cover for C. H. R. Marriott's 'The Banting Quadrille' (1866).
Chromolithograph by Concanen and Lee and Siebe. Illustrated cover for Harry
Clifton's 'Have you Seen the Ghost?'. Chromolithograph by Siebe.

the crowded streets, and in the foreground an elaborately dressed gentleman flanked by two ladies and watched by a third. There are a number of
Concanen's usual flourishes: a jester chats with two soldiers on the right-
hand side of the composition; a comically attired small boy tries to catch a
dog trailing his lead; the medieval ladies wear medieval headgear, but are
wearing dresses that look suspiciously like crinolines. This seems to not so
much conjure up the medieval past as meld past and present in a dialectic

23. (*Cont.*)

24. Illustrated cover for Frank Musgrave's 'Bow Bells Polka' (1863).
Chromolithograph by Concanen and Lee.

image not unlike that of *The Colleen Bawn*, in which the present projects itself into a costume-drama heterotopia, in this case a version of 'Merrie Englande' rather than eighteenth-century Ireland.

* * *

There are in fact so many striking illustrated covers that an account as selective as this can only scratch the surface. We might conclude by looking at one of the most unusual topical covers, Concanen and Lee's illustration for C. Godfrey's 'Popular Tunes Quadrille' (1862), which takes as its theme the sheer volume of popular illustrated music that was being published in the 1860s. Self-reflexivity is often an aspect of the work of Concanen and his peers, with the names of the music publishers, for example, often slipped into the composition somewhere (e.g. 'Oxford Street', 'The Gorilla Quadrille'). Here such self-referentiality is taken a stage further. The cover represents a man in tails playing an overstrung piano with considerable vigour, his rather long hair flying with the exertion. But we are not in one of the domestic interiors that Concanen did so well, or in a music hall, as the musician's tails might suggest (though he is also wearing slippers): this is a much more stylized composition, with the pianist framed in abstract space by the sheets of music that are falling from the pile on top of the piano, as if shaken loose by his playing. The piano itself is of interest, since it bears the motto 'Prize . . . Medal', suggesting that it is some kind of newly patented instrument, perhaps one put on show at the 1862 Exhibition. The real appeal of the piece, though, is the series of falling covers, since they are perfect miniatures of many of Concanen's own works: among them it is possible to identify 'The Perfect Cure', 'The Lord Dundreary Galop', 'Champagne Charlie', 'The Burlesque Galop', 'Captain Jinks of the Horse Marines' and 'The Popular Tunes Quadrille' itself.

Here we have a form of popular visual culture that goes beyond its own comic mode to comment self-consciously upon it. The cascading covers suggest Concanen's own consciousness of being part of a particular culture industry, one that produced an avalanche of music that could be marketed by the use of bright chromolithographic illustrations, by linking it to current events, or popular plays, or by trading on the charisma of music-hall stars (while also providing them with advertising). The wild hair and frenzied playing of the pianist, like the overflowing music sheets, suggests a pace of cultural production that threatens to exhaust player and audience alike – and perhaps the illustrator too. But as with all the covers we have considered, what strikes one above all is the vitality of the piece: this is no plea for a return to classical restraint.

In one of the classic accounts of the mid-Victorian period, *The Age of Equipoise*, W. L. Burn argues that the period 1852 to 1867 demonstrates a certain stability and cohesiveness, but he criticizes the 'selective Victorianism' that sees the period only as a vanished age of stability in contrast to later, more turbulent times. Those who take the black-and-white group portraits of the period for the reality ignore the selectivity and the representational

25. Illustrated cover for C. Godfrey Jr's 'Popular Tunes Quadrille' (1862).
Chromolithograph by Concanen and Lee.

limits of such images. He imagines one such group photograph in front of
a country house:

It is perhaps as well, for instance, that this is not a coloured photograph. If it
had been, the rather dreadful clash of colours into which fashion and aniline
dyes have led the daughters would have been obvious. Their Zouave jackets, of
magenta and solferino, are worn over pink chemisettes with mauve stripes; their

crinolines are of light green with olive-green chevrons around the hems; their hats are of pale yellow with a tiny garden of artificial red roses on top.[89]

The point is well made: the 1860s was as far from being an age of stable rural tranquillity as it was from being one of classic restraint in clothing and colour. In this study I have tried to suggest that the impact of social and political modernity in this period created doubts as to who exactly the middle classes were. If this was a decade of great cultural vitality, as we have seen, that was not least because figures as different as Wilkie Collins, Dion Boucicault and James McNeill Whistler were wrestling with the questions of how the attention of the reader or viewer might be held in an age of distraction, and who those readers and viewers were – in short, the question of how to come to some accommodation with the power of the masses. The popular illustrated sheet music of the period shows us a somewhat different modernity, and perhaps one more reflective of the lifeworld of the group who were enfranchised by the 1867 Reform Act. As we see in a piece like the 'Popular Tunes Quadrille', Concanen and his fellow popular artists were at least as self-conscious as their better-known peers about the cultural work they were doing. But their orientation to the nebulous mass market is rather different, and this appears most clearly in their treatment of the city, and in their topical covers. The modern, urban environment, with its distracting noise, overcrowding and commercialized amusements is seen here as an inviting (if often deceptive) place. As in music-hall song, it is a place of fugitive sexual promise, of masculine as well as feminine pleasure in display and self-presentation, but also of a wry form of self-awareness. What appear at first to be cautionary tales about urban snares often have more to say about the endlessly vital appeal of the streets than about their perils. The kaleidoscopic covers of Concanen, Hamerton, Packer and the others, with their magentas, mauves and solferinos, their deluded swells, assertive women and endlessly renewed fashions, endorse and fill out this vision of modern urban life. We see an almost affectionate investment in the sheer energy represented by the variegated amusements of the day rather than critical distance and biting satire. In his essay in praise of Constantin Guys, Baudelaire remarks on the art of everyday life:

But there is in this trivial life, in the daily metamorphosis of exterior things, a rapid movement which demands from the artist an equal speed of execution ... From the moment lithography made its appearance, it was immediately found to lend itself very well to this enormous and apparently frivolous task.[90]

Only apparently frivolous, of course, for Baudelaire, since he sees a particular value in the efforts of a man of the crowd, like Guys, to capture the energy and beauty of everyday life. The chromolithographic work of Concanen, Lee, Siebe, Packer, Hamerton and their peers, possesses, I would argue, this same value. Their work is certainly replete with socio-logical significance, not only in its visual content, but in its negotiation of a path among the stratifications of cultural taste. From a different per-spective, we can see it as offering a glimpse of a material unconscious, or an insight into the structure of feeling of mid-Victorian London. But we should also recognize in it, as Sitwell did, and as Baudelaire did in the art of Guys, a glimpse of something beyond its recording of its own historical moment, whether we choose to see that as a hint of eternal beauty, as he does, or as something else – perhaps a modest utopianism, an optimism of the will, or a distillation of sheer delight from the mixed stuff of modern-ity itself.

Conclusion: Pepper's Ghost and the presence of the present

Since this book has attempted to bring together cultural and other histories, it may be as well to conclude by saying something about the 'presence of the present', to use Richard Altick's term, in the literary, dramatic and visual artefacts of the 1860s. That is to say, I want to finish with a more direct account of mediation, or the relationship between historical and quotidian materials on the one hand, and aesthetic forms on the other. Refracted by literary, dramatic or painterly form, the history of the 1860s cannot appear in these novels, plays and paintings untransformed. Even the most ephemeral of materials, such as illustrated sheet music, does not provide a clear window onto the past. What kind of 'presence' are we talking about, then?

Perhaps it is easier to begin by rejecting some possible answers. I do not, for example, consider that they primarily offer us a glimpse into the 'material unconscious' of the 1860s, to use Bill Brown's felicitous phrase for 'literature's repository of disparate and fragmentary, unevenly developed, even contradictory images of the material everyday', which he outlines in one of the most impressive contributions to a theory of the 'presence of the present' in recent years.[1] (Modelled on Walter Benjamin's idea of the 'optical unconscious' of the photograph, Brown's concept seems to imagine the cultural artefact as a verbal or painterly amber in which the lived experience of the past is somehow preserved from the hand of history, to be brought to consciousness again by the critic.) Nor am I suggesting that these artefacts express a Jamesonian 'political unconscious', in the sense of a narrative or stylistic solution to the ideological contradictions of their historical moment, though that is, perhaps, a little closer to what I have in mind. In fact what I want to stress about these 1860s cultural artefacts is their high level of self-consciousness about their own procedures. I believe the texts, performances and images under consideration here feature self-conscious theorizations and fantasies of their relationship to the changing nature of British society in the 1860s. This self-consciousness appears in various guises. *The Woman in White*, for example, is, among other things, a meditation on the role of the artist in the age of crowds at the same time that it is itself a device for securing the attention of the crowd; in *Symphony in White, No. 1* Whistler deliberately sets out to challenge the tyranny of the 'Subject' (i.e. the idea that paintings should have some obvious narrative or thematic content) and to retrain an elite audience for a different sort of visual experience. Even the melodramatic *Colleen Bawn* displays a high level of self-awareness that it is adapting religious spectacle for melodramatic purposes, with its Lourdes-like grotto, and its self-conscious references to distilling spirits.

As a less abstract way of thinking about the presence of the present, or the question of mediation, in the literature, drama and visual arts of the 1860s, we might examine the history of one of the foremost 'sensations' of the decade, a secular spectre that we have already encountered, Pepper's Ghost, or the Ghost Illusion, and its subsequent manifestation in a novel of 1865, Charles Dickens's *Our Mutual Friend*. Henry Dircks, a civil engineer, had read a paper to the British Association in October of 1858 on how to produce 'spectral optical illusions', and subsequently published an article on the same topic in the *Mechanics' Magazine*.[2] He recognized that his idea might have a commercial application, and tried to persuade the theatres to adopt it, but with little success, until John Henry Pepper, the chief lecturer and Honorary Director of the Royal Polytechnic Institution in Regent Street, recognized the spectacular possibilities of Dircks's ghostly special effect. Pepper, usually styled Professor Pepper, was a well-known lecturer on popular science, and had been at the Polytechnic since 1848. He was renowned for making science and technology into entertainment: one of his other successes demonstrated the fire-retardant nature of a kind of patented starch by showing a crinoline-clad woman walking a fiery path, with the flames licking at her hem. In the winter of 1862 audiences were dwindling at the Polytechnic, part of the more general downturn in business after the departure of the crowds that had come to London to see the 1862 Exhibition.[3] Dircks's spectral invention, as adapted by Pepper to fit an ordinary stage, came as a welcome new attraction. The new illusion was given its first airing in the Polytechnic's smaller theatre in a private performance for friends and members of the press on 24 December, just in time for the annual Christmas flurry of competing entertainments. Soon it appeared in public shows, and its success was rapid: the *Times* round-up of seasonal entertainment of 27 December 1862, makes no mention of it; but by Easter of 1863, when the same paper gave its usual seasonal summary of holiday entertainment, it felt that Pepper's show was now so familiar that there was little need to describe it in any detail. (Pepper and Dircks patented their ghost in February 1863.[4]) A writer for *Once A Week* gives us a sense of what made the Ghost Illusion such a hit. The audience (the account suppresses at first the fact that he is at the Polytechnic) sees a white-clad apparition appear in a room:

the furniture of the room, the pictures on the wall ... showing plainly through its form ... Then slowly the white robes parted, the gleaming veil was lifted from the head. The folded arms flung back their covering and stretched themselves as though to fold us in their grasp. And it stood confessed. A skeleton! Were none of us startled then? Did no one in that throng, but now so joyous, thrill with unutterable horrors now? One at least retained his courage. Grasping the first weapon that came to hand, he rushed forward and aimed a fearful blow at the spectre. The blow fell harmless upon the empty air. Again he struck; this time with slower and surer aim, and again the heavy weapon passed harmlessly through the terrible figure. He rushed recklessly forward, and strove to grasp the spectre with his hands! He passed again and again over the very spot where the hideous apparition still waved in triumph its bony arms and grinned horribly with its fleshless lips. It was nothing – a vision – impalpable as the air from which it grew ... It was gone! But it had been there. I saw it myself. We all saw it. Here in this very London, in which I write. Here, at – well, 'in point of fact' ... at the Polytechnic![5]

In its first manifestation at the Polytechnic the Ghost was used in a dramatized excerpt from Bulwer Lytton's recently published *A Strange Story* (1862), presumably illustrating the scene in Chapter 39 in which the magician, Margrave, appears to Dr Fenwick as a 'a spectrum, a phantasm'.[6] Subsequent shows (that which *Once a Week* describes) revolved around the appearance of a skeleton, excerpts from Charles Dickens's *The Haunted Man* (his Christmas story from 1848), and a comic mime called *Cupid and the Love Letter.*[7] Pepper carefully guarded the technical side of his adaptation of Dircks's apparatus, and *Once a Week* could only reveal that 'nothing can be more ingenious than the optical arrangements by which this singular delusion is effected' (p. 543). Some contemporary commentators assumed that the trick was done with mirrors, and indeed a mirror could be used below stage to relay the actor's image to the second reflecting surface at stage level, but the primary surface was not a mirror, but simply a large sheet of plate glass.[8] The key to the illusion is the way in which plate glass can be made to act as a mirror, or as a transparent medium, or a combination of the two, as the lighting determines. In fact the illusion can be produced quite effectively without any mirror, and using just one sheet of highly polished plate glass at an angle of forty-five degrees to the stage, and a darkened room adjacent to the stage but hidden from the audience.

At the right moment, the onstage lights are brought down a little, and a bright light is shone on the desired person or object in the hidden room, causing it to appear as a 'spectral', semi-transparent reflection in the invisible plate glass on stage, and making the off-stage person or object appear to occupy the same three-dimensional space as the on-stage characters.

Audiences had long been used to some very sophisticated spectral illusions, of course, including the magic-lantern Phantasmagoria of Paul Philidor and, most famously, Étienne-Gaspard Robert (known as Robertson), which terrified audiences in the 1790s with ghostly moving images.[9] Pepper described the Ghost as the 'New Phantasmagoria', but in fact the new illusion took spectrality a stage further by allowing three-dimensional actors to interact with the reflected image, in effect creating a space that married the substantial to the supernatural (the patent application of 5 February states that 'the object of our said Invention is by a peculiar arrangement of apparatus to associate on the same stage a phantom or phantoms with a living actor or actors, so that the two may act in concert').[10] By using a real (offstage) actor as the origin of its projection rather than a painted slide, Pepper's effects made its ghosts extremely, well, lifelike.

Whether it was inspired by the events of Lourdes or by Dickens's Christmas story, Dircks and Pepper's illusion was modern industrial magic, depending on the availability of large sheets of highly polished plate glass and powerful lights (the Drummond Light, also known as oxy-hydrogen light or limelight, was developed in the 1820s, and was first used in London theatres in 1837). This was an illusion, then, that derived at least part of its power from the phantasmagoria of the market, or to be more precise, from commercial window displays. Wolfgang Schivelbusch suggests that plate glass windows appeared in London for the first time in the 1850s, but in fact a version of this glass, which shows none of the imperfections of blown glass, was available in England at the beginning of the nineteenth century, and its limited use in shop windows dates from this period, as we see from the descriptions of 'large panes of plate glass' in the windows of the London shops in Robert Southey's *Letters from England* (1807).[11] Plate glass remained hugely expensive, though by the 1830s, as Richard D. Altick notes, writing of the West End, 'all the best shops were fronted with plate glass' (p. 227), and an American visitor of 1833–4 describes panes of up to forty-five inches in width (sheets large enough to fit an entire shop-front appear for the first time in the 1870s). In Regent Street, then as now one of London's most prestigious retail streets, as well as the home of the Polytechnic (and, for a time in the 1860s, Dion Boucicault, who lived more or less across the road from the Polytechnic), plate glass would have been relatively common. Andrew H. Miller describes how new manufacturing techniques as well as the repeal of the glass tax in 1845 led to the more widespread adoption of plate-glass windows in shops, so that by 1847 there are contemporary descriptions of 'walls of plate glass' to enchant the visitor to London; the glass itself as much as the goods displayed behind it initially acted as a draw, but the lasting effect of the new material was to 'present the commodity fetish in all its glory'.[12] The Great Exhibition of 1851 brings the use of glass for the enhanced display of goods to a new level: the fairy-tale effect produced by the convergence of an endless if unavailable array of commodities, and the use on an unprecedented scale of plate glass, is captured in the term 'Crystal Palace'. By the 1850s, large plate-glass display windows become typical – the appearance of firms offering plate glass insurance offers one index of their spread.[13] By then, too, visitors to the Crystal Palace had fully learned the pleasures of looking without buying, and window-shopping had developed into a common West End activity.[14] The effect was to turn the streets into aisles of the department stores themselves: uncovered arcades that blurred the distinction between interior and exterior, walking and consuming. (As we have seen, one unexpected side effect of the creation of such consumer fairylands was the arrival of the middle-class shoplifter, soon pathologized as the kleptomaniac.[15])

The resemblance between shop-window and stage effect was not lost on at least one contemporary commentator. Sensitized by the Polytechnic ghost to the optics of everyday life, W. Bridges Adams noted that the Ghost was a creature of the times, not so much a special effect as an emanation of the fabric of the modern city itself:

This very day I have seen some hundred ghosts, and scores of people saw them with me, though not consciously. It was in an omnibus, passing from Charing Cross to the city. The plate-glass in the shops had dark backgrounds, and became thus the dark chambers of Porta [*sc.* Giovanni Battista Della Porta, the sixteenth-century writer on optics, then thought to have invented the camera obscura] and everything that passed by was projected by the vision into the shops. It was a perfect phantasmagoria, and it was the plate-glass that produced the effect ... I had occasion afterwards to enter a butcher's shop, the front open, and a counting-house in the interior, glazed with plate-glass. Projected into this glass were dozens of ghosts of the sheep and beeves hanging up in front. They were as clean as photographs, and with a similar effect.[16]

The gas-lit street became a theatre; the lime-lit theatre drew on the magic of commercial display. Descriptions of the phantasmagoric aspect of nineteenth-century urban experience are familiar to readers of Baudelaire and Benjamin, but we have not always seen how literally the term applies.

The Ghost was a powerful draw for the Polytechnic, attracting, among others, the Prince and Princess of Wales, who visited on 19 May 1863, and who were entertained by seeing some of their retinue appear in ghostly form. Box-office takings at the Polytechnic realized some £12,000 for Pepper, but the scientist-cum-showman also supplemented this income by licensing a number of music halls to put on their own ghost shows, including the London Pavilion and the Canterbury: one used it to mount a mimed dream sequence, the other to enhance a fairy spectacle. One of the working-class theatres, the Brittania, put on the first actual play to be written around the new special effect. This was *Faith, Hope and Charity*, by C. H. Hazlewood, which opened on 6 April 1863, and in which a ghost appears to the wicked baronet who has murdered her. It was succeeded by a number of other forgotten plays. The first really successful play to put the Ghost to work followed Pepper's example by utilizing Charles Dickens's 1848 story *The Haunted Man*. Written for the Christmas market like its better-known predecessor, *A Christmas Carol* (1843), *The Haunted Man* describes the visitation of its protagonist by a ghost: in this case the haunted man is a misanthropic but good-hearted chemistry lecturer tortured by his past, and the spirit is his second self. The ghost offers to take away the chemist's painful memories of 'sorrow, wrong, and trouble', and gives him a sort of Midas touch so that everyone he touches is similarly deprived of the memories of past pains. The net effect, it turns out, is a general hardening of hearts rather than the relief sought, and the chemist has to plead with the spirit to take back his dubious gift so that memories and human sympathies are restored in time for Christmas morning. On 22 June 1863, *The Times* noted that the Polytechnic Ghost had moved house, as it were, and, after a series of delays, was now manifesting itself at the Adelphi Theatre to a crowded house:

'The Ghost! The Ghost! The Ghost!' With this triple exclamation repeated in print for nearly a fortnight has the manager of the Adelphi announced the appearance at his theatre of the spectre that has almost earnt [*sic*] for the Polytechnic Institution the reputation of a haunted house.[17]

The review goes on to explain the peculiar nature of the special effect, and to praise its effectiveness :

Many of our readers will recollect how the ghost is represented in the pictorial illustration to Mr. Dickens's book. The impression produced by that illustration is exactly that which is produced on the Adelphi stage – namely the impression of a person clearly visible and capable of appearing as one of a party, but wholly impervious to the sense of touch. The manner in which the figure suddenly vanishes, literally seeming to go nowhere, is most startling; still more surprising is its disappearance, when it gradually melts away, assuming a more filmy look, till it has attained absolute nonentity. Sometimes, in passing from one side of the reflecting surface to the other, it becomes slightly distorted at its extremities, but altogether the maintenance of the illusion on so large arena as the stage of the New Adelphi Theatre may be regarded as a great triumph on the part of Mr. Pepper's shadowy protégé.

While some reviews complained that the vivid special effects were rather better than the play itself, the *Haunted Man* ran for a respectable eighty-five nights.[18]

The Ghost was quickly pegged as part of the cult of sensation, and it began to appear in other cultural forms. In Harry Clifton's *Have You Seen the Ghost*, for example, it is represented as another novelty to keep the pot of sensation simmering:

> Where ignorance is bliss, 'tis folly to be wise
> But in this age prolific so many things arise
> Exciting curiosity, of wonders we've a host
> Another new Sensation – 'Have you seen the Ghost?'[19]
> *Chorus:*
> All round town, on ev'ry wall and post
> Go where you will it's 'Have you seen the Ghost?'
> To profit by excitement our countrymen contrive
> Here's another new sensation to keep the game alive.

The Ghost also provides much of the tortured linguistic fun of F. C. Burnand's annual Christmas burlesque, *1863; or, The Sensations of the Past Season* (1863), in which the Ghost from the *Haunted Man* appears and relates how Pepper and Dircks protected their intellectual property:

> You recollect how very well I went;
> Well, hosts of copies rose around about
> The speculation paying past a doubt,
> . . .
> Still, Pepper said I should protected be;
> He's now, like Horniman's, a patent-tea.
> The Chancellor did grant it – it's a bore
> To those who rather dread the chance o' law
> The others are ex-spectres now, you see,
> Which they did not, of course exspecter be.

A number of the other theatrical ghosts who face extinction at the hands of special effects also put in an appearance. Banquo's ghost is eloquent on the subject of his usurpation:

> The Ghost of Pepper means
> To take my place at future banquet scenes.

> Limelight and glass contrive to overthrow
> The flesh and blood of defunct Banquo.
> This for the drama's an unlucky age,
> When thus they *cast reflections* on the stage.[20]

Behind the recurring jokes about the older theatrical spectres who will be displaced by the limelight ghost, there is a suggestion that forms of entertainment that depend more on the audience's acceptance of theatrical conventions might lose their capacity to enthrall, part of a more general set of discourses about the nature of attention and modern spectacle. The ghost was an 'effect' rather than a piece of theare. Even Dion Boucicault, rarely behindhand when it came to pioneering stage illusions, complained in an essay, 'The Decline of the Drama', that 'ghosts are now secured by patent and produced by machinery by Professor Pepper'.[21]

The ghost was tracked by a variety of ephemeral forms, but he also made his way into the nineteenth century's dominant cultural mode, the novel. If Dickens inspired the dramatic use of the plate-glass apparition, he also seems to have been inspired by it, and Pepper's Ghost enters into the imaginative fabric of his novel of the mid-1860s, *Our Mutual Friend*, a narrative equally occupied with actual revenants and the spectral wealth produced by stocks and shares: bubbles of the earth, and bubbles of the market.[22] (There is an etymological neatness to this, since spectre and speculation are cognates.) There is no single source to the novel's ghostly tropes, of course: for example, the inspiration for the description of the tortured face of the schoolteacher, Bradley Headstone – 'he went by them in the dark, like a haggard head suspended in the air' – may derive from the magic-lantern phantasmagoria of Philidor and Robertson.[23] But the description of the home-life of the Lammles, where the spectral presence (*sc.* the secret of their loveless marriage) appears 'as one of a party' between the characters, seems pure Polytechnic:

In these matrimonial dialogues they never addressed each other, but always some invisible presence that appeared to take a station about midway between them. Perhaps the skeleton in the cupboard comes out to be talked to, on such domestic occasions? ... 'I have never seen any money in the house,' said Mrs. Lammle to the skeleton, 'except my own annuity. That I swear.' ... After this, Mrs Lammle looked disdainfully at the skeleton – but without carrying the look on to Mr Lammle – and drooped her eyes. After that, Mr Lammle did exactly the same thing, and drooped his eyes. A servant then entering with toast, the skeleton retired into the closet, and shut itself up.[24]

There is a moral point to this semi-comic haunting: the Lammles – a lesser species of the Veneerings – have lived so long on the mere appearance of being wealthy, despite a clear lack of 'substance', that they have become peculiarly susceptible to haunting by insubstantiality.

The metaphorical register of the novel attempts, inter alia, to capture the parallel between over-valuation in society and in the financial markets, and in doing so seems to hesitate between the idea of deceptive surfaces, like veneers, or silver-plating, and the idea of glass as something that can assume a deceptive solidity under certain conditions. We see this hesitation in action, for example, in Silas Wegg's tirade against Noddy Boffin, which moves from silver-plating to smeared glass by way of the (unmentioned) silvering of mirrors:

'Bof-fin,' replied Wegg, turning upon him with a severe air. 'I understand your new-born boldness. I see the brass underneath your silver plating ... Why, you're just so much smeary glass so see through, you know!' (p. 786)

It is this same idea of opacity/transparency that underlies the ultimate fate of the Veneerings after Mr Veneering's financial 'smash', and their retirement to Calais, 'there to live on Mrs Veneering's diamonds', which turn out to be, unlike their owners, the real thing: that which may appear to be glass, or paste as jewellers call it, may be something more durable. Although Bradley Headstone is not, like the Lammles and the Veneerings, a financial deceiver, his respectable occupation and restrained demeanour only barely conceal the fire devouring him from within. But in his case too Pepper's Ghost puts in an appearance in an oblique form:

Rigid before the fire, as if it were a charmed flame that was turning him old, he sat, with the dark lines deepening in his face, its stare becoming more and more haggard, its surface turning whiter and whiter as if it were being overspread with ashes, and the very texture and colour of his hair degenerating ... Not until the late daylight made the window transparent did this decaying statue move. Then it slowly arose, and sat in the window looking out. (p. 800)

This is Pepper's ghost in a curiously domestic form: the limelight has been replaced by an ordinary fire; and there is no one – except for the reader and Bradley himself – to see his white and spectral reflection in the window, before the light of the dawn makes the window transparent again. The immediate effect is to render the already strange Bradley even more uncanny, but the passage also contributes to the construction of him as a complex, self-divided character, an entity possessing the deep, layered subjectivity that the nineteenth-century novel so successfully constructs, as Nancy Armstrong has shown.[25] In Dickens, of course, that 'depth' is always revealing itself to be something staged, a theatrical production. (Perhaps as a signature of such theatricality, Pepper's Ghost is not the only

1860s stage hit that finds its way into *Our Mutual Friend*, a novel that also echoes the watery themes and the love triangle of *The Colleen Bawn*. In Dickens, it is the plucky working-class woman, Lizzie Hexam, who in the nick of time saves her aristocratic lover, Eugene Wrayburn, from drowning at the hands of her lower-middle-class would-be lover, Bradley Headstone. As in *The Colleen Bawn*, the novel's plot depends on the reappearance of one thought to be dead by drowning, in this case John Harmon.)

What does all this tell us about the 'presence of the present'? Dickens does not *describe* Dircks and Pepper's optical illusion in *Our Mutual Friend*. His novel is not an overt commentary on the new sensation, in the way that *Have You Seen the Ghost* and *1863* are. Nor does his novel, I think, unconsciously register the ghost as part of the popular (and materially based) sensation culture of the time by incorporating it into its own structures. Indeed, the Ghost is not a *thing* to be registered, consciously or unconsciously – it is an optical effect created by a series of relationships among lights, actors, glass and the audience. What the Ghost illusion offers Dickens is a means of figuring the deceptive, smoke-and-mirrors world he is consciously trying to evoke, a world distorted by the commodity form, but also a *mise en abyme* figure of his own illusion-making activity. The appearance of his earlier story on stage, transformed by the use of the plate-glass Ghost, seems to have provided the author with a scenario adequate to a world of polished and deceptive surfaces. This is a world in which the market can conjure up the chimerical wealth and substance of the Veneerings, as plate glass produces both the Arabian Nights delights of the dioramic window display and the patented illusion of the Ghost. In a very direct sense, then, the Ghost represents to Dickens a series of figures through which to capture some of the more phantasmagoric aspects of London in the mid-1860s, a city in which the Limited Liability Acts appeared to him to have altered fundamentally the degree of shareholders' responsibility, making financial speculation and the creation of new companies more attractive.[26] Nor is this Age of Paper the only source of discontinuity between appearance and reality: Dickens imagines another version of appearance/reality in which the self-discipline and self-denial of an upwardly mobile Bradley Headstone create curious effects of self-alienation when they come up against the counter-force of his consuming desire for Lizzie Hexam. (Dickens will imagine an even more extreme version of this split between a dutiful self and a desiring self in the Gothic *Mystery of Edwin Drood* (1870), where John Jasper recapitulates the role of Headstone.)

But, of course, the Ghost must also have reminded him of the extent to which he was himself engaged in the conjuring of a ghost-illusion, the creation of depth and the prestidigitation of movement and life out of a flat verbal surface. Just as the shop window aimed to captivate customers, his own showmanship was put to work to interpellate that same unknown public identified by his collaborator, Wilkie Collins: his experiments with monthly part-publication and with serialization were in pursuit of just this project. As we saw earlier, *All the Year Round*, which began in 1859, just in time for the decade of Reform, was a weekly magazine priced at two pence, not an expensive quarterly or monthly. To this extent, Dickens must have felt his own imbrication in the Age of Paper, and his own kinship to Professor Pepper: no novel is immaculately conceived.

Dickens's novel, then, allows us to discuss some of the less familiar aspects of the popular culture, and the material world, of the 1860s, and it opens onto the more general field of the transformation of the lived environment by expansion of consumer culture in the period. But Pepper's Ghost is not part of some textual or optical unconscious: it has not been fixed within his text in the way that a random background detail is inadvertently captured by a camera; rather we are allowed to catch fleeting glimpses of it because Dickens recognized in the patented spectre a correlative for his own illusion-making activity, and he was prompted to do so by the fact that his own earlier story was being used to provide a frame on which to hang the Ghost. We can go beyond the vestigial presence of Pepper's illusion in the novel to the material culture that underwrote it (plate glass and strong lighting, with their links to the glamour of the great exhibitions, the department stores and the shopping streets themselves) only if we have access to other historical sources. These connections may have been available to some of Dickens's readers, though certainly not to all. But whether they were so available or not, there is no sense in which they have been repressed by the text, to be brought to consciousness by us. The idea of a material unconscious, or textual analysis as historiography, seems in this light to be fantasy of recovering from the text what in fact has to be supplied to it. Rather than being 'in' the text, this material has to be pursued down long syntagmatic chains from the novel itself.

Indeed, notwithstanding his title, such 'a strong form of metonymic reading' is, as Elaine Freedgood has pointed out, very much what Bill Brown practices in *The Material Unconscious*, and Freedgood's own readings in *The Ideas in Things* (2006) also show how powerful such metonymic readings can be. These readings start with some minor textual detail (e.g. in Brown, toy stoves in Stephen Crane; in Freedgood, mahogany furniture in *Jane Eyre*), and pursue it outward from the text, before returning to the text itself.[27] I have no wish to underplay the importance of the work these critics have done in insisting on the need for a materialist reading practice to move beyond immanent or symptomatic analysis of the things in texts. But I am not sure that their approach works for the case we have been considering. There is, for one thing, the methodological issue: it would be, I think, very difficult to happen upon Pepper's Ghost, plate-glass windows, and consumer phantasmagoria by starting with *Our Mutual Friend*, since unlike mahogany furniture in *Jane Eyre*, or the toy stove in Stephen Crane, the ghost is not 'there' in the text, except as a disposition of characters in a few particular scenes, the reference to a mirror in one place, and a skeleton in another. Nor is this exclusively true of something like the Ghost illusion, which is by definition not really there, and which I have, of course, deliberately chosen as a particularly vivid example of how an orientation towards the things in texts may fail us. One would also, for example, scour in vain *The Woman in White* to find even displaced references to Reform. As most historicizing critics will grant, such determining absences are only found by endless 'background' reading, or by pure or mixed happenstance; metonymic lines from the text to such extra-textual factors are usually constructed in reverse. As with detective fiction, one creates the solution first. Only if one had already read accounts of Pepper's illusion, and was in fact looking for it in other forms, would one ever find its vestiges in *Our Mutual Friend*. Fiction on its own will not lead us into this world.

Perhaps the most significant difference between my practice here and 'strong metonymic reading' is that I am less interested in what these artefacts consciously or unconsciously memorialize, and more in what they *did* to contemporary audiences. Dickens includes a cameo of Pepper's Ghost because he is thinking through issues of audience, spectacle and belief; of the suspensions of disbelief involved in optical illusions, in financial markets, and in reading fiction. But the important aspect of these scenes, in my view, is their disposition towards effect. As his letters to Collins, inter alia, tell us, Dickens always has an eye to 'effect', and these representations of the Lammles and of Bradley Headstone deploy carefully contrived effects that are essentially theatrical or optical, orientating the reader in a particular way towards the characters and the action. In the first, what is staged in a little closet drama is the curious disconnect between husband and wife, a disconnect that derives from the commercial nature of their 'partnership'; but to have impact this must be shown, not told to us. In the Headstone passage, the effect aimed for is that of a dioramic transformation scene, complete with lighting. We are being shown the change for the worse in his character caused by his obsession, but at this point Dickens wants us to see this rather than be told, and this is the point of the effect. The Pepper's Ghost references should remind us above all else of Dickens's self-conscious participation in an expanding marketplace of commodity experiences of various kinds. In the case of sensation, audience and effect are crucial: what we need to read these cultural artefacts is not so much a depth model of consciousness/unconsciousness as an 'affects', or a vocabulary that might capture their self-consciously deployed devices for soliciting and capturing attention.[28] To adapt Tom Gunning's famous description of early cinema, this is a 'culture of attractions', one in which the writer or artist deploys, and the audience comes to expect, certain eye-catching techniques.[29] This is not to say that issues of cultural memory are insignificant in the 1860s (they are crucial, as we have seen, in *The Colleen Bawn*, for example), but my primary focus here has been on how authors and writers in the 1860s understood their place in an age of crowds, and how they attempted to capture those crowds, or, as in the case of aestheticism, to shut the crowd out. The other major difference between my approach and those of Brown and Freedgood perhaps goes without saying: I have been interested here in producing an account of the 1860s rather than a theory of fiction, and drama, fine art and more ephemeral forms have been at least as important to that account.

It remains to say something about the subsequent history of the cultural tendencies we have examined here. The 'Leap in the Dark' did not, of course, mean the end of the hegemony of the middle and landed classes. There was no revolt of the masses after 1867 any more than there was a servile insurrection during the American Civil War. Relationships between taste and class continued to be contested, though neither the three-decker novel nor the West End theatre by any means collapsed, or gave themselves over wholeheartedly to 'transpontine effects'. Indeed, in the case of the novel, the power of the circulating libraries, which lingered until the 1890s, ensured high levels of consistency in the kinds of literary fare on offer. Collins's fiction would continue to sell well, but his vision of the possibilities offered by the unknown public were not realized until a book-renting public was replaced by a book-buying public – *The Woman in White* sold more than 100,000 copies upon its release in a sixpenny format by Chatto and Windus in 1895.[30] Sensation fiction more generally lingered at least until the end of the century; even when it lost its novelty in the three-volume novel, it survived in newspaper and magazine formats.[31] The attention-engineering techniques of mystery and suspense popularized by the sensation novel can be traced through subsequent popular and middle-brow fictional forms, from the 'revival of the romance' in the 1880s, through various avatars of the detective story and the thriller in the twentieth century, as well as across various media. Some of the spectacular techniques of stage melodrama acquired a new lease of life through the medium of cinema, and subsequently television and other visual platforms. The advent of all these visual technologies would be attended by moral panics similar to those of the 1860s, as well as by fantasies of audience control.

Aestheticism mutated into an easily mocked lifestyle in the 1870s and 1880s, parodied by George Du Maurier in *Punch*, by W. S. Gilbert and Arthur Sullivan in *Patience* (1881), and in such popular comic songs as Robert Coote's 'Quite Too Utterly Utter: New Aesthetical Roundelay' (1882). But Whistler's attempts to retrain a select audience attentive to the nuances of form above content would have many impressive sequels, the most obvious being the various strands of high modernism, from post-Impressionism onwards. Many twentieth-century artists forsook figuration, the better to focus the visual experience of the viewer. In this light, one might see such works as Kazimir Malevich's *Suprematist Composition: White on White* (1918), Josef Albers's *Homage to the Square: Apparition* (1959) and Robert Ryman's minimalist *Surface Veil* series as all legitimate offspring of Whistler's art. While the techniques of modernism have long been used by popular visual culture, the 'difficulty' and exclusivity of non-academic art have come to be a cliché. (While I have been writing this Conclusion, the Italian minister for culture has gone on record to the effect that he does not understand contemporary art.[32])

The music halls that inspired the chromolithographic sheet music covers of the 1860s would also have a long afterlife, though many of the less well-capitalized halls closed in the 1870s in the wake of regulatory legislation. By the end of the century the music hall, with its roots in urban working-class experience, had yielded to a less class-specific and more 'respectable' Variety theatre. Comic chromolithographic music covers in the style of Concanen (e.g. those of H. G. Banks) continued to appear until the end of the century, when other styles, and photographic methods of reproduction, displaced them. At least some aspects of their exuberance lingered in other popular forms, from saucy seaside postcards, to cinematic shorts (the firm of Bamforth and Company was active in the production of both of these), to comics. Since Sitwell's *Morning, Noon and Night in London*, Concanen himself has been periodically rediscovered. In 1962 an exhibition was devoted to his work, now seen as vernacular art rather than advertising. Museums and libraries now regularly showcase their holdings of sheet music covers.[33] While it has as yet, perhaps, to receive the academic attention it deserves, his work and that of his peers has increasingly come to be recognized as providing a valuable countervision of the Victorian period, one that saw the vitality of the streets, and the pleasures of the crowd.

Notes

INTRODUCTION: WHITE YEARS

1 Boucicault was born in Dublin, but made his career in London and the United States; his plays appear in anthologies of nineteenth-century American as well as British drama. Whistler was born in Massachusetts, but made his career in Paris and London. Melodrama has French as well as English origins; black-face minstrelsy is complexly related to African-American culture as well as to Euro-American immigrant culture, and it mutates in various ways when imported into Britain.

2 Thérèse Taylor, *Bernadette of Lourdes: Her Life, Death and Visions* (London: Continuum, 2003), pp. 60, 65. See also Ruth Harris, *Lourdes: Body and Spirit in the Secular Age* (London: Penguin, 1999).

3 The doctrine of the Immaculate Conception, the idea that Jesus's mother, Mary, had been born without original sin, had been pronounced by Pope Pius IX in 1854, and is often perceived as a determined effort by the Catholic Church to stem the tide of modernity by defiantly embracing the supernat-ural and miraculous. That the apparition at Lourdes declared itself to be the Immaculate Conception probably led the Church to take a more enthusiastic attitude to Soubirous's story than it would otherwise have done – other appa-ritions of this period were not greeted so warmly. Harris, *Lourdes*, p. 14.

4 For the *Times* coverage of the story see 'France in 1858', *The Times*, 26 August 1858, 10. See also 'Police Interference with "Miracles"', *The Times*, 21 May 1858, 12; 'France', *The Times*, 6 September 1858, 8; Leader, *The Times*, 10 September 1858, 6; and 'France', *The Times*, 18 September 1858, 8. The earliest reference I have been able to find is in May, though this cites an earlier story that I have not been able to locate.

5 See *Adelphi Theatre Project*, 1862–3 Season Commentary, www.emich.edu/public/english/adelphi_calendar/acphome.htm (accessed 30 June 2008).

6 Alfred Rosling Bennett, *London and Londoners in the 1850s and 1860s* (London: Fisher Unwin, 1924), pp. 306–7.

7 Harvey Peter Sucksmith, ed., *The Woman in White* (Oxford University Press, 1992), p. 15.

8 Wilkie Collins, 'The Unknown Public', reprinted in *My Miscellanies* (London: Chatto and Windus, 1875), pp. 249–64. Lorna Huett argues that in

this essay Collins is erecting a cordon sanitaire between readers of *Household Words* and those of the penny papers. I would argue that he may also covet that public. See her 'Among the Unknown Public: *Household Words, All the Year Round* and the Mass-Market Weekly Periodical in the Mid-Nineteenth Century', *Victorian Periodical Review*, 38.1 (2005), 61–82.

9   Peter Brooks argues that melodrama can be understood as a form imbued with a strong drive to resacralize the modern world at the same time that it acknowledges that such sacralization can now only appear in personal forms. See his *The Melodramatic Imagination: Balzac, Henry James, Melodrama, and the Mode of Excess* (1976; New Haven and London: Yale University Press, 1995), p. 16.

10 Cited in Elizabeth R. Pennell and Joseph Pennell, *Life of James McNeill Whistler* (London: William Heinemann, 1920), p. 74.

11 Cited in Stanley Weintraub, *Whistler: A Biography* (London: Collins, 1974), p. 86.

12 For an argument that the 'sensation novel' is not a subgenre at all, but entirely a product of a critical discourse anxious to police the boundaries of class, see Bradley Deane, *The Making of the Victorian Novelist: Anxieties of Authorship in the Mass Market* (London: Routledge, 2003), pp. 59–90.

13 Jonathan Loesberg, 'The Ideology of Narrative Form in Sensation Fiction', *Representations*, 13 (Winter 1986), 115–38.

14 On Lee, see Gregory W. Bush, *Lord of Attention: Gerald Stanley Lee and the Crowd Metaphor in Industrializing America* (Amherst: University of Massachusetts Press, 1991). For the crowd in the earlier part of the nineteenth century, see John Plotz, *The Crowd: British Literature and Public Politics* (Berkeley: University of California Press, 2000).

15 Cited by Walter Benjamin in 'Paris, Capital of the Nineteenth Century', in Peter Demetz, ed., *Reflections: Essays, Aphorisms, Autobiographical Writings*, trans. Edmund Jephcott (New York: Schocken, 1986), pp. 146–62, p. 151.

16 Cited in Peter Bailey, 'The Victorian Middle Class and the Problem of Leisure', in his *Popular Culture and Performance in the Victorian City* (Cambridge University Press, 1998), pp. 13–30, p. 18.

17 Andrew Maunder, ed., *Varieties of Women's Sensation Fiction*, vol. I: *Sensationalism and the Sensation Debate* (London: Pickering and Chatto, 2004), p. xiv.

18 Reprinted in Maunder, *Varieties of Women's Sensation Fiction*, pp. 32–56, p. 51.

19 Quoted in ibid., p. 157.

20 Quoted in ibid., p. xxxvii.

21 'Attention engineering' is a term used by preacher-turned-pundit Gerald Stanley Lee (1862–1944). See Bush, *Lord of Attention*. On Bernadette Soubirous's own handling of crowds see Harris, *Lourdes*, pp. 66–71.

22 Lieven de Cauter, 'The Panoramic Ecstasy: On World Exhibitions and the Disintegration of Experience', *Theory, Culture, And Society*, 10 (1993), 1–23.

23 Jonathan Crary, *Suspensions of Perception: Attention, Spectacle, and Modern Culture* (Cambridge: MIT Press, 2001), p. 4. Crary's argument is not entirely of a piece with earlier accounts of distraction and modernity in Simmel, Benjamin and others, especially in his insistence that distraction and concentration are not opposites but parts of a continuum (p. 51).

24 Tony Bennett, *The Birth of the Museum: History, Theory, Politics* (London: Routledge, 1995).

25 For an account of the lead-up to the 1867 Reform Act see Catherine Hall, Keith McClelland and Jane Rendall, *Defining the Victorian Nation: Class, Race, Gender and the Reform Act of 1867* (Cambridge University Press, 2000).

26 For an account of the China War and some of Britain's other less well-known military exploits during the 1860s see Ian Hernon, *Britain's Forgotten Wars: Colonial Campaigns of the 19th Century* (Stroud: Sutton, 2005).

27 On *Our English Coasts* and the fear of invasion see Jonathan P. Ribner, 'Our English Coasts, 1852: William Holman Hunt and the Invasion Fear at Midcentury', *Art Journal*, 55.2 (Summer 1996), 45–54.

28 There had been other reminders of the Mutiny, of course, including a mutiny of East India Company troops in 1860.

29 For the events of 1865 see Hernon, *Britain's Forgotten Wars*, pp. 76–100; see also Catherine Hall, 'Jamaica', in *Defining the Victorian Nation*, pp. 192–204.

30 See, for example, Sir John Clapham, *An Economic History of Modern Britain*, vol. II: *Free Trade and Steel, 1850–86* (Cambridge University Press, 1967), pp. 450, 466.

31 Some historians have suggested that the cotton famine was due more to over-production and other factors. At any rate, there seemed little protest among cotton-district MPs about the War's effects. See below, Chapter 4.

32 See Clapham, *An Economic History*, pp. 333–85, for the general trends in banking and investment in these years.

33 The background of the illustrated cover makes the point of the song clearer. Two characters are conducting some kind of financial transaction; that they are Jewish stereotypes, complete with hooked noses, suggests fears of Jewish control of the market.

34 See, for example, Walter L. Arnstein, *Britain Yesterday and Today: 1830 to the Present* (Lexington: D. C. Heath, 1988), pp. 75–6.

35 See David Skilton, ed., *The Early and Mid-Victorian Novel* (London and New York: Routledge, 1993), p. 1. For an analysis of this dominance see, for example, Kate Flint, 'The Victorian Novel and Its Readers', in Deirdre David, ed., *The Cambridge Companion to the Victorian Novel* (Cambridge University Press, 2001), pp. 17–36.

36 See Richard Stang, *The Theory of the Novel in England, 1850–1870* (New York: Columbia University Press, 1959), p. 5. See also Flint, 'The Victorian Novel', p. 18.

37 On Dunlop see Stang, *The Theory of the Novel*, pp. 6–7.

38 Flint, 'The Victorian Novel', p. 31.

39 E. S. Dallas, review of Dickens's *Great Expectations*, *The Times* (17 October 1861), 6, reproduced in Skilton, ed., *The Early and Mid-Victorian Novel*, pp. 30–33, p. 32.

40 On the place of Lloyd's in the fictional marketplace see Deane, *Making of the Victorian Novelist*, pp. 59–66.

41 See Simon Eliot, 'The Business of Victorian Publishing', in Skilton, ed., *The Victorian Novel*, pp. 37–60, pp. 51–2.

42 See Linda Williams, *Playing the Race Card: Melodramas of Black and White from Uncle Tom to O. J. Simpson* (Princeton University Press, 2001), p. 16.

43 Catherine Gallagher, *The Industrial Reformation of English Fiction: Social Discourse and Narrative Form, 1832–1867* (Chicago University Press, 1985).

44 On the sensation novel as a species of Gothic see, for example, Lyn Pykett, 'Sensation and the Fantastic in the Victorian Novel', in Deirde David, ed., *The Cambridge Companion to the Victorian Novel* (Cambridge University Press, 2001), pp. 192–211.

45 I am offering a somewhat overstated version of a familiar narrative, which rarely appears in quite so bald a form. For example, a classic work of scholarship on the Victorian theatre, Allardyce Nicoll's *A History of Late Nineteenth-Century Drama, 1850–1900*, vol. I (Cambridge University Press, 1946), provides a far more sophisticated account, while still keeping to this basic narrative of progress. For the summary of the theatre of the 1860s that follow, I have drawn on Nicoll as well as more recent accounts such as Michael R. Booth's *Theatre in the Victorian Age* (Cambridge University Press, 1995) and Simon Trussler's *Cambridge Illustrated History of British Theatre* (Cambridge University Press, 1994).

46 See Booth, *Theatre in the Victorian Age*, pp. 63–4. Booth gives a valuable account of many aspects of the mid-Victorian stage, from performance to lighting.

47 On the importance of Victoria's attendance at the theatre and the Windsor theatricals (up to Albert's death in 1861) see Nicoll, *Nineteenth-Century Drama*, pp. 9–10.

48 Bishop Colenso had controversially asserted in his *The Pentateuch and the Book of Joshua Critically Examined* (1862) that parts of the Bible, including the story of the Flood, could not be taken as historical facts.

49 According to Allardyce Nicoll, James Planché introduced the first stage transformation scene in *The Golden Branch* (Lyceum, 1847). Louis Daguerre perfected the dioramic transformation scene. *Spooner's Transformations* and *Spooner's Protean Views* were a series of small prints that changed when held up to strong light. In *Transformation No. 9*, for example, 'The Queen on her Charger' changes to 'A Review of the Troops in Windsor Park'.

50 Towsend Walsh, *The Career of Dion Boucicault* (1915; New York: Benjamin Blom, 1967), p. 120.

51 For a summary of the different types of drama on the Victorian stage see Booth, *Theatre in the Victorian Age*, pp. 189–202.

52 John Ruskin, *Modern Painters: Their Superiority in the Art of Landscape Painting to All the Ancient Masters* (London, 1843), vol. I, section 1, ch. 2, p. 14.

53 'F. T. P', 'The British School of Oil Painting', *The International Exhibition, 1862: Official Catalogue of the Fine Art Department* (London, 1862), pp. 3–9.

54 Lambourne, *Victorian Painting* (London: Phaidon, 1999), pp. 27–9.

CHAPTER 1 THE WOMAN IN WHITE AND THE CROWD

1 Oliver Wendell Holmes, a toast composed for Wilkie Collins in 1874. See William Baker and William M. Clarke, eds., *Letters of Wilkie Collins*, vol. II, *1866–1890* (Houndmills: Macmillan, 1999), p. 394, n.1.

2 Thérèse Taylor, *Bernadette of Lourdes: Her Life, Death and Visions* (London: Continuum, 2003), p. 60.

3 As noted in the introduction, this puts it in the same league as such popular weekly newspapers as *Lloyd's Weekly Newspaper* and the *News of the World*. On sales of the more popular papers see Patricia Anderson, *The Printed Image and the Transformation of Popular Culture* (Oxford: Clarendon Press, 1991), p. 171.

4 Examples include Alphonse Leduc's 'Sensation Polka' (1862), Robert Coote's 'A Sensation Polka' (1863), Nicholas Henderson's 'Sensation Quadrille' (1862) and Eugène Duval's 'Great Sensation Galop' (1863).

5 Contemporary reviewers do not always see Collins as the first of the sensation school. Mrs Oliphant, for example, in a much-cited review, points to Nathaniel Hawthorne, Edward Bulwer-Lytton and Charles Dickens himself as having anticipated him, though she considers Collins to be the first to produce sensation by more 'legitimate' means, that is to say without the use of fantastic, grotesque or supernatural means. See her unsigned review, 'Sensation Novels', *Blackwood's Magazine*, 91 (May, 1862), 565–74, reprinted in Norman Page, ed., *Wilkie Collins: The Critical Heritage* (London and Boston: Routledge and Kegan Paul, 1974), pp. 110–21, p. 112.

6 As Nancy Armstrong points out, the realist novel has always depended on various complementary modes – Gothic, sensation, adventure, romance – to reinforce its own claims to mature referential stability. See *How Novels Think: The Limits of Individualism from 1719–1900* (New York: Columbia, 2005), p. 22. The most useful accounts of the sensation novel include Winifred Hughes, *The Maniac in the Cellar* (Princeton University Press, 1980); Patrick Brantlinger, 'What is Sensational about the "Sensation Novel"?', *Nineteenth-Century Fiction*, 71.1 (1982), 1–28; D. A. Miller, *The Novel and the Police* (Berkeley and Los Angeles: University of California Press, 1988); Jenny Bourne Taylor, *In the Secret Theatre of Home: Wilkie Collins, Sensation Narrative and Nineteenth-Century Psychology* (London and New York: Routledge, 1988); Lyn Pykett, *The Improper Feminine: The Women's Sensation Novel and the New Woman Writing* (London: Routledge, 1992); Ann Cvetkovich, *Mixed Feelings: Feminism, Mass Culture, and Victorian Sensationalism* (New Brunswick: Rutgers University Press, 1992). For a perspective that steps outside fiction to look at 'sensation culture' more generally see, for example, Richard D. Altick, *Deadly Encounters: Two Victorian Sensations* (Philadelphia: University of Pennsylvania Press, 1986) and Michael Diamond, *Victorian Sensation* (London: Anthem, 2003). Among the recent interventions on sensation that I have found useful are articles by Eva Badowska on sensation fiction and the commodity, and by Lynn Voskuil on sensation melodrama and the public sphere.

7 For a checklist of some of the 'sensations' of the early 1860s, see 'Sensation! A Satire' in the *Dublin University Magazine* for January 1864, reprinted in Andrew Maunder, ed., *Varieties of Women's Sensation Fiction*, vol. I: *Sensationalism and the Sensation Debate* (London: Pickering and Chatto, 2004), pp. 85–9.

8 Henry Morley takes this line in his 1865 critique of Watts Phillips's *Woman in Mauve*: 'Using the popular Americanism introduced by Mr Boucicault,

his play is meant as wholesome ridicule of what are called "sensation" novels and "sensation" plays.' See his *Journal of a London Playgoer* (1866; Leicester University Press, 1974), pp. 301–3. Earlier he describes '"sensation" scene' as 'the new term in theatrical slang, which Mr Boucicault imported for us from the other side of the Atlantic' (p. 234).

9 Italy may also have provided Dickens more directly with material: Dr Manette may have been in part inspired by those Neapolitan political prisoners released in 1859 after ten years' incarceration by King Ferdinand, and who became the object of great public interest in London. Dickens, like many others, was very sympathetic towards them (see *Letters*, 1859).

10 J. G. Millais, *Life and Letters of Sir John Everett Millais*, 2 vols. (London, 1899), vol. I, pp. 278–82, cited in Gasson, *Wilkie Collins an Illustrated Guide*.

11 Peters, *The King of Inventors*, (Harvard: Princeton University Press, 1993) pp. 102–4.

12 Brandling provided the lithographs for Collins's travelogue, *Rambles Beyond Railways, or Notes in Cornwall Taken A-foot* (1851). When Collins completed *The Woman in White* in August of 1860, he held a celebratory dinner attended by Egg, Ward and Holman Hunt, among others. Egg was also a friend of Dickens, and it was through him that Dickens and Collins first met.

13 Catherine Peters, *The King of Inventors*, p. 102. See also William E. Fredeman, ed., *The Correspondence of D. G. Rossetti, The Formative Years: 1835–1862* (Cambridge: D. S. Brewer, 2002), vol. I, pp. 209–10.

14 Gasson, *Wilkie Collins*, p. 30.

15 The novel purported to contain 'a genuine biographical sketch of the celebrated original and eccentric genius, the late George Morland'. The *British Critic* was not impressed, and claimed that it had 'no more to do with Morland than with Bonaparte [and was] very poor stuff indeed'. See the entry for William Collins (1740–1812) in Rolf Loeber and Magda Loeber, *A Guide to Irish Fiction, 1650–1900* (Dublin: Four Courts Press, 2006), pp. 283–4.

16 I am using the term 'habitus' here in Pierre Bourdieu's sense of a set of learned dispositions, including such things as intellectual and aesthetic attitudes, and taken-for-granted and seemingly 'natural' career paths.

17 None of this, of course, takes us much beyond the Foucauldian approach to Collins's novel first opened up by D. A. Miller some twenty-five years ago in *The Novel and the Police*. Miller was the first to argue that the sensation novel played a significant role in the modernization of the subject at mid-century.

18 For a somewhat different account of the novel's relationship to the mass market see Bradley Deane, *The Making of the Victorian Novelist: Anxieties of Authorship in the Mass Market* (London: Routledge, 2003), pp. 59–90.

19 See, for example, Walter Kendrick, 'The Sensationalism of The Woman in White', in Lyn Pykett ed., *Wilkie Collins: A Casebook* (Basingstroke: Palgrave, 1998).

20 Henry James, from an unsigned review, 'Miss Braddon', in *The Nation*, 1 (9 November 1865), 593–5, reproduced in Page, ed., *Wilkie Collins: The Critical Heritage*, pp. 122–4, pp. 122–3.

21 It is tempting to think that this passage recaptures the mental strain experienced by Collins when he was finishing the novel at Broadstairs.

22 J. Davis, 'The London Garrotting Panic of 1862: a Moral Panic and the Creation of a Criminal Class in Mid-Victorian England', in V.A.C. Gatrell, Bruce Lenman and Geoffrey Parker (eds.), *Crime and the Law: The Social History of Crime in Western Europe since 1500* (London: Europa, 1980). On Morant Bay and Governor Eyre see, for example, Catherine Hall, Keith McClelland and Jane Rendall, *Defining the Victorian Nation: Class, Race Gender and the Reform Act of 1867* (Cambridge University Press, 2000).

23 On responses to Fenianism see, for example, Patrick Quinlivan and Paul Rose, *The Fenians in England, 1865–1872* (London: John Calder, 1982).

24 If Collins's novel echoes that of Dickens, *A Tale of Two Cities* also owes something to Collins: one source for this episode of personal sacrifice was the plot of Collins's 1857 play *The Frozen Deep*, which gives a heroic spin to the doomed Franklin expedition to the Arctic. Dickens collaborated with Collins on the script, and acted in it in a performance for charity. See George Woodcock's introduction to the Penguin edition, pp. 9–25, pp. 9–11.

25 On the disciplinary function of museums and other forms of national display, see Tony Bennett, *The Birth of the Museum: History, Theory, Politics* (London: Routledge, 1995).

26 The private asylum is explored at greatest length in Charles Reade's *Hard Cash*, but it is also a significant presence in many other novels of the period, including Braddon's *Lady Audley's Secret* and Le Fanu's *The Rose and the Key*.

27 See *The Woman in White*, Appendix E, pp. 599–600.

28 To Mrs Harriet Collins, 13 September 1845, in William Baker and William M. Clarke, eds., *Letters of Wilkie Collins*, vol. I: *1838–1865* (Houndmills: Macmillan, 1999), p. 27.

29 To Mrs Harriet Collins, 16 October 1853, *Letters*, I, pp. 98–101, p. 98.

30 *Letters*, I, p. 23. Also cited in Kenneth Robinson, *Wilkie Collins: A Biography*, (London: Chatto and Windus, 1951) pp. 37–8.

31 To Harriet Collins, 24 September 1845, *Letters*, I, p. 32. Robinson, *Wilkie Collins*, p. 40.

32 Charles Baudelaire, 'The Painter of Modern Life', trans. P. G. Konody, in C. Geoffrey Holme, ed., *The Painter of Victorian Life: A Study of Constantin Guys* (London: The Studio, 1930), p. 48.

33 Baudelaire, 'The Painter of Modern Life', p. 67. Cf. Guys's ink/watercolour *The Lady in Black*, at the Minneapolis Institute. Besides his 'painting of modern life', Guys produced sketches of the Crimean War for the *ILN* between 1854 and 1856.

34 At another level, perhaps, we can see the dead body of the Count as a figure for the bloated three-decker itself, now drawing to its close, just as Anne Catherick had represented all of the airy promise of its beginning.

35 See John Plotz, *The Crowd: British Literature and Public Politics* (Berkeley: University of California Press, 2000) on the nineteenth-century crowd in relation to the 'representativeness' of fiction itself.

36 Jonathan Loesberg, 'The Ideology of Narrative Form in Sensation Fiction', *Representations*, 13 (Winter 1986), 115–38 (117).

37 Cvetkovich, *Mixed Feelings*, pp. 71–96.

38 See Holme, *The Painter of Victorian Life*, p. 12.

39 After the success of *The Woman in White* and *No Name*, Collins was lured off by Smith and Elder to write a serialized novel for one of the more prestigious new magazines, *The Cornhill*. A letter to his mother suggests that he was not over-impressed with his new literary surroundings. 'Did you get the Cornhill? Was there ever such a dull magazine? I wonder anybody reads it', 1 April 1866. *Letters*, II, pp. 273–4. This may, of course, be an April Fool's joke.

40 Cf. Deane, *The Making of the Victorian Novelist*, pp. 59–90.

41 6 January 1867, *Letters*, II, pp. 281–2.

42 To Mrs Harriet Collins, 8 January 1867, *Letters*, II, p. 282.

43 See Deane, *The Making of the Victorian Novelist*, p. 63.

44 Altick, *The Shows on London*, pp. 470–2; Bailey, *Popular Culture and Performance in the Victorian City, passim*.

45 15 August 1859, cited in Peters, *King of Inventors*, p. 209.

46 Martin Meisel, *Realizations* (Princeton University Press, 1983), pp. 69–83. Meisel suggests that the theory of effect marks a departure from neoclassical ideas of the harmony of the work.

47 Unsigned review, *The Times*, 30 October 1860, reprinted in Norman Page, ed., *Wilkie Collins*, pp. 95–103, p. 101; unsigned review, the *Spectator*, 28 December 1861, *Critical Heritage*, p. 109; unsigned review [Mrs Oliphant], *Blackwood's*, May 1862, *Critical Heritage*, pp. 110–21, p. 113; unsigned review, *Saturday Review*, 25 August 1860, *Critical Heritage*, pp. 83–7, p. 85.

48 Unsigned review, *Saturday Review*, 10 (25 August), 249–50, 83–7 (83–4).

49 *Critical Heritage*, p. 119.

50 'King Sensation', reprinted in Maunder, ed., *Varieties of Women's Sensation Fiction*, p. 395.

51 Harry Quilter, 'A Living Story-Teller', *Contemporary Review*, April 1888, reprinted in *Critical Heritage*, pp. 229–47, p. 235. We will meet Quilter again in Chapter 3, as the purchaser of Whistler's 'White House' in Chelsea.

52 Unsigned obituary article, *Spectator*, 28 September 1889, *Critical Heritage*, pp. 249–52, p. 250.

53 On the dialectic between distraction and the fixing of attention in modernity see Jonathan Crary, *Suspensions of Perception: Attention, Spectacle, and Modern Culture* (Cambridge: MIT Press, 2001).

54 See Susan M. Griffin, 'The Yellow Mask, the Black Robe, and the Woman in White: Wilkie Collins, Anti-Catholic Discourse, and the Sensation Novel', *Narrative*, 12.1 (2004), 55–73. Such anti-Catholicism is, of course, a link between Collins and his eighteenth-century Gothic predecessors. That the sensation novel 'preaches to the nerves' was the accusation of H. L. Mansel in 'Sensation Novels', *Quarterly Review*, 113 (1863), 481–514 (482).

55 See Introduction.

56 For the *Times*'s coverage of the story see 'France in 1858', *The Times*, 26 August 1858, 10. See also 'Police Inteference with "Miracles"', *The Times*, 21

May 1858, 12; 'France', *The Times*, 6 September 1858, 8; Leader, *The Times*, 10 September 1858, 6; and 'France', *The Times*, 18 September 1858, 8. The earliest reference I have been able to find is in May, though this cites an earlier story which I have been unable to find.

57 As Thérèse Taylor puts it, 'The shrine of Lourdes sprang from the crises of the nineteenth century – the decline of traditional rural life, unemployment, rising populations, and the confrontation between the worlds of tradition and modernity.' *Bernadette of Lourdes*, p. 12.

58 The Catholic church's interest in spectacular apparitions also drew it to the early science of spectacle: the Jesuit Athanasius Kirchner's *Ars Magna Lucis et Umbrae in Decem Librem* (1645, 1646), in which he describes various optical effects (though not, as is sometimes thought, the magic lantern), is 'a true monument in pre-cinema history'. See Laurent Mannoni, *The Great Art of Light and Shadow: Archeology of the Cinema*, trans. Richard Crangle (Exeter University Press, 2000), p. 21.

59 Leader, *The Times*, 10 September 1858, 6.

60 The latter reference is to a supernatural entity in Sir Walter Scott's *The Monastery* (1820).

61 See Introduction.

CHAPTER 2 THE MANY LIVES OF THE COLLEEN BAWN: PASTORAL SPECTACLE

1 See Richard D. Altick, *Deadly Encounters: Two Victorian Sensations* (Philadelphia: University of Pennsylvania Press, 1986), pp. 137–9; Henry Morley, *Journal of a London Playgoer* (1866; Leicester University Press, 1974), pp. 234, 301–3.

2 Henry Morley seems to believe that in fact the better classes were no longer being courted by the theatres: 'what's on offer in theatres this week [*sc.* 13 April 1863] would be an insult to the taste of the town if it did not indicate a lamentable change in the class to which drama looks for patronage'. See his *Journal of a London Playgoer*, p. 244.

3 Ibid., p. 245.

4 *The Times*, Monday, 1 October 1860, 6. Good writers, he considers, now write novels rather than plays.

5 *Illustrated London News*, July–December 1860, December 8, 536. For an overview of the play's success and the 1860–1 season at the Adelphi, see the Adelphi Theatre 1800–1906 website at www.emich.edu/public/english/adelphi_calendar/m60d.htm (accessed 24 November 2005).

6 'Our Roving Correspondent', *Punch*, 39 (3 November 1860), 171.

7 A popular subgenre of Victorian melodrama in which the action turns on the financial vulnerability of the central characters.

8 In the operatic adaptation of the *Colleen*, *The Lily of Killarney*, the heroine's hair is described as brown, and all of the coloured images of the play that I have seen represent Eily as having dark hair, which suggests that Boucicault

interpreted the phrase Colleen Bawn as meaning fair-skinned or simply 'fair' (these two meanings are condensed in the term 'Lily of Killarney'). In Irish as in English, fair colouring is often synonymous with attractiveness or goodness (and cf. the term 'white-headed'). Gerald Griffin's 1829 novel *The Collegians*, the major source for Boucicault's play, features a fair-haired Eily.

9 Peter Brooks, *The Melodramatic Imagination: Balzac, Henry James, Melodrama and the Mode of Excess* (New Haven and London: Yale University Press, 1976).

10 The playbill for the first London performances of the play seems to suggest that 'O'Donoghue's Stables' and the Water Cave are two distinct settings, but the action of II.vi and Father Tom's comments in III.i indicate that they are the same place.

11 Acting editions of the *Colleen* were produced by Lacy, French and Dicks in the nineteenth century. Here I have used the version of the play in Andrew Parkin, ed., *Selected Plays of Dion Boucicault* (Gerrards Cross: Colin Smythe, 1987), pp. 191–251.

12 The term 'Adelphi effects' is used by Henry Morley in his review of the play for *The Examiner*, reproduced in his *Journal of a London Playgoer* (Leicester University Press, 1974), pp. 213–4, p. 214. The circulation of illustrated Colleen Bawn sheet music, clearly intended for domestic rather than professional use, indicates the popularity of the play, but also reminds us that the piano was now firmly ensconced in the middle-class home, making 'carpet dancing' a popular amusement.

13 Richard Fawkes, *Dion Boucicault: A Biography* (London: Quartet, 1979), pp. 122–3. Morley also notes that 'upon the scenery ... pains have been spent'. See his *Journal*, p. 234. Henry Crabb Robinson, apparently commenting on the Drury Lane version rather than that of the Adelphi, remarks on the pretty scenery, and compares it to the Neapolitan Blue Lake, but felt that the chief scene had been 'mutilated, and had not the primitive attraction' (presumably of the Adelphi production). See Elured Brown, *The London Theatres 1811–66: Selections from the Diary of Henry Crabb Robinson* (London: Society for Theatre Research, 1966), pp. 208–9.

14 Queen Victoria to her daughter Princess Victoria (Vicky), 6 February 1861, cited in James H. Murphy, *Abject Loyalty: Nationalism and Monarchy in Ireland During the Reign of Queen Victoria* (Cork University Press, 2001), p. 126, from Roger Fulford, *Dearest Child, Private Correspondence of Queen Victoria and the Princess Royal, 1858–61* (London: Evans, 1977), p. 305.

15 There are copies of these in the Calthrop Collection at the Templeman Library, University of Kent at Canterbury. The Queen had earlier commissioned a portrait of Boucicault as the vampire in *The Vampire* (1852).

16 Writing in December 1862, Henry Morley laments that 'at the minor houses, including, alas! Drury Lane, *The Colleen Bawn*, in licensed reproduction or unlicensed burlesque, is to be seen in all directions'. See his *Journal*, p. 234.

17 *The Colleen Bawn, or The Collegian's Wife, A Popular Melodrama in 3 Acts as Performed at the London Theatres* appeared in Purkess's Penny Pictorial Plays

(London, n.d.). *Cushla Ma Chree* was a rewrite of the *Colleen* obtained by the manager of the Theatre Royal, Preston. Boucicault sued. See '*Boucicault v. Delafield*', *The Times*, 25 May 1864. Calthrop clippings file. On the burlesque versions see Richard W. Schoch, ed., *Victorian Theatrical Burlesques* (Aldershot: Ashgate, 2003), pp. 3–8. Morley gives the title of the Dutnall piece as *The Coolean Drawn* (p. 234).

18 See Morley, *Journal*, pp. 237–9, p. 238 and p. 265. R. H. Hutton saw Fechter's 'intellectual' approach to acting to be his major strength. In a review of *The Duke's Motto* in *The Spectator*, he passes over the athletics, but criticizes the intermingling of 'spectacles' like the dancing Zingari maidens with serious acting. The effect, he suggests, is like 'eating trifle with your roast beef'. See R. H. Hutton, *A Spectator of Theatre: Uncollected Reviews by R. H. Hutton*, ed. Robert Tener (University of Calgary Press, 1998), p. 23.

19 Morley, *Journal*, p. 301.

20 On the vogue of the cloaks see Townsend Walsh's *The Career of Dion Boucicault* (1915; reprinted New York: Benjamin Blom, 1967), pp. 79–80.

21 'The Philosophy of "Sensation"', *St. James's Magazine*, 5 October 1862, reprinted in Maunder, *Varieties of Women's Sensation Fiction*, pp. 16–26, p. 18.

22 'Our Dramatic Correspondent', *Punch*, 40 (13 April 1861), 150.

23 'Our Dramatic Correspondent', *Punch*, 40 (4 May 1861), 186.

24 *Punch*, 40 (1 June 1861), 226.

25 The vogue of speed and novelty was satirized throughout the early 1860s, and not just in *Punch*. See, for example, Kate Harley's *Making a Sensation* (1862), in which she sings 'A humdrum life I could not bear, my motto is keep moving', strikes a similar note, and Frank Hall's 'The Great Sensation Song' (1863), performed by J. H. Stead: 'Politics and accidents / And scandalizing too sir / Either's all the same to me / As long as it is new sir'.

26 *Punch*, 41 (20 July 1861), 31.

27 Ibid., 23. The reference to Webster's being transported puns on current debates about the need for prison reform.

28 Henry James Byron (1835–84) was the author of more than 150 pieces for the theatre, many of them burlesques featuring the excruciating puns at which he excelled. He also wrote for *Fun*, rival to *Punch*, and edited a number of other comic journals.

29 *Miss Eily O'Connor: A New and Original Burlesque, founded on the Great Sensation Drama of The Colleen Bawn*, bound with *The Introductions and Alterations in the Burlesque of Miss Eily O'Connor as Represented at The Royal Strand Theatre* (Lacy's Acting Edition; London, 1862).

30 As Alfred Rosling Bennett recalls, 'About 1860 came Stead with his *Perfect Cure*, which raged through the land like an influenza.' See his *London and Londoners in the Eighteen-Fifties and Sixties* (London: Fisher Unwin, 1924), p. 66, and for a detailed description of the act, p. 187. See also Dickens's account of the act in 'Managers and Music-Halls', *All the Year Round*, 4 (23 March 1861), 558–61 (558–9).

31 'Sensation! A Satire', *Dublin University Magazine*, 63 (January 1864), reprinted in Maunder, *Varieties of Women's Sensation Fiction*, pp. 88–96, p. 91.

32 'The Philosophy of "Sensation"', p. 18.

33 See Schoch, *Victorian Theatrical Burlesques*, p. 3.

34 *Athenaeum*, 15 February 1862, 232–3.

35 For biographical accounts of Boucicault's career in these years see Fawkes's *Dion Boucicault*, Townsend Walsh's *Career of Dion Boucicault*, and Sven Eric Molin and Robin Goodefellowe, *Dion Boucicault, The Shaughraun*, 2 vols., *Part II: Up and Down in Paris and London* (Newark: Proscenium Press, 1983).

36 'In the Days of My Youth', Calthrop clippings file.

37 Walsh, *Career of Dion Boucicault*, p. 72, n.1.

38 It is sometimes assumed that Scanlan – and Cregan in the novel and stage versions – was a member of the Protestant Ascendancy, but in fact it seems more likely that the Scanlans were well-to-do Catholics. Scanlan's employment of the Catholic barrister Daniel O'Connell as his advocate makes more sense if Scanlan was, like O'Connell, a member of Munster's 'Catholic semi-gentry', to use Oliver MacDonagh's phrase. See Oliver MacDonagh, *The Hereditary Bondsman: Daniel O'Connell, 1775–1829* (London: Weidenfeld and Nicolson, 1988), p. 189. The gap that yawned between Ellen Hanley and John Scanlan, then, was more likely one of class than of religion. It is noteworthy in this respect that the *Times* reportage makes no mention of religion, and neither does a broadside version presumably aimed at a more popular audience, 'A True and Particular Account of the Bloody and Cruel Murder of Ellen Hanly, on the River Shannon' [1820], now in the National Library of Scotland, which recounts the events of the story and gives Stephen Sullivan's confession in full.

39 It has sometimes been suggested that Griffin himself acted as a court reporter at Scanlan's trial, but this seems unlikely. John Cronin suggests that Griffin's later work as a reporter may have led to this confusion. See his *Gerald Griffin, 1803–1840: A Critical Biography* (Cambridge University Press, 1978), p. 51. In a letter to his wife, O'Connell records his lack of sympathy for his client's fate:

> It is very unusual with me to be so satisfied, but he is a horrid villain. In the first place he got a creature, a lovely creature of 15, to elope with him ... she was not heard of afterwards for near 2 months when a mutilated carcase floated on shore, or rather was thrown, which was identified to be hers from some extremely remarkable teeth. He will be hanged tomorrow unless being a gentleman prevents him. (*The Correspondence of Daniel O'Connell*, ed. Maurice R. O'Connell, 8 vols. (Dublin: Irish University Press for the Irish Manuscripts Commission, 1972), vol. II, p. 243).

The circumstantial evidence against Scanlan and Sullivan was damning: they had been the last ones seen with the dead girl; a local man identified the rope around the body's neck as one he had sold to Scanlan; Sullivan was found to have given articles of Hanley's clothing, including her mantle, to his sister, while Scanlan had given some to his landlady. See 'Limerick City Assizes: Horrible Murder', *The Times*, Friday, 4 August 1820, 3. See also the accounts reproduced in W. MacLysaght and Sigerson Clifford, *Death Sails the Shannon: The Tragic Story of the Colleen Bawn, the Facts and the Fiction* (Tralee: Anvil Books, 1953), pp. 166–7.

40 Sullivan fled to Kerry, where he lived under an assumed name, until he was arrested the following year at Castleisland for uttering forged bank notes, and was recognized in jail as the absconded boatman. Arraigned before Charles Kendall Bushe on 21 July 1820, he was found guilty and hanged the following week (unlike his employer, he had no legal counsel). As in the case of Scanlan, his body was given to the County Hospital for dissection.

41 The *Times* review of *The Colleen Bawn* recalls such an adaptation at the minor theatres. See 'Adelphi Theatre', *The Times*, Tuesday, 11 September 1860, 10.

42 On the links between the *Colleen* and the *Octoroon* see Scott Boltwood, ' "The Ineffable Curse of Cain": Race, Miscegenation, and the Victorian Staging of Irishness', *Victorian Literature and Culture*, 29.2 (2001), 383–96. Boltwood assumes that Cregan is a Protestant, and Eily is a Catholic, but this is never made clear in the play, and the novel version suggests otherwise.

43 'Mr Boucicault's Oration to the Public', published in the 'Dramatic Feuilleton' of the *New York Saturday Press*, 31 March 1860, 3. Reproduced in *The Vault at Pfaff*'s, http://digital.lib.lehigh.edu/pfaffs/sat/press/ (accessed 28 October 2008). My thanks to Virginia Jackson for drawing my attention to this invaluable resource on nineteenth-century New York.

44 Ada Clare, 'Thoughts and Things', *New York Saturday Press*, 7 April 1860, 4. Reproduced in *The Vault at Pfaff's*, http://digital.lib.lehigh.edu/pfaffs/sat/press/ (accessed 28 October 2008).

45 'Amusements', *New York Times*, 31 March 1860, 8. The newspaper refers to him as Bourcicault, a version of his name that Boucicault himself used at times.

46 'Amusements', *New York Times*, 7 April 1860, 5.

47 'Princess's Theatre', *The Times*, 12 February 1868. Calthrop clippings file.

48 Brooks, *The Melodramatic Imagination*. On the relationship of melodrama to the social modernity of the city see, for example, Ben Singer, *Melodrama and Modernity: Early Sensational Cinema and its Contexts* (New York: Columbia University Press, 2001), who also argues that Brooks is drawing on an older tradition of interpretation of melodrama. Discussing Boucicault's Walter Scott adaptation, *The Trial of Effie Deans* (1863), Lynn M. Voskuil has argued that what sensation melodrama offers is a consumer-culture version of the modern public sphere. See her 'Feeling Public: Sensation Theater, Commodity Culture, and the Victorian Public Sphere', *Victorian Studies*, 44.3 (Spring 2002), 245–74. She does not suggest why this should take the form it does in *Effie Deans*, which like *The Colleen Bawn* seems to live the present through the past. See also Matthew Buckley, 'Sensations of Celebrity: Jack Sheppard and the Mass Audience', *Victorian Studies*, 44.3 (Spring 2002), 423–63.

49 Wolfgang Schivelbusch, *The Railway Journey: The Industrialization of Time and Space in the Nineteenth Century* (1977; Berkeley: University of California Press, 1986).

50 I have discussed *After Dark* in relation to the industrialization of time and space in 'Blood on the Tracks: Sensation Drama, the Railway, and the Dark Face of Modernity', *Victorian Studies*, 12.1 (Autumn 1998/9), 47–76.

51 Walter Benjamin, 'Paris, Capital of the Nineteenth Century', in Peter Demetz, ed., *Reflections*, trans., Edmund Jephcott (New York: Schocken, 1986), pp. 146–62, p. 148.

52 Susan Buck-Morss, *The Dialectics of Seeing: Walter Benjamin and the Arcades Project* (Cambridge and London: MIT Press, 1991), pp. 110, 111.

53 Benjamin, 'Paris, Capital of the Nineteenth Century', p. 148.

54 For a rather different reading of Boucicault's staging of Ireland in relation to modernity see Luke Gibbons, 'Modernism, Montage, and the City', in *Transformations in Irish Culture* (Cork University Press, 1996), pp. 165–9, p. 168. Gibbons suggests that Ireland's colonial status brings about the same 'disintegration of experience' (p. 168) in the countryside that elsewhere registers in the city. As I hope is clear, I see the play's sensational aspect as relating to metropolitan experience, though its origins do lie in the violent events of the Irish countryside.

55 The wearing of Colleen Bawn cloaks is not a unique incident of such cross-cultural identification, of course. There was a vogue for 'Gipsey parties' in the 1850s and 1860s, a form of excursion-cum-camping which may have offered similar pleasures. See, for example, the Harry Clifton song 'Charity Crow' (1865).

56 This in turn originated from Thomas Moore's poem of the same name, which describes a jilted Irishwoman who is about to drown herself in her despair and thus turn herself into Ireland's national instrument: Irish art, it would seem to suggest, comes out of emotional upheaval, out of betrayal and suffering – a distinctly Romantic conception of the origins of art. Not so the Colleen Bawn, who by surviving death creates a different sort of allegory, one of a cross-class reconciliation of peasant and gentry that foils the predatory middle-man, Corrigan. The water-cave scene also echoes some of the familiar Victorian treatments of the 'fallen woman', such as the last picture in Augustus Egg's *Past and Present* series (1858).

57 Gaston Bachelard, *The Poetics of Space*, trans. Maria Jolas (1958; Boston: Beacon Press, 1969), pp. 18–24.

58 Anna-Maria Hall and Samuel Carter Hall, *Hall's Ireland: Mr and Mrs Hall's Tour of 1840*, ed. Michael Scott, 2 vols. (1841; London and Sydney: Sphere, 1984), vol. I, p. 74.

59 Luke Gibbons, 'Topographies of Terror: Killarney and the Politics of the Sublime, *South Atlantic Quarterly*, 95.1 (Winter 1996), 23–44 (33–4). The general argument of this article is that Killarney becomes such a highly charged locus of the sublime because of the conflation of aesthetic and political aspects to its 'wildness'.

60 On the famine as a topic that required a revision of the formulas of melodrama see Julia Williams and Stephen Watt, 'Representing a "Great Distress": Melodrama, Gender, and the Irish Famine', in Michael Hays and Anastasia Nikolopoulou, *Melodrama: The Cultural Emergence of a Genre*

(New York: St. Martin's Press, 1999), pp. 245–65. Williams and Watt argue that *The Colleen Bawn* reinforces the imperial vision of a benign landlord class, but I believe that the play's politics and its treatment of historical memory are more complex than this suggests.

61 'Theatre Royal – *The Colleen Bawn*', Calthrop clippings file.

62 This was not the only version of the play published by Purkess. The Templeman Library has a cover image of a different version in which we see Myles shoot Danny.

63 'Execution', *The Times*, Tuesday, 8 August 1820, 3.

64 Fawkes, *Dion Boucicault*, p. 122; 'Royal English Opera', *The Times*, 11 February 1862, 12.

65 J. Pittman, ed., *The Lily of Killarney, Opera in 3 Acts by Sir Julius Benedict, the Words by Dion Boucicault and John Oxenford* (London and New York: Boosey, n.d.).

66 For a suggestive analysis of two earlier Irish playwrights in whose work the ritual/representation issue arises see Claire Connolly, 'Theater and Nation in Irish Romanticism: The Tragic Dramas of Charles Robert Maturin and Richard Lalor Sheil', *Eire-Ireland*, 41.3 and 4 (Fall/Winter 2006), 185–214.

67 'In the Days of my Youth'.

68 On theatre, performance, and memory see, for example, Joseph Roach, *Cities of the Dead: Circum-Atlantic Performance* (New York: Columbia, 1996).

CHAPTER 3 THE WHITE GIRL: AESTHETICISM AS MESMERISM

1 Patricia De Montfort also identifies her as the model for some of Whistler's magazine illustrations of this period. See her 'White Muslin: Joanna Hiffernan and the 1860s', in Margaret F. MacDonald *et al.*, eds., *Whistler, Women, and Fashion* (New York, New Haven and London: The Frick Collection and Yale University Press, 2003), pp. 76–91, p. 80. The catalogue raisonné for Whistler's paintings is Andrew McLaren Young, Margaret MacDonald and Robin Spencer, with the Assistance of Hamish Miller, *The Paintings of James McNeill Whistler*, 2 vols. (New Haven and London: Yale University Press, 1980). Heffernan is the normal form of the Irish name, but many of the contemporary sources name her as Hiffernan, so this is the form of her name I have used.

2 See John Gage, *Colour and Meaning: Art, Science and Symbolism* (London: Thames and Hudson, 1999), pp. 15, 196–208.

3 For example, a handbook of 1864 identifies 'Zinc White No. 1' as a possible replacement for the better-known lead white. Cited by Hermann Kuehn, 'Zinc White', in Robert L. Feller, ed., *Artists' Pigments: A Handbook of Their History and Characteristics*, vol. 1 (Washington: National Gallery of Art and Oxford University Press, 1986), pp. 169–86, p. 172.

4 For the mixed reviews of these paintings see Elizabeth R. Pennell and Joseph Pennell, *Life of James McNeill Whistler* (London: William Heninemann, 1920), pp. 59–60.

5   Daphne Du Maurier, ed., *The Young George Du Maurier: A Selection of his Letters, 1860–67* (London: Peter Davies, 1951), pp. 14–17, p. 16. Henceforth abbreviated *L*.

6   De Montfort, 'White Muslin', p. 80.

7   The primary victims of lead poisoning were, of course, the workers engaged in the manufacture of lead white, not the artists. Symptoms ranged from shortness of breath to blindness and paralysis. See R. D. Harley, *Artists' Pigments, c. 1600–1835* (London: Archetype, 2001), p. 168.

8   Gordon Fleming, *The Young Whistler, 1834–66* (London: George Allen and Unwin, 1978), p. 173.

9   'F. T. P', 'The British School of Oil Painting', *International Exhibition of 1862, Official Catalogue, Fine Art Department* (London, 1862) B2–B9 (B3). See also Lionel Lambourne, *Victorian Painting*, p. 132.

10 Elizabeth Pennell and Joseph Pennell, *Life of James McNeill Whistler*, p. 58. Whistler's description of the typical Royal Academy genre painting closely resembles an actual painting exhibited at the 1861 Royal Academy Exhibition, C. S. Lidderdale's *The Inventor*.

11 Letter to George Lucas, June 1862, cited in Margaret MacDonald, ed., *James McNeill Whistler: Drawings, Pastels, and Watercolours: A Catalogue Raisonné* (New Haven and London: Yale University Press, 1995), p. 10.

12 *The Times*, 16 June 1862, 1. Such advertisements were not unusual, of course: the same page carried advertisements for W. P. Frith's *Derby Day* at the Upper Gallery, Pall Mall and his *Railway Station* at the Fine Art Gallery in the Haymarket, as well as works by Rosa Bonheur, John Leech and others.

13 'Fine Art Gossip', *Athenaeum*, 28 June 1862, 859.

14 Wilkie Collins, *The Woman in White*, edited with an introduction by Harvey Peter Sucksmith (Oxford University Press, 1992), p. 15.

15 Leonée Ormond, *George Du Maurier* (University of Pittsburgh Press, 1969), pp. 145–8. As Ormond points out, the drawing is in part a parody of an illustration that Du Maurier had produced for another sensation novel, *The Notting Hill Mystery* (1862–3).

16 *Athenaeum*, 5 July 1862, 23.

17 Elected to the presidency in 1848, Louis Napoléon assumed dictatorial powers in 1851, creating the Second Empire in 1852. In the 1860s he relaxed his control over the press to some extent and permitted some expression of political opposition.

18 Stanley Weintraub, *Whistler: A Biography* (London: Collins, 1974), pp. 85–6. Henceforth abbreviated *WB*.

19 Elizabeth R. Pennell and Joseph Pennell, *Life of James McNeill Whistler*, p. 74.

20 H. L. Mansel, 'Sensation Novels', *Quarterly Review*, 113 (1863), 481–514, 482. See also Nicholas Daly, *Literature, Technology, and Modernity, 1860–2000* (Cambridge University Press, 2004), pp. 40–2.

21 Mrs Oliphant, 'Sensation Novels,' *Blackwood's*, 91 (1862), 564–84, 572. Cf. Nicholas Dames, 'Wave-Theories and Affective Physiologies: The Cognitive Strain in Victorian Novel Theories', *Victorian Studies*, 46.2 (Winter 2004),

206–16, for a more wide-ranging account of such 'somatic' readings of Victorian fiction.

22 On the role of the commodity experience in nineteenth-century culture see Anne Friedberg, *Window Shopping: Cinema and the Postmodern* (Berkeley: University California Press, 1993).

23 On historical accounts of modernity as a form of sensory overload see Ben Singer, *Melodrama and Modernity: Early Cinema and Its Contexts* (New York: Columbia University Press, 2001), pp. 59–99; on the 'training' given by the sensation novel and sensation drama see my *Literature, Technology, and Modernity*.

24 Cited in Elizabeth Pennell and Joseph Pennell, *Life of James McNeill Whistler*, p. 100, from Bierstadt Tuckerman, *Book of the Artists* (1867).

25 Gage, *Colour and Meaning*, p. 22.

26 Ibid., p. 208.

27 On the lifelong Whistler–O'Leary friendship, which began in Paris in the 1850s, see Ronald Anderson, 'Whistler, an Irish Rebel and Ireland: The Political Implications of an Undocumented Friendship', *Apollo*, 123 (April 1986), 254–8.

28 Cited in Elizabeth Pennell and Joseph Pennell, *Life of James McNeill Whistler*, 101, from Moncure Conway, *Reminiscences*.

29 See David Park Curry, *James McNeill Whistler at the Freer Gallery of Art* (New York and London: Freer Gallery and the Smithsonian in Association with W. W. Norton: Norton, 1984), pp. 38–9.

30 On the more general significance of female figures in aestheticism as mediating between the claims of autonomous art and commodity culture, see Kathy Alexis Psomiades, *Beauty's Body: Femininity and Representation in British Aestheticism* (Stanford University Press, 1997), especially pp. 108–13 on *Symphony in White, No. 2*.

31 Both plays are loosely derived from Mrs S. C. Hall's tale of an English landowner caught up in agrarian violence, *The Whiteboy: A Story of Ireland in 1822* (1845). An early adaptation was staged in New York in 1848 as *The White Boy; or, MacArty's Fate*. See Allardyce Nicoll, *A History of Late Nineteenth-Century Drama, 1850–1900*, vol. I (Cambridge University Press, 1946), and Rolf Loeber and Magda Loeber, *A Guide to Irish Fiction, 1650–1900* (Dublin: Four Courts, 2006), pp. 541–2.

32 The *Times* critic complained in 1878 that Whistler titled his paintings as if 'young ladies had no right to feel aggrieved at being converted into "arrangements"'. Cited in *WB*, p. 195.

33 Ormond, *George Du Maurier*, pp. 413–14; see also Henry James, *Notebooks*.

34 Daniel Pick, *Svengali's Web: The Alien Enchanter in Modern Culture* (New York and London: Yale University Press, 2000).

35 Du Maurier appears to have borrowed the name from Charles Nodier's eponymous fairytale of 1820.

36 Pick, *Svengali's Web*, p. 27.

37 Cited in Showalter's introduction to *Trilby*, p. xiv.

38 See, for example, Ed Rogers's *My Gal's Got Trilby Feet*; and Vesta Tilley's *I'm Looking for Trilby* ('Trilby the sweet, Dear Little feet / Fix'd up in sandals remarkably neat'). See Frederick Denny's *Encyclopedia of the British Music Hall*, oldtimemusichall.net (accessed 22 May 2007).

39 On Wilde as Svengali see, for example, Jonathan Grossman, 'The Mythic Svengali: Anti-Aestheticism in *Trilby*', 28 (Winter 1996), 525–42 and Pamela Thurschwell, *Literature, Technology, and Magical Thinking, 1880–1920* (Cambridge University Press, 2001), pp. 37–64. Pick is more circumspect in *Svengali's Web*, and leaves the question of originals open.

40 *Trilby*, *Harper's Monthly Magazine*, 27 (December 1893–May 1894), 577.

41 In other respects life seemed to be imitating art. Whistler had returned to Paris in the 1890s, and had even acquired a studio in the Rue Notre Dame des Champs, the same street on which Poynter, Lamont and Armstrong once had their studio/apartment, and where he and Du Maurier had visited so often.

42 Felix Moscheles, *With Du Maurier in Bohemia* (London, 1896).

43 E. R. Pennell and J. Pennell, *The Whistler Journal* (Philadelphia: Lippincott, 1921), p. 161.

44 See *Trilby*, act I, in George Taylor, ed., *Trilby and Other Plays* (Oxford University Press Classics, 1996).

45 Pennell and Pennell, *Journal*, p. 157.

46 If *The Picture of Dorian Gray* and 'The Facts in the Case of M. Valdemar' are some of the pre-texts for Du Maurier's sensational plot, *The Woman in White* is another: the foreign genius steals Trilby's identity as surely as Count Fosco does that of Laura Fairlie.

47 Robert Fernier, *La Vie et L'Oeuvre de Gustave Courbet: Catalogue Raisonné*, 2 vols. (Lausanne and Paris: Fondation Wildenstein and La Bibliothèque des Arts, 1977), vol. I, pp. 244–5; vol. II, pp. 6–10; and Petra ten-Doesschate Chu, *Letters of Gustave Courbet* (University of Chicago Press, 1992), p. 682. On Jo's work as a model, and on other Irish models of this period, see also Fintan Cullen and R. F. Foster, *Conquering England: Ireland in Victorian London* (London: National Portrait Gallery, 2005), pp. 61–5. I am grateful to Fintan Cullen for recommending a number of sources on Ireland and Victorian art.

48 Jean-Jacques Fernier, 'Courbet, reves d'homme', in *Courbet, L'Amour: Catalogue de l'exposition estivale 1996* (Ornans: Musée Gustave Courbet, 1996), pp. 13–33, p. 28.

49 See also Jack Lindsay, *Gustave Courbet: His Life and Art* (Queen Square Bath, Somerset: Adams and Dart, 1973), pp. 216–17.

50 Cited in Lindsay, *Gustave Courbet*, p. 216.

51 On the painting's chequered career see Fernier, *La Vie et L'Oeuvre de Gustave Courbet* and Bernard Teyssèdre, *Le Roman de l'Origine* (Paris: Gallimard, 1996), and, since I wrote the first version of this chapter, Thierry Savatier, *L'Origine du monde: Histoire d'un tableau de Gustave Courbet* (Paris: Bartillat, 2006). Savatier thinks that Hiffernan is unlikely to have been the painting's model, and argues for a photograph as the 'original'. Nochlin records her

failed attempts to locate the painting in 'Courbet's *L'Origine du monde*: The Origin without an Original', *October*, 37 (1986), 76–86.

52 Sophie Monneret, *L'Impressionisme et son époque: Dictionnaire internationale illustré* (Paris: Denoël, 1978). Chantal Humbert 'L'Amour du progress, ou Courbet chez le photographe' in *Courbet, L'Amour*, pp. 137–58, p. 145.

53 De Montfort, 'White Muslin', p. 80.

CHAPTER 4 BLACK AND WHITE IN THE 1860S

1 *Punch*, 41 (20 July 1861), 31.

2 Contributions to the debate include Robert C. Toll, *Blacking Up: The Minstrel Show in 19th-Century America* (New York: Oxford University Press, 1974); Eric Lott, *Love and Theft: Blackface Minstrelsy and the American Working Class* (New York: Oxford University Press, 1993); David R. Roediger, *The Wages of Whiteness: Race and the Making of the American Working Class* (London: Verso, 1991); W. T. Lhamon, ed., *Jump Jim Crow: Lost Plays, Lyrics, and Street Prose of the First Atlantic Popular Culture* (Cambridge: Harvard University Press, 2003). The place of the immigrant Irish in blackface has been a controversial topic in Irish studies. See, for example, Robert Nowatzki, 'Paddy Jumps Jim Crow: Irish Americans and Blackface Minstrelsy', *Eire-Ireland*, 41.3 and 4 (Fall/Winter 2006), 162–84.

3 See J. S. Bratton, 'English Ethiopians: British Audiences and Blackface Acts, 1835–65', *The Yearbook of English Studies*, 11 (1981), 127–42; and Michael Pickering, 'White Skin, Black Masks: "Nigger" Minstrelsy in Victorian England', and 'John Bull in Blackface', *Popular Music*, 16.2 (May 1997), 181–201. See also J. S. Bratton, ed. *Music Hall: Performance and Style* (Milton Keynes: Open University Press, 1986), pp. 71–91.

4 The classic study is L. P. Curtis's *Apes and Angels: The Irishman in Victorian Caricature* (Washington: Smithsonian Institution Press, 1971). On the Fenians, see Patrick Quinlivan and Paul Rose, *The Fenians in England, 1865–1872* (London: John Calder, 1982).

5 Of course, the title 'Symphony in Black' has been used more than once: for example, by Erté and by Duke Ellington.

6 See Cora Kaplan, 'White, Black and Green: Racialising Irishness in Victorian England', in Peter Gray, ed., *Victoria's Ireland: Irishness and Britishness, 1837–1901* (Dublin: Four Courts, 2004), pp. 51–68.

7 Catherine Hall, 'The Nation Within and Without', in Catherine Hall, Keith McClelland and Jane Rendall, *Defining the Victorian Nation: Class, Race, Gender and the Reform Act of 1867* (Cambridge University Press, 2000), pp. 179–233.

8 See, for example, Sarita Malik's entry for the show on the Museum of Broadcast Communication's online *Encyclopedia of TV*, www.museum.tv/publicationssection.php (accessed 8 August 2007).

9 Jim Crow, *A Celebrated Nigger Song, Sung by Mr T. Rice, With the Most Unbounded Applause at the Surrey Theatre* (London: B. Williams, 1837?), Lester S. Levy Collection, http://levysheetmusic.mse.jhu.edu (accessed 16 August 2007).

10   See Eric Lott, *Love and Theft*.

11   See Lhamon, *Jump Jim Crow*, pp. 35–40.

12   Bratton, 'English Ethiopians', pp. 133–4.

13   Lhamon sees Rice as a pioneer of a subversive form of blackface that appealed to and brought together various opponents of official culture, in a 'demotic commingling of white and black' (p. 12). He points to the character of O'Leary, an Irish servant, in *The Virginia Mummy*, as an example of the cross-ethnic scope of Rice's rebellious project.

14   Adelphi Theatre Project, 'Seasonal Summary' for 1836–7.

15   In the same piece a Miss Mott played the part of Zip Coon, 'a mulatto help'. Zip Coon becomes a common character in blackface performances, but usually it is a male part, that of a black dandy.

16   Pickering, 'White Skin', p. 74. See also Bratton, 'English Ethiopians'.

17   They extended their tour to Dublin in 1844.

18   The authorship of Dixie has long been a matter of dispute. Most recently, see Howard L. Sacks and Judith Rose Sacks, *Way Up North in Dixie: A Black Family's Claim to the Confederate Anthem* (Washington, DC: Smithsonian Institution Press, 1993).

19   See, for example, Toll, *Blacking Up*, pp. 51–7, and Pickering, 'White Skin', pp. 75–6.

20   For an example of the theatrical incorporation of minstrel materials see Boucicault's *After Dark* (1868).

21   At the end of the nineteenth century the Mohawk Minstrels incorporated some of the Moore and Burgess troupe, and became the Mohawk, Moore and Burgess Minstrels, performing at St James's Hall. The Mohawk Minstrels also published a long-running series of the *Mohawk Minstrels Magazine of Favorite Songs and Ballads: as Sung by Them at the Agricultural Hall, London*.

22   Pickering, 'John Bull', p. 181.

23   See the sheet music to 'Limerick is Beautiful', 'originally sung in New York with great success by Dan Bryant, in his great character of Myles na Coppaleen', with *The Colleen Bawn* in large superscript, published by Pond, Broadway.

24   Michael Kilgarriff, *Sing Us One of the Old Songs: A Guide to Popular Song, 1860–1920* (Oxford University Press, 1998), p. 48.

25   Cf. *Complete Repertoire of the Songs, Ballads, and Plantation Melodies Sung by the Christy Minstrels* (London: Hopwood and Crew, 1860). The British Library has an edition that claims to be the 'three hundred and fourth thousand' edition.

26   The chromolithographed cover, by Concanen, Lee and Siebe, shows a pair of crossed Confederate flags.

27   'Easter Amusements', 7 April 1863, 12. The St James's and Polygraphic Halls were in Islington, and were long associated with Moore and Burgess Minstrels.

28   Frank Hall, *In the Strand; Or, I wish I was with Nancy* (London: Foster and L'Enfant, 1861).

29 Bratton, 'English Ethiopians', pp. 139–42. Bratton also cites a former black-face performer, Harry Reynolds, on the trade distinction between acts that used plantation blackface, and those that used blackface as a sign that they would be relying on certain comic conventions (p. 138).

30 G. W. Hunt, *Am I Right, Or any Other Man* (London: L'Enfant and Hodgkins, 1862).

31 Charles Haddon Spurgeon attracted enormous audiences to his sermons at such venues as the Crystal Palace at Sydenham, and the Surrey Music Hall. His own purpose-built church, the Metropolitan Tabernacle, with seating for 5,000, was completed in 1861.

32 Pickering, 'White Skin', p. 84. See also Hall, *Defining the Victorian Nation*, pp. 184–5.

33 'The Kelts of Ireland', *Journal of Anthropology*, 1.2 (October 1870), 117–31. Stepan, *Idea of Race*. But see also Chris Morash, 'Celticism: Between Race and Nation', in Tadhg Foley and Seán Ryder, eds., *Ideology and Ireland in the Nineteenth Century* (Dublin: Four Courts, 1998), pp. 206–13 on Beddoes and the coexistence of linguistic and physiological ideas of race in this period.

34 Henry Hudson, 'On the Irish Celt', *Journal of the Anthropological Society of London*, 1.8 (1870), clxxviii–clxxxi.

35 Class is as important as religion here: to take a fictional example, there is little sense that Phineas Finn, the Catholic Irish MP in Trollope's Palliser novels, is in any way the inferior of his English peers – he is, in fact, represented as a man who has risen through his abilities.

36 *The Octoroon*, II.i. When Zoe dies, we are told that her eyes change colour, as 'her soul's gwine do' (V.iv).

37 On the play's sources see Jules Zanger, 'The Tragic Octoroon in Pre-Civil War Fiction', *American Quarterly*, 18.1 (Spring 1966), 63–70. The earliest example adduced is R. Hildreth's novel, *The Slave, or Memoirs of Archy Moore* (1836).

38 'Theatre Royal, New Adelphi', *The Times*, 15 November 1861, 6.

39 Joseph Roach, *Cities of the Dead: Circum-Atlantic Performance* (New York: Columbia, 1996), p. 215.

40 Ibid., p. 181.

41 For a full account of Boucicault's changes, see John A. Degen, 'How to End the Octoroon', *Educational Theatre Journal*, 27.2 (May 1975), 170–8.

42 'The Octoroon', *New York Times*, 15 December 1859 (accessed through the *New York Times*'s electronic archive, 31 October 2008).

43 See, for example, 'Law Reports: The *Octoroon* Copyright', *New York Times*, 20 December 1859; 'Law Reports: The *Octoroon* War', *New York Times*, 26 December 1859.

44 The actor Joseph Jefferson gave evidence that the audiences for the *Octoroon* were extremely well behaved, and there is nothing in the *New York Times*'s accounts of reactions to the play to suggest that audiences were excited to violence. For a sceptical reaction to Robertson's claims see 'Dramatic', *New York Times*, 16 December 1859.

45 'Adelphi Theatre', *The Times*, 12 December 1861, 12.

46 'Adelphi Theatre', *The Times*, 19 November 1861, 12.

47 'Letters to the Editor, The Octoroon', *The Times*, 20 November 1861, 5.

48 Degen, 'How to End the Octoroon', p. 173.

49 Quoted in ibid., p. 173.

50 'Letters to the Editor, The Octoroon', p. 5.

51 This was an exhausting schedule for both of them. Boucicault was replaced by Delmon Grace as Scudder for part of the run; his wife was replaced by Cecilia Ranoe as Eily. See Adelphi Theatre Project, Daily Calendar for 1861–2, by Alfrida Lee.

52 Christine Bolt, *Victorian Attitudes to Race* (London: Routledge and Kegan Paul, 1971); Douglas Lorimer, *Colour, Class, and the Victorians: English Attitudes to the Negro in the Mid-Nineteenth Century* (Leicester University Press, 1982); Nancy Stepan, *The Idea of Race in Science: Great Britain 1800– 1960* (Oxford: Macmillan/St Antony's College, 1982). Subsequent references in parentheses in the text.

53 'On the Negro's Place in Nature', *Journal of the Anthropological Society of London*, 2 (1864), xv–lvi. In the ensuing debate, Winwood Reade agreed, but argued that the coastal Negroes were a degraded people who should be distinguished from other Africans. J. Reddie wondered if the Negroes who were enslaved were atypical, as Reade had suggested, and pointed out that England had its own 'refuse population' who had not proved susceptible of improvement: 'even among our own criminal population there is supposed to be a sort of hereditariness … and therefore we may have an easy explan- ation of the proverbial thievery of the Negro' (xxi).

54 See, for example, Leslie M. Harris, *In the Shadow of Slavery: African Americans in New York City, 1626–1863* (University of Chicago Press, 2003), pp. 279–88.

55 On Anglo-American relations in this period see Douglass Ephraim Adams, *Great Britain and the American Civil War*, 2 vols. (London: Longmans, 1925). Subsequent references in parentheses in the text are to vol. II. See also H. C. Allen, *Great Britain and the United States: A History of Anglo-American Relations* (New York: Archon, 1969), pp. 452–517.

56 See also Allen, *Great Britain and the United States*, pp. 476–7.

57 On the hunt by British travellers for the American gentleman, see Christopher Mulvey, *Transatlantic Manners: Social Patterns in Nineteenth-Century Anglo-American Travel Literature* (Cambridge University Press, 1990), pp. 19–32.

58 For an account of the events see Ian Hernon, *Britain's Forgotten Wars: Colonial Campaigns of the 19th Century* (Stroud: Sutton, 2003), pp. 76–100.

59 Hall, 'The Nation Within and Without', p. 203.

60 Ibid., p. 197.

61 Mandelstam, 'Du Chaillu's Stuffed Gorillas and the Savants from the British Museum', *Notes and Records of the Royal Society of London*, 48.2 (July 1994), 227–45. I am indebted to this article for the account of du Chaillu in London that follows.

62 Where the villain, Frollo, tells his Caliban-like slave, Quasimodo:

'Well really, Quasimodo, I must say
You seem to grow more hideous every day;
Why, if you go on in this frightful way,
'Twixt you and the Gorilla there will be
The very strongest similarity.'(I.i).

63 Cf. Charles Kingsley's often-quoted description of the Irish poor as 'white chimpanzees'. See, for example, Kaplan, 'White, Black and Green', p. 54.

64 Sheridan Gilley gives a detailed account of the riots and their context in 'The Garibaldi Riots of 1862', *The Historical Journal*, 16.4 (December 1973), 697–732. Subsequent references in parentheses in the text.

65 Things are more complicated than this, in fact: the play's villain, Corry Kinchela, knows a Fenian amnesty is imminent, and connives at the hero's escape in the hope that he will be shot in the attempt.

66 Dinitia Smith, 'Getting that Monkey off his Creator's Back', *New York Times*, 13 August 2005, www.nytimes.com/2005/08/13/movies/ MoviesFeatures/13kong.html (accessed 26 September 2008). Smith cites Mark Cotta Vaz, *Living Dangerously: The Adventures of Merian C. Cooper, Creator of King Kong* (New York: Villard, 2005).

67 The most recent remake of the film (2005, dir. Peter Jackson) complicates the original narrative in various ways, not least by devoting a long sequence to the sympathetic interaction with the beast of the heroine, vaudeville actress Ann Darrow (Naomi Watts) – the film's original animal/human ethos does not play well at a time when gorillas are among the most prominent endangered species. Nonetheless, some of the original linkage of Kong and the crowd survives, with Carl Denham (Jack Black) telling Darrow that you have to kill a vaudeville crowd or be killed by them; the film's last line – 'it was beauty killed the beast' – also goes to Black.

CHAPTER 5 THE CHROMOLITHOGRAPHERS
OF MODERN LIFE

1 Maurice Willson Disher, *Victorian Song: From Dive to Drawing Room* (London: Phoenix House, 1955), p. 14. See also John M. Garrett, *Sixty Years of British Music Hall* (London: Chapell, 1976), Chapter 1 (unpaginated).

2 Actually it is not quite clear that he was really among the living when she first met him either.

3 Sacheverell Sitwell, *Morning, Noon, and Night in London* (London: Macmillan, 1948). Subsequent references will be given in the text in parentheses.

4 Alfred Concanen (1835–86), the son of the artist Edward Concanen (who illustrated *Remembrances of the Great Exhibition*), produced a wide body of lithographic work, including theatrical posters and panoramic views. See, for example, his poster for the 1867 production of F. C. Burnand and Arthur S. Sulivan's *Cox and Box*, reproduced in Simon Trussler, *The Cambridge Illustrated History of British Theatre* (Cambridge University Press, 2000), p. 239. John Brandard was the brother of the engravers Edward and Robert

Brandard, and he too produced lithographs in a variety of genres, including topographical views, naval subjects and portraits. Thomas Packer also worked in a number of genres, producing views of the Crimean War, inter alia.

5 As it happens, 'The Bond Street Beau', written by F. W. Green (d. 1884) to a melody by Alfred Lee (d. 1906), is probably a song of the early 1870s rather than the 1860s. Green, a prolific lyricist, wrote many other popular songs from the late 1860s to the early 1880s, including 'Clicquot' (1870), sung by Alfred 'The Great' Vance, 'Cool Burgundy Ben' (1868) and 'Dolly Varden' (1870), and blackface minstrel songs such as 'Ten Little Niggers' (1869).

6 Martin Hardie, *English Coloured Books*, with an introduction by James Laver (1906; Bath: Kingsmead Reprints, 1973), p. 234.

7 See Bamber Gascoigne, *How to Indentify Prints: A Complete Guide to Manual and Mechanical Processes from Woodcut to Inkjet* (London: Thames and Hudson, 2004), p. 19d.

8 Quoted in Gordon N. Ray, *The Illustrator and the Book in England from 1790 to 1914* (New York: Pierpont Morgan Library and Oxford University Press, 1976), p. 51; on the early and subsequent adventures of lithography see pp. 51–8 and 143–8. There are also useful accounts in Hardie, *English Coloured Books*, pp. 96–116 and 233–43, and in Michael Twyman, *Early Lithographed Music* (London: Farrand Press, 1996), pp. 19–24 and 25–34; and spirited comments on the resistance to lithography in England in Elizabeth Robins Pennell and Joseph Pennell, *Lithography and Lithographers* (London: T. Fisher Unwin, 1915), pp. 109–22.

9 On the dubious originality of Baxter's process see R. M. Burch, *Colour Printing and Colour Printers* (London, 1910), p. 125.

10 See Burch, *Colour Printing*, p. 196.

11 This is not to say that the lithograph in France always enjoyed more prestige. Among other things, it became the vehicle for cheap erotic prints that for a largely male audience linked the promise of urban modernity to sexual promise. See Abigail Solomon-Godeau, 'The Other Side of Venus: The Visual Economy of Feminine Display', in Victoria de Grazia and Ellen Furlough, eds., *The Sex of Things: Gender and Consumption in Historical Perspective* (Berkeley: University of California Press, 1996), pp. 113–50.

12 Cited by Ronald Pearsall, *Victorian Sheet Music Covers* (Newton Abbot: David and Charles, 1972), p. 10.

13 See his *Elements of Drawing* (London, 1857), pp. 257–59, p. 259. See also Ray, *Illustrator and the Book*, p. 51, and Pennell and Pennell, *Lithography*, pp. 109–10. Earlier he warns that 'in these days of cheap illustration, the danger is always rather of your possessing too much than too little' (p. 254).

14 Hardie, *English Coloured Books*, pp. 240–1.

15 On attitudes to the cheap availability of images see also Patricia Anderson, *The Printed Image and the Transformation of Popular Culture* (Oxford: Clarendon, 1994). On the currency of similar attitudes in the twentieth century, see D. L. LeMahieu, *A Culture for Democracy: Mass Communication and the Cultivated Mind in Britain Between the Wars* (Oxford: Clarendon, 1988). For a

detailed account of the disruption of existing visual hierarchies by the arrival of photomechanical images at the end of the Victorian period, see Gerry Beegan, *The Mass Image: A Social History of Photomechanical Reproduction in Victorian London* (Basingstoke: Palgrave, 2008).

16 *The Nation*, 1874, cited in Peter C. Marzio, *The Democratic Art: Chromolithography 1840–1900, Pictures for a Nineteenth-Century America* (London: Scolar Press and the Amon Carter Museum of Western Art, Fort Worth, 1980), p. 1.

17 Marzio, *The Democratic Art*, p. 209. He also notes that 'chromo' means 'vulgar' in French, and is Australian slang for a prostitute (pp. 209–10).

18 Gascoigne, *How to Identify Prints*, p. 28b.

19 R. J. Hamerton should not be confused with Philip Gilbert Hamerton, the art critic and etcher, whom we encountered in Chapter 3 as a contemporary commentator on Whistler.

20 Lynda Nead, *Victorian Babylon: People, Streets, and Images in Nineteenth-Century London* (London: Thames and Hudson, 2000), pp. 122–5 and 132–4. The cover on p. 134 attributed to J. Hamerton is by R. J. Hamerton. The term 'frenzy of the visible' is Jean-Louis Comolli's.

21 Derek B. Scott, 'Music and Social Class in Victorian London', *Urban History*, 29.1 (May 2002), 60–73 (65).

22 Ibid., p. 65. Scott describes the promenades as 'petit bourgeois in character'.

23 Cited in Pearsall, *Victorian Sheet Music Covers*, p. 16.

24 See, for example, Catherine Haill, *Victorian Illustrated Music Sheets* (London: HMSO, 1981), p. 3, and the more detailed account of the evolution of illustrated music in A. Hyatt King, 'English Pictorial Music Title Pages: Their Style, Evolution, and Importance, 1820–1885', *Library*, 1950, s5-iv, 262–72.

25 See King, 'English Pictorial Music', p. 265.

26 See Burch, *Colour Printing*, p. 200.

27 See Pearsall, *Victorian Sheet Music Covers*, pp. 14–24.

28 Nonetheless, the broadside form lingered long after this. They were certainly still a feature of 1860s street life, as is suggested by the presence of broadside seller Silas Wegg in Dicken's 1864 novel of contemporary life, *Our Mutual Friend*.

29 Dagmar Kift, *The Victorian Music Hall: Culture, Class and Conflict* (Cambridge University Press, 1996), pp. 18–21, 26, 31–2.

30 As Richard Altick points out, from 1856 the Canterbury also featured an eighty-foot-long art gallery, which featured paintings (or more likely copies or engravings) by Haydon, Maclise, Frith and Gainsborough, among others, which suggests that the division of taste by class in these years is at the very least complicated, as I have tried to suggest in earlier chapters.

31 Charles Dickens, 'Managers and Music-Halls', *All the Year Round*, 4 (23 March 1861), 558–61 (558–9).

32 Disher, *Victorian Song*, p. 137. As Alfred Rosling Bennett recalls, 'About 1860 came Stead with his "Perfect Cure", which raged through the land like an

influenza.' See his *London and Londoners in the Eighteen-Fifties and Sixties* (London: Fisher Unwin, 1924), pp. 66, 187.

33 Kift, *Victorian Music Hall*, pp. 141–2. That Morton received a small fine suggests that the courts did not relish the policing of such disputes. Successive Select Committees failed to produce any legislation to end such cultural turf wars.

34 The complexity of music-hall audiences informs two related collections of essays from the 1980s: J.S. Bratton, ed., *Music Hall: Performance and Style* (Milton Keynes: Open University Press, 1986) and Peter Bailey, ed., *Music Hall: The Business of Pleasure* (Milton Keynes: Open University Press, 1986).

35 Kift, *Victorian Music Hall*, p. 62. Alfred Rosling Bennett, who grew up in a middle-class family, writes that he was 'discouraged' from attending music halls, and knew the songs of the 'lion comiques' through 'burlesques and barrel organs'. Yet while still in his teens he did attend Weston's with a French guest in 1868. See his *London and Londoners in the 1850s and Sixties*, p. 342. The author of *London in the Sixties, by One of the Old Brigade* (London: Everett, 1914), who mixed in aristocratic and military circles, claims (inaccurately) that 'London in the sixties possessed no music-halls as at present [in 1908] except the London Pavilion and a transpontine establishment unknown to the West End' (p. 25), though he warmly describes Evans's in Covent Garden (pp. 63–4).

36 S. M. Ellis, ed., *A Mid-Victorian Pepys: Letters and Memoirs of Sir William Hardman, MA; FRGS* (London, 1923).

37 Anon., 'An Opinion of Music Halls', *The Tomahawk*, Saturday, 14 September 1867, cited from arthurlloyd.co.uk (accessed 4 April 2007).

38 Anon, 'Music Halls: Second Notice', *The Tomahawk*, Saturday, 21 September 1867.

39 Peter Bailey, 'Champagne Charlie and the Music Hall Swell Song', in his *Popular Culture and Performance in the Victorian City* (Cambridge University Press, 2000), pp. 101–27, p. 123. For valuable insights into the 'business of pleasure' and the ideological dimension of the halls, see in the same collection his 'Business and Good Fellowship in the London Music Hall', pp. 80–100, and 'Music Hall and the Knowingness of Popular Culture', pp. 128–51.

40 See also, for example, Sir John Clapham, *An Economic History of Modern Britain*, vol. II: *Free Trade and Steel, 1850–86* (Cambridge University Press, 1967), pp. 450, 466.

41 Bailey, 'Champagne Charlie', p. 107.

42 Cited in ibid., p. 102.

43 See below, note 86.

44 Martin Meisel, *Realizations: Narrative, Pictorial, and Theatrical Arts in Nineteenth-Century England* (Princeton University Press, 1983).

45 See, for example, Clapham, *Economic History*, pp. 462–5.

46 Jacky Bratton, *The Victorian Popular Ballad* (London: Macmillan, 1975), p. 202.

47 The illustrated sheet music I have been able to collect has often been disbound from such volumes; one assumes that this was done early in the twentieth century, when people began to collect music covers, or more recently. W. E. Imeson published his *Illustrated Music-Titles and their Delineators: A Handbook for Collectors* in 1912. His recommendation to keep the illustrations and discard the sheet music may in part be responsible for the covers that one still finds in that condition.

48 Pearsall, *Victorian Sheet Music Covers*, pp. 108–9.

49 See her 'Jones and the Working Girl: Class Marginality in Music-Hall Song 1860–1900', in Bratton, ed., *Music Hall*, pp. 23–48. Her research in the British Library, Harvard Theatre Collections and other sources found that 70 out of 500 comic songs assume a middle-class audience or market.

50 For a short account of the economics of music publishing see Garrett, *Sixty Years of British Music Hall*, Chapter 2 (unpaginated).

51 This advertisement appears on the back cover of George Roe's 'Up in a Balloon Schottische' (1868). Other subdivisions existed, of course, and many publishers divided songs into Gentlemen's Comic Songs and Ladies' Serio-Comic Songs. John Blockley, in an advertisement of 1871 on the back cover of 'Mrs Watkin's Evening Party', offers 'patriotic, convivial, and comic songs'. An advertisement by Edwin Ashdown on George Leybourne's 'After the Opera' (1871) offers 'popular comic, serio-comic, and motto songs'.

52 Clifton's career as a singer started outside the world of the halls, and he was marketed to a more genteel audience than such lions comiques as Leybourne. An advertisement on the back of his 'Have You Seen the Ghost' describes him as having 'worked against the vulgar taste' that has 'sprung up for a class of songs of a very questionable character'.

53 On the comic ballad in Victorian Music Hall see Bratton, *The Victorian Popular Ballad*, pp. 155–202. 'Real' pastoral ballads were also to be heard in the 1860s, of course. Agnes Robertson, as the Colleen Bawn, sings a version of 'The Pretty Girl Milking Her Cow', or *Cailín Deas Crúite na mBó* in *The Colleen Bawn*.

54 As Janet Traies points out, the 'spree' is a working-class topos that is sometimes appropriated to middle-class use in the these songs. See Traies, 'Jones and the Working Girl'.

55 *The Properest Thing to Do, Comic Song Written and Sung by Frank Hall* (London: L'Enfant and Hodgkins, 1863).

56 Bratton, *Victorian Popular Ballad*, pp. 10–11, 184–5.

57 Frank Hall, 'I Really Couldn't Help It' (London, 1863).

58 Presumably a more dramatic version of 'killing glances'. To 'Burke' is literally to suffocate or strangle; the term derives from the infamous pair, Burke and Hare, who murdered their victims so that they could sell the bodies to medical students.

59 *Down in Piccadilly, Written and Sung With Immense Success by Frank Hall* (London: Foster and King, 1863). Illustrated by Concanen and Lee.

60 See Traies, 'Jones and the Working Girl', p. 32. On the 'swell' see Bailey, 'Champagne Charlie'. For middle-class commentators the sartorial borrowings of the 'gent' represented simple counter-jumping. But we might also theorize such a reinterpretation of the urban gentleman as a more tactical activity, not unlike the twentieth-century stylistic appropriations described by Dick Hebdige in *Subculture: The Meaning of Style* (1979).

61 Harry Clifton, *The Dark Girl Dress'd in Blue, sung by Kate Harley and Harry Clifton* (London: B. Williams, 1862).

62 This is not a motif confined to music-hall song, of course. The protagonist of Wilkie Collins's *Basil* (1859) falls in love at first sight on an omnibus in much the same way, also with unfortunate consequences. For a discussion of this trope, and its relation to the public intimacy of the railway compartment, see Christopher Matthews, 'Love at First Sight: The Velocity of Victorian Heterosexuality', *Victorian Studies*, 46.3 (Spring 2004), 425–54.

63 According to Peter Bailey, milliners were associated with casual prostitution throughout the nineteenth century. See his 'Musical Comedy and the Rhetoric of the Girl', in *Popular Culture and Performance*, pp. 175–93, p. 183.

64 In Greene's work and others of its type, we are told the story by the confidence trickster, not the victim.

65 According to Michael Kilgarriff, the last song was part of repertoire of The Great Vance. See *Sing Us One of the Old Songs: A Guide to Popular Song, 1860–1920* (Oxford University Press, 1998), p. 20. My edition of this song says it was sung by Nat Ogden and A. B. Hollingsworth.

66 Traies, 'Jones and the Working Girl', pp. 40–3.

67 W. H. Cove, 'The Charming Young Widow I met in the Train' (London, 1863).

68 George Ware, 'She'd a Black and a Rolling Eye (London, ?)

69 'Sewing Machines', *Once a Week*, 8 (December 1862–June 1863), 202–4 (204).

70 The first practical sewing machines were developed in the 1830s, though the first British firm appears in 1852. According to sewmuse.co.uk the Thomas No. 2 was a sewing machine first manufactured by the Thomas Sewing Machine Company of Birmingham in 1860; it was also manufactured by other firms.

71 Frank Hall, *The Sewing Machine* (London, 1864).

72 Lord Dundreary was the feather-brained aristocrat made famous by E. A. Sothern's performance in Tom Taylor's *Our American Cousin*. See below. As Peter Bailey notes, Gladstone had given cigar sales a boost by dramatically cutting the duty on tobacco. See 'Champagne Charlie', p. 116. Presumably this was related to the entente between France and Britain.

73 Bailey, 'The Victorian Barmaid as Social Prototype', in *Popular Culture and Performance in the Victorian City*, pp. 151–74.

74 Benjamin's account of the *flâneur* as the crowd-surfer of modernity appears in 'On Some Motifs in Baudelaire', in *Illuminations: Essays and Reflections*, ed. Hannah Arendt, trans. Harry Zohn (New York: Schocken, 1969), pp. 155–200. Major contributions to the debates around gender and *flâneur*ship

include Janet Wolff, 'The Invisible *Flâneuse*: Women and the Literature of Modernity', *Theory, Culture, and Society*, 2.7 (1985); Anne Friedberg, *Window Shopping: Cinema and the Postmodern* (Berkeley: University of California Press, 1993); and Mica Nava, 'Modernity's Disavowal: Women, the City and the Department Store', in Mica Nava and Alan O'Shea, eds., *Modern Times: Reflections on a Century of English Modernity* (London: Routledge, 1996).

75 John Harvey, *Men in Black* (London: Reaktion, 1995), pp. 151–93. Flugel uses the term 'the Great Masculine Renunciation' in *The Psychology of Clothes* (1930).

76 Frank Hall, *Kleptomania* (London, 1863).

77 In terms of the psychopathology of shopping, the classic historical study is Elaine Abelson, *When Ladies Go A-Thieving: Middle-Class Shoplifters in the Victorian Department Store* (Oxford University Press, 1989). Abelson cites another song of kleptomania: 'Ladies, Don't Go Thieving' (London, 1860?).

78 The Spellman Collection identifies this as a dressing-gown, but we can see that Dundreary is fully dressed beneath it, which makes a smoking jacket seem more likely.

79 There is also a version in the Spellman collection that places Nelly [*sic*] Power's name on the balloon. Michael Kilgarriff notes that a ladies' version of the song was written for her by Power's mother, and was also sung by Annie Adams, Alice Dunning and Louie Sherrington. See *Sing Us One of the Old Songs*, p. 95.

80 Advertisement on the back of 'Up in a Balloon'.

81 On cultural responses to the perceived threat see Jonathan P. Ribner, 'Our English Coasts, *1852*: William Holman Hunt and Invasion Fear at Midcentury', *Art Journal*, 55.2 (1996), 45–54. As Ribner notes, Tennyson's 'Britons, Guard Your Own' (1852) and 'Riflemen Form!' (1859) are among the literary responses to the perceived threat.

82 Henry Walker, *The Awkward Squad* (London, 1859).

83 See T. W. Robertson and E. P. Hingston, *Artemus Ward's Panorama* (New York: G. W. Carleton, 1869), which includes the *Times* review as an Appendix, pp. 201–2, p. 202.

84 See the entry for Banting in the online *Oxford Dictionary of National Biography*, oxforddnb.com (accessed 9 January 2007).

85 Bennett, 'London and Londoners', p. 263.

86 Although this optical effect is often attributed to John Henry Pepper, its English version was largely devised by Henry Dircks. See George Speaight, 'Professor Pepper's Ghost', *Theatre Notebook*, 43.1 (1989), 1–24; *Oxford Dictionary of National Biography* entry for J. H. Pepper; and Pepper's own *A True History of Pepper's Ghost and All About Metempsychosis*, with a new introduction by Mervyn Heard (1890; London: The Projection Box, 1996). One of the working-class theatres, the Brittania, put on the first actual play to be written around the new special effect. This was *Faith, Hope and Charity*, by C. H. Hazlewood, which opened on 6 April 1863, and in which the ghost of

a woman appears to the wicked baronet who has murdered her. It was succeeded by a number of other forgotten plays, but the first really successful
play to put the Ghost to work followed Pepper's earlier example by utilizing
Charles Dickens's 1848 *Christmas story* (Adelphi, June 1863).

87 The copy of this galop that I possess was published in London by John
Blockley. The British Library does not have a copy, and I have been unable to
locate one elsewhere, but it is presumably also from the 1860s. Curiously, the
stamped signature of 'Concanen, Lee and Siebe' appears in mirror writing.

88 It may be related to John Hollingshead's *Under Bow Bells* (1860), a series of
stories and sketches compiled from *Household Words*, or from the short-lived
literary periodical, *Bow Bells* (1862–4). It may also, of course, be a scene from
a play that I have failed to identify, or related to a song that I have not been
able to find.

89 Walter L. Burn, *The Age of Equipoise: A Study of the Mid-Victorian Generation*
(London: Allen and Unwin, 1964), p. 27.

90 C. Geoffrey Holme, ed., *The Painter of Victorian Life: A Study of Constantin
Guys with an introduction and a translation of Baudelaire's Peintre de la Vie
Moderne by P. G. Konody* (London: The Studio, 1930), p. 29.

CONCLUSION: PEPPER'S GHOST AND THE
PRESENCE OF THE PRESENT

1 The 'material unconscious' is a term introduced in Bill Brown's *The Material
Unconscious: American Amusement, Stephen Crane, and the Economics of Play*
(Cambridge: Harvard University Press, 1996), p. 4.

2 On Dircks, John Henry Pepper and the Ghost, see George Speaight,
'Professor Pepper's Ghost', *Theatre Notebook*, 43.1 (1989), 1–24; the *Oxford
Dictionary of National Biography* entry for J. H. Pepper; and Pepper's own
A True History of Pepper's Ghost and All About Metempsychosis, with a new
introduction by Mervyn Heard (1890; London: The Projection Box, 1996).

3 See Pepper, *True History*, p. 1.

4 Their patent was disputed in France by the magician Henri Robin, where a
toy called the Polyscope, invented by Pierre Séguin in 1847, was held to have
used the effect at an earlier date. See Speaight, 'Professor Pepper's Ghost',
p. 22. However, see also Mannoni, *The Great Art*, pp. 248–50, on the differences between Séguin's invention and the stage Ghost.

5 *Once a Week*, 9 May 1863, 543.

6 There is a certain appropriateness to this choice, since Lytton's narrator, Dr
Fenwick, compares the image he sees to 'some exhibition in London' with 'a
curious instance of optical illusion; at the end of a corridor you see, apparently in strong light, a human skull'. *A Strange Story: An Alchemical Novel*
(1862; Berkeley and London: Shambala, 1973), p. 222.

7 Pepper, *True History*, pp. 3, 12, 29–30; Speaight, 'Professor Pepper's Ghost', p. 19.

8 A contemporary aficionado of projection effects, Abbé Moigno, saw the illusion when Pepper took it to Paris for a highly successful show at the Théâtre
Impérial at Le Châtelet and gave a detailed account of how he thought the

illusion was staged, in which he assumes that the effect was achieved with 'three enormous two-way mirrors, about 5 m square, costing almost 4000 Francs'. See Laurent Mannoni, *The Great Art of Light and Shadow: Archeology of the Cinema,* translated and edited by Richard Crangle (University of Exeter Press, 2000), p. 249. According to Pepper, the use of a mirror below stage was a refinement of Pepper and Dircks's patent added by a magician called Silvester. The patented illusion required the actor to recline at an angle below stage, and for the plate glass to be similarly angled to catch the reflection.

9   See Mannoni, *The Great Art*, pp. 136–75.

10   Pepper, *The True History*, p. 5.

11   Wolfgang Schivelbusch, *The Industrialization of Light in the Nineteenth Century,* trans. Angela Davies (Berkeley: University of California Press, 1995), pp. 146–7. See Richard D. Altick, *The Shows of London* (Cambridge: Belknap Press, 1978), pp. 226–7.

12   Andrew H. Miller, *Novels Behind Glass: Commodity Culture and Victorian Narrative* (Cambridge University Press, 1995), pp. 1–4, pp. 2, 4. See also his excellent account of the impact of the Great Exhibition, pp. 50–90. In New York, a sensation was created in 1848 by the opening of A. T. Stewart's dry-goods bazaar on Broadway, known as the Marble Palace, which featured plate-glass windows and huge, thirteen foot high mirrors. See Elaine S. Abelson, *When Ladies Go A-Thieving: Middle-Class Shoplifters in the Victorian Department Store* (New York: Oxford University Press, 1989), p. 67.

13   Altick, *The Shows of London*, pp. 226–7. See also Alison Adburgham, *Shops and Shopping 1800–1914: Where and in What Manner the Well-dressed Englishwoman Bought her Clothes* (London: George Allen and Unwin, 1964), p. 96.

14   Miller, *Novels Behind Glass*, p. 65.

15   The OED traces the first use of the term 'cleptomania' to 1830. The first medical use is thought to be by C. C. Marc in 1846. The London *Times* uses it in 1855, and in 1862 an article entitled 'Kleptomania' by J. C. Bucknill, MD, appears in the *American Journal of Insanity*. See Abelson, *When Ladies*, p. 278, n. 88. As we have seen, a comic song of that name appears in 1863.

16   W. Bridges Adams, 'Patent Ghosts', *Once a Week*, 19 September 1863, 361–2, 362.

17   'Adelphi Theatre', *The Times*, 23 June 1863, 5.

18   See *Adelphi Theatre Project*, 1862–3, Season Commentary.

19   Harry Clifton, *Have You Seen the Ghost* (London: Hopwood and Crew, 1865).

20   Henry J. Byron, *1863; or, The Sensations of the Past Season, With a Shameful Revelation of Lady Somebody's Secret* (London: Lacy, 1863), scene i.

21   Dion Boucicault, 'The Decline of the Drama', *North American Review*, 125 (September 1877), 239, cited by Allardyce Nicoll, *A History of Late Nineteenth-Century Drama, 1850–1900*, vol. I (Cambridge University Press, 1946), p. 42, n. 2.

22   Cf. *Macbeth*, one of the Shakespearean plays quoted in the novel, in which Banquo, later a ghost himself, tells Macbeth that the 'earth hath bubbles like the water', and the witches appear from and disappear back into such bubbles. John Harmon's return from death by drowning as John Rokesmith

suggests one kind of spectre; the wealth of the Veneerings suggests the other. For a sophisticated account of *Our Mutual Friend* as Dickens's meditation on the reifying effects of commodity culture, as well as a symptom of his own place within it, see Miller, *Novels Behind Glass*, pp. 119–58.

23 Charles Dickens, *Our Mutual Friend* (1865; Oxford University Press Classics, 1998), p. 544.

24 Ibid., pp. 556–7.

25 Nancy Armstrong, *How Novels Think: The Limits of Individualism from 1719–1900* (New York: Columbia, 2005).

26 Richard Price argues that in fact the 1856 and 1862 limited liability acts remained more or less unused until after 1866, when the collapse of the discount brokerage of Overend and Gurney drove firms to look to new ways of raising capital. See Price, *British Society, 1660–1880: Dynamism, Containment and Change* (Cambridge University Press, 1999), p. 82. For a different literary take on liability see Andrew H. Miller, 'Subjectivity Limited: The Discourse of Limited Liability in the Joint-Stock Companies Act of 1856 and Gaskell's Cranford,' in *ELH*, 61 (1994), 139–57.

27 Elaine Freedgood, *The Ideas in Things: Fugitive Meaning in the Victorian Novel* (University of Chicago Press, 2006), pp. 11–12.

28 On the somatic aspect of Victorian theories of the novel, see Nicholas Dames, 'Wave-Theories and Affective Physiologies: The Cognitive Strain in Victorian Novel Theories', *Victorian Studies*, 46.2 (Winter 2004), 206–16.

29 Tom Gunning, 'The Cinema of Attractions: Early Film, Its Spectator and the Avant-Garde,' in Thomas Elsaesser and Adam Barker, eds., *Early Film* (British Film Institute, 1989). Cf. Crary, *Suspensions of Perception*, p. 25, n.34.

30 (Anon.), *Sixpenny Wonderfuls: 6d Gems from the Past* (London: Chatto and Windus and the Hogarth Press, 1985), p. 26.

31 Andrew Maunder, ed., *Varieties of Women's Sensation Fiction*, vol. I: *Sensationalism and the Sensation Debate* (London: Pickering and Chatto, 2004), p. xiii.

32 'I just don't get modern art, says Italy's culture minister', *The Guardian*, 13 August 2008, www.guardian.co.uk/artanddesign/2008/aug/13/architecture.art (accessed 3 September 2008).

33 See *The Art of Alfred Concanen: An Exhibition of Victorian Lithograph Song Covers*, April–June 1962 (London: Museum Street Galleries, 1962). In 2005, the Bodleian Library in Oxford used its extensive collection of illustrated sheet music as the basis for the exhibition *The British Music Hall Song, 1850–1920*. In 2006, the Harris Museum and Art Gallery in Preston featured the work of Concanen, Brandard and others in *Odd Pieces: Illustrated Music of the Victorian and Edwardian Era*. At the time of writing both the Victoria and Albert Museum and the British Library showcase illustrated sheet music, the latter displaying quite an extensive collection online in their Collect Britain section. The Spellman Collection at the University of Reading makes all of its collection of illustrated sheet music available online, as does the Lester S. Levy Collection at Johns Hopkins University in the United States.

Index

CAMBRIDGE STUDIES IN NINETEENTH-CENTURY
LITERATURE AND CULTURE

General editor
Gillian Beer, *University of Cambridge*

Titles published

Lightning Source UK Ltd.
Milton Keynes UK
UKOW04f1824110314

227931UK00010B/251/P

9 781107 630208